FASHION MARKETING & THEORY

Access Press UK
1 Hillside Gardens
Darwen
Lancs
BB3 2NJ

First Edition

British Library Cataloging-in-Publication data
A Catalogue record for this book is available from the British Library

ISBN 978-0-9562471-1-7

BIOGRAPHICAL NOTE

From Left to Right: Gianpaolo Vignali, Prof. Claudio Vignali

Gianpaolo Vignali

Gianpaolo is a graduate from UMIST with his first degree in Mathematics. Later adding a Masters in Strategic Management his career first started as a part-time Lecturer and Researcher at Manchester Metropolitan University before moving to full-time employment in the department of Retail at Leeds Metropolitan University. He is now the Programme Leader for Fashion Buying at Manchester Metropolitan University where he delivers on both undergradute and post graduate programmes.

Prof. Claudio Vignali

Professor Vignali joined Leeds Metropolitan University on 1st September 2003 from the School of Consumer, Tourism and Hospitality Management at Manchester Metropolitan University, where he had been the Consumer Section and Research Head for the past three years. Prior to this he was the postgraduate diploma course leader in the department of Retailing and Marketing.

He has written more than 50 articles and books in the field of Retailing and Marketing and is the editor of two academic journals, The British Food Journal and the International Journal of Management.

In the past Professor Vignali has worked for Crown Berger Paints, part of Akzo Nobell, and Benetton, where he has held positions from brand manager to export director and developed distribution and retail operations in Europe and the Middle East.

AWKNOWLEDGEMENTS

We have worked on this book for a SHORT time.

It was at a CIRCLE [Centre for International Research in Consumers, Locations, and Environments;www. circleinternational.co.uk], conference were a series of papers were presented in a fashion track, that the original seeds were gathered for this book. A series of academics saw the need for a simple but effective gathering of information so that readers could understand the Principles of Fashion Marketing.

It has been a pleasure to work with all the contributors whom you will see, have dedicated their own research results to dedicated chapters.

I would also like to thank my fiancée Gemma Barlow for listening to me explaining concepts which were not too clear and sitting next to me whilst I stamped the context of the book out on my Mac. I would like to thank my father for his guidance and ever critical demands on my time.

I [senior] would like to praise my wife Sylvana for her patience, my grand daughter Rachel and grandson Gianluca for deleting so much material from my lap top. I too would like to thank my son for his listening to my suggestions.

We hope that the reader will appreciate the essence and the backbone knowledge we have tried to collect.

Gianpaolo Vignali, Darwen, UK   21.2.2010

Claudio Vignali, Zagreb, Croatia   21.2.2010

PREFACE

The survival of fashion, its constant changes, development and decline, its connection with all historical events (wars, revolutions, scientific discoveries, change of customs, flourishing of art) indicate its importance.

Although there are many definitions of fashion, it generally refers to new, frequently perishable, ways of life in all areas of human activity in a determined time period such as science, politics, art, behaviour, entertainment and similar.

Fashion is only one of the most important social and economic manifestations of our time. It also indicates and serves as a measure of psychological and socio-economical motivations of the humankind, and in a way the indicator of human ambitions and wish to compete.

Fashion began when mankind left the 'savage' ages – when the fulfilment of only existential needs and needs for security is left behind, when the 'esthetical' needs appeared, often resulting from an additional need to be different, and later on from psychological and social motives to show social status. Decoration of body is visible already in the cavemen ages, when the so called fashion event was motivated by sexual needs and in this sense it still has existential importance for the natural, biological motive for the survival of the species. The decoration of caves with painted surfaces may also be characterized as fashion, although the true motivation for such an activity had existential character describing fight against natural disasters or good hunt and protection of hunters.

Luxury and splendour in fashion belong to the most prominent status symbols of the past until the middle of the eighteen-century. Luxury dresses worn in castles, public, religious and political ceremonies of all times witness to it.

The real fashion, or what we call fashion these days, has existed from the time of Enlightenment, the breakthrough of bourgeoisie. Only with the breakthrough of bourgeoisie, the fashion, at least partially, ceased to be only the expression of the social status of an individual, although numerous varieties still provided differentiation between the individuals, but this difference had socio-economic not caste or class character any more.

The governing classes always dictated the fashion trends in the past and there were no authentic fashion of the common people, whose clothes were mainly national garbs. This relation could and had to be more direct in the periods when each civilization was locked within its territorial borders of one nation, when exchanges between nations were difficult and very rare. Nowadays national fashion is declining (except what is left of folklore and regional customs), as well as the fashion of artistic and artisan's works bearing national characteristics, while internationalization and universalisation of clothing fashion, decoration and internal design happens more often.

Modern times are best explained by Yves Saint Laurent's statement that 'it is no longer fashionable to be fashionable'. Today people who want to be fashionable must create their own image, and must not accept the influences from the 'above'. We can assume that in the near future the fashion phenomena will cease to be necessary equivalent to social constitution, but it will become only esthetical choice. The basic direction of the fashion will be that it will become more personal, more connected to the wants and taste of individuals and it will adjust to the wants of individuals for their differentiation within the community based on their taste.

The fashion is most frequently connected with the presentation of a person through his clothes. The level of technical modernization of the textile and clothes manufactories and constant stimulation of needs to buy clothes made the fashion into a big and very profitable business.

Clothes present material made primarily to protect the human body. The shape of the clothes and kind of material, from early beginnings, primarily depended on the climate of the area where it developed and the level of technological development for its production. In the efforts to improve living conditions men has been constantly refining the materials and developing the shapes of clothes in order to be more and more comfortable and better protect the body.

With time clothes ceased to have only protective function and more and more esthetical elements were entering the clothes design. For example, clothes were coloured and more harmonious relations between colours and design were sought. Here we see the esthetical function of clothes besides the original protective one. This function has been loosing and gaining importance depending on the social and ethical conflicts. In the societies that showed conflicts at all levels, the fashion was loosing importance, and in those where there were established sets of values, clothes and fashion dominated as an indicator of economical and social values, driver of a whole industry sector as well as characterizing nations as dominant drivers of certain fashion styles.

Besides the protective and esthetical functions, since the earliest times the clothes has had also an important religious character. Event today there is an obvious connection between religious rituals and clothes in the uniforms of religious groups, as symbol of expressing mourning, or important religious events such as wedding, Communion and similar. Clothes are used to cover certain physical defaults or point out some physical characteristics, having certain sexual-esthetical function, as it has had through the human history.

Special clothes express belonging to certain social group; therefore one of the functions is to express social status. With bigger and various offer on one hand, and ideologization of life on the other hand, the clothes nowadays become deliberate communication media. This communicative function of clothes is expressed by the choice of clothes from a variety of offers and the way it is placed in the context of men's chosen or imposed environment. In this communicative function clothes often clearly express social roles. Based on their clothes we can recognise men and women, the rich and the poor, an introvert and an extrovert, supporters of traditional and alternative cultural forms or followers of various ideologies, homosexuals, whores, fetishists, artists, solicitors and similar. These communicative signs shall not be taken for granted, but there shall always be a possibility of a favourable impression, which a person with his clothes wants to give to the surroundings.

Changes of fashion trends with the production of fashion clothes stimulate production of new and different kinds of fabrics, various additional material, shops and new school programs for education of professionals for textiles and designers. With continuous development and changes in production of clothes also develop the techniques of its sales. With the aim to create needs for always new and fashionable clothes, there are numerous magazines having function to establish certain fashion trends and awareness, fashion designer as profession is established, which today has a status of an artist and many other activities are established relating to changes of clothes, fashion itself, but also other activities relating to changes of fashion.

The fashion industry itself has been market oriented and directed to end consumption; therefore, marketing is inevitable for a successful business operation in accordance with the needs and market trends.

The basic role of marketing in the fashion industry is to:

• Investigate needs for textile and clothes

• Offer products that various consumers need and want

• Facilitate the choice of goods and affordable purchase through the best sales channels

• Give sufficient information in constant communication with the customers in order to facilitate their choice of goods and final decision

The basic task of marketing in the fashion industry is to connect the production and consumption of clothes in the way that the suppliers achieve positive business results and get customers' satisfaction in the consumption of these products.

This book will begin with a section on the clothing market, a section on consumer behaviour, and followed by a section of cases regarding fashion clothes retailers. They are all global retailers, some on them dominate on the UK market and some of them have maintained for a long time world known brands, which have experienced ups and downs in their lifecycle, and some of them are still expanding.

The aim was to consider the main points of each case and to determine if they are where they wanted to be. To highlight market position Porter's Generic strategy has been used. As the UK clothing economy is in growth, the UK has an attractive clothing market for retailers. The fashion industry is continuing to grow at an enormous rate, while the large retailers are leading the way for the ever-changing styles and trends. Therefore, we believe that many who read this book will find a lot of useful information on the fashion market in the UK, many fashion clothing retailers and methods of solving their future problems.

*"Family is the core. There is
 nothing that can mean more for
those who have been, are being
and who are yet to come."*
GianpaoloVignali

FASHION MARKETING & THEORY

GIANPAOLO VIGNALI

&

CLAUDIO VIGNALI

CONTENTS

CHAPTER 1: FASHION CONCEPTS

GIANPAOLO VIGNALI

Modernity & Fashion

The definite roots of modernity cannot be accurately placed but many authors discuss this commencing in the 17th century. It further gathered pace and momentum in the 18th century in France and Britain, furthermore the further acceleration of this method was push by the industrial and political revolutions in these countries. The drive of innovation and pioneers allowed for unique new forms of not only clothing but industrial developments too. This diversity in society and the concept of the "new" allowed cities to create their own identities and thus modernity in turn favored the modern/urban settings as opposed to the traditional and rural ways. It also favored the artificial compared to the natural.

The main emphasis of this era was based on progress and improvement as new ideas and concepts were forever being push forward to compete with the previous. The fact that many new ideas that were created were of a novelty value it exposed the living at the time and the new wealth gearing to constant new change. The shift was also felt as craft production moved to a new automated production. But the new shifts were not always welcome and in turn the way at which modernity was evolving did this pose a problem?

In turn Breward (1994: 146) supports this school of though and further denotes that:

"if there is one major theme amongst many in which…a discussion of Victorian

clothing can be situated, it is this problem or idea of "modernity".

and this is further supported by Wilson (1985: 63) who suggested that modernity:

"seems useful as a way of indicating the restless desire for change characteristic

of cultural life in industrial capitalism, the desire for the new that fashion expresses

so well".

This "newness" and it expression through fashion also allowed modernity to become a catalyst in the development and rise of industrialisation, the growth of capitalism, urbanisation, individualism and the development of mass culture/customisation.

As a result these developments were interlinked and synonymous with the times asa new capitalist class emerged. Their wealth was tied to the factories that they developed, the capital that was employed in their industries and the associated merchandise too. This new class culture challenged the existing setup as the traditions and expectations linked to this approach were being changed. (Entwistle 2000: 106), depicts this very well by suggesting that these challenges were provided, "less with swords than through symbols."

The most major of these symbols as suggested by Entwistle (2000) was of course dress. This is further denoted and explained by Slater (1997: 70) who suggests that:

"new money buys landed estates, it can wear the clothes of court and society, it can indulge in the leisure pursuits of the aristocracy".

This contravined the suggested normal practice as fashion trends had traditional been set by the Royals and wealthy aristocrats. These members of society were looked up to and were the celebrities of their day. The transformation of the focus between the traditionalists and the new capitalist class was never forseen and as a result it was this new money who now set the trend.

This allowed modernity to provide an, " expanded stage for the public drama of modern life," (Steele, 1988:135) and therefore fashion was allowed to prevail as its catwalk emerged. The modern city also allowed for this to develop. This allowed for the consumer society to evolve and a greater emphasis on the way in which people presented themselves began.

Therefore modernity was related to the new the progress and development, novelty and change and as a result this wealth helped create the cities of today. as fashion can be associated with modernity it comes to reason that by default fashion is linked to cities too.

Individualisation

Individualisation created an interesting approach when linked to fashion. Essentially fashion allowed for creativity and also this created the demand for identity and uniqueness. This stimulated tension between clothes that were revealing and clothes that were concealing as each had a purpose and a necessary time. Sennett (1977) and Finkelstein (1991) furthered this appraoch by distinguishing that identity is immanent in appearance and that it can be hidden behind a disguise.

An explanation of this concept is that when we meet someone for the first time initially thecliche of first impressions count and we can refer to ones clothes as a way of deciepheringwho the individual may be. This gives the individual their identity and as a result we canslot the individual into their place and role in society. This also poses another interestingpart of where this individual fits into society and who this individual may be?

This individualisation resulted in popular demand and in the 19th century this process of modernity changed social life and the emergence of the city. Cites expanded as more and more people moved their for work and the wealthy moved their to socialise. These cities became bustling and full of life. On the other hand this led to congestion too. Cities provide a place for people to conveine and this led to the modern drama or catwalk where citizens could stage their life (Steele, 1991). This city life created an awareness on oneself and their role as an individual in this society. And in this case the ones who survived in the city were the ones who could blend in but also stand out when they had to.

Fashion acted as to satisfy one persons needs to be accepted by society and allowed the person to adapt to differing social situations. Fashion also allowed for diversity to be explored exploring the differing elements of contrast and the need of change. Fashion allowed for individuals to conceal their identity and dress acted as a form of protection. In Victorian times it wasn't rare for city inhabitants to read into your appearance and identity as this was in the era when existing class structures were being challenged with the introduction of new wealth. Fashion allowed for the distance to be put between what one was and what they really were and can be viewed as being ones armour or disguise that artistically deonted them from the other (Entwistle, 2000). Senet (1977) suggested that until the middle of the 18th century one would accept the other on face value but as the rise of new wealth emerged it was sought that come the 19th century society would probe beneath the identity to expose the truth. The 19thh century saw the rise of the individual. This also led to the classifications of stereotypes through the development of physiognomy and examples of this included crooked mouths being linked to criminality and full lips indicating viciousness.

Individualisation comes to argue the difference between the authentic self and the artificial self and fashion is what forms the base of discussion.

The Fashion City - From Paris to Madchester

As we have established the development of modernity has been linked to the evolution in particular of novelty, progress and change. The development is also linked to the change from craft production to automated production and therefore this involves artificialpractices, it favours the urban over the natural. As a result this began to see the uprising of subcultural differences as fashion was used as a physical means to exploit this. From the 19th Century the main fashion cities emerging were Paris, London, Vienna, Berlin, Brussels, Milan and even New York at this stage had an influence on fashion.

There are several factors that contribute to the evolution of these fashion cities in the 19th century. The initial movement was through the international trade networks. Those who were well travelled were able to see how differing cultures presented themselves and acted through fashion. The superior clad individuals of the city would often acclaim a higher status and this was envied by many from all walks of life. The draw of labour to the cites allowed for the bustling industries to set up. As such immigrants were able to be exploited in the use of sweatshops and this allowed the industry to develop at the pace it needed. This then became a way in which the cities would compete against one another.

This developed in the the 20th century and Paris was branded as the fashion capital of the world, whilst New York promoted itself as a city of modern commercial culture and London was the location for conservatism and tradition and as Breward (2000) explains it was the place of fog shrouded streets. Cities have their own identity and ways of characterising themselves and this can been seen through many films period and modern with the stereotypical characters associated in them from Audrey Hepburn in Paris and Sherlock Holmes in London.

Paris was a city linked to tradition but style and it is argued that they even set up the first fashion design house in the mid 1800's. They did have a thriving fashion industry pre WWII and designers like Dior synonymous with Paris were encouraged to design the "New Look" ranges in 1949. This New Look range single handedly revived Paris post WWII and propelled them to the summit of the fashion city league table. Dior was described as being able to consider the feminist ideal ads his explanation for the design of the New Look was due to women longing to look like women again.

London was considered to be the "Aristocratic bohemianism" (Breward 2003 p182) in the 1960's and this developed in the 70's and 80's as having a thriving underground of subcultures. The most recognisable fashion landmark of London is probably Savile Row which dates back to 18th Century. Facilitating and supply the gentlemen of this era through to now has been the remit of the individual tailors on this famous street.

Queen Elizabeth in Norman Hartnell in 1939

The 1960's brought some flamboyance to the streets of London and was classified as thenew age. It was described as the new spirit of youth profiling artisits such as Mary Quant, The Beatles and Twiggy. The 60's inspired a generation and the relaxation of many walks of life including the introduction of the female contraception pill saw a relaxed approach to sexuality and lifestyle. As the 60's turned into the 70's one of the most noted changes to the London scene was the introduction of the punk subculture.

Twiggy in the 1960's

The main catalyst of this subculture was a unique concoction between a designer and a musical genius. When Vivienne Westwood opened up her shop 'sex' on the Kings Road in conjunction with Malcolm McLaren its mix of sado-masochistic and nazi influence took off and the linkage to the Sex Pistols propelled the movement across the Atlantic and once again London had its own look. This subculture or micro system facilitated a need on the streets of London but this eventually grew to be a much bigger phenonemum and eventually Punk became a macro fashion competing with the tradition and prestige of Savile Row.

McRobbie (1998) mentions that this movement started in the sweaty clubs of the underground London scene and eventually cam to maturity when theses club goers would make clothes for friends creating a demand and recognition which saw many market stall opening to feed this need.

The progression of the 70's into the 80's saw the introduction of the discount fashion retailer and as a result Britain could not compete with the manufacturing demands seeing the mass shift of production to countries like India and China. Mass global outsourcing was born at a time where inner Britain was undergoing inner city regeneration.

Given these examples of Fashion Cities would Manchester fit the mould? As it was the worlds first industrial city and the centre of the industrial revolution this city did have an influence but whereas the others focussed on fashion Manchester was very much focussed on industry and it lost its place as being a main fashion city. But a micro culture did appear during the 80's and Madchester was born. The club scene allowed for sartorial experimentation and social display. The Hacienda attracted people from all over the UK.

Sex and Punk in 1970's London

Peter Saville a graphic designer pioneered a new look to this scene an d bands such as the Happy Mondays and New Order allowed for a fast recognition to this scene. This creative culture allowed for fashion designers to prosper and for the flow of these ideas that would inspire a generation. These designers too had the opportunity to rent retail space at relatively low prices and Afflecks Palace became a mecca for this movement and helped to support the tradition and history of small design businesses.

Tony Wilson 1950-2007

The main figurehead of this change was Tony Wilson who had become a guru for the city. Tony passed away in 2007 and his pioneering approach allowed for the city to be recognised on a European and World Level from Detroit to Paris. This club scene allowed for the fashion industry in Manchester to thrive as everybody needed something new to wear every week, (Haslam, 2004).

18th Century

When we discuss Modernity there are always at least three permutations to its development namely; the art movement, the spirit of character and the historical era and these gave rise to the three most important developments of the last 300 years including industrialisation, urbanisation and individualism. But often there can be a crisis linked to modernity and instantly arguments arise linked to a machine inspired de-humanisation, greed, capitalism etc.

An example of the demise of modernity in the UK can be linked to Lancashire cotton during the industrial revolution. Textile trade in the UK rose during the 17th and 18th Centuries and one of the main fundamentals here to this rise was the productiona and utilisation of Lancashire cotton. This cotton allowed for great leaps in the production linked to the industrial revolution as the cotton industry was founded on the cottage system of lancashire and the North West.

By the turn of the 18th century trade had expanded into fustians, linens and small wares. Pre 1760 would see individual spinners, usually women who would work in their front rooms whilst their husband would work the land. Added help would be implied once the men had returned fro the fields and additional support provided. These cottage industries developed so that between 1760 and 1820 mills started to dominate the landscape of the North West as wealthy business men would start production into this area. The expansion can be put down to the increased amount of export to the new world and products were specifically designed and produced to cater for exotic markets. Cooler weavers and brighter colours sustained this demand.

Technology also developed and a range of production tools improved the production of raw cotton such as:

Kay's Flying Shuttle (1733)

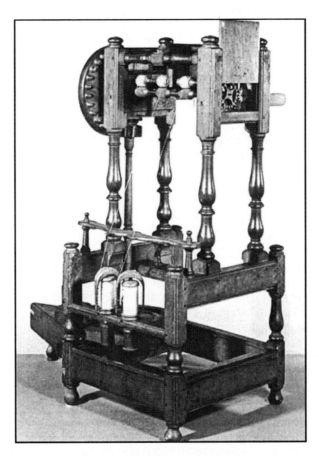

Arkwright's Water Frame (1769)

Hargreaves Spinning Jenny (1770)

Crompton's Mule (1779)

All of these tools allowed for increased production to the extent that it outstripped demand. These technological advances allowed for the development of the textile industry and the rise of the fashion industry in the North West and UK as a whole. Having said this this drive was also powered by another factor and the emergence of the fashion consumer. This willingness of the fashion concious population allowed for the first aspects of marketing to be noticed as these consumers started to buy luxuries as opposed to necessaties fuelled by the industrial revolution.

Modernity provided an 'expanded stage for the public drama of modern life' (Steele, 1988; 135) Modernity roots from the 17th century and gathered momentum in both France and Britain in the 18th century. Driven by the industrial and political revolution, modernity favoured the; artificial, modern and urban, over the; natural, traditional and rural.

Manchester was at the for-front of the industrial revolution, and was classed as one of the world's first industrial cities. It allowed the factories and machines take over the farming land. A painting of Flints Farm in Moss side by James Hey Davies (1844-1930) shows the changes which were occurring. With the painting set in the 19th century, it shows that there was once a lot of open farm land in and around the city centre. Manchester city centre has now crept within a mile of Moss side. In an area of dense housing estate and bustling nonstop traffic such as the Princes Park way.

Another painting which conveyed such a drastic change would be the 'Southwest prospect of Manchester and Salford' set about 1734. This was constructed by an artist called John Harris (1680-1740). Again his rural landscape portrayed Manchester and Salford on the brink of industrial revolution. The painting shows buildings such as the Royal exchange seen as it was first built in 1729. It has now been rebuilt and transformed to reflect Manchester's changing focus and fortune.

The architecture of Manchester in the present day reflects the industrial development of the early 20th century. Cotton production was a thriving industry in Manchester up to the pre Second World War period which contributed to the emerging fashion industry. In addition to this the development of Large department store previously only seen in London help contribute to the urbanisation and mass consumption of fashion in Manchester.

Advances in technology meant that fashion and garments could be produced in high quantities. The inventions of machines such as the Power Loom allowed for fashion to develop and form, in addition new fashionable silhouettes could be achieved. This growth in the fashion industry changed the world of consumption and in addition it increased Individualism and the expressions of ones self through the clothes in with they wore.

Cotton allowed for the change between cottage and factory production. The increase of fashionable dress was not only down to technological advancements either as the fashion consumer arrived onto the scene. This growth in consumer demand also allowed fro more fashionable fabrics to be created as sophisticated consumers demanded a wider choice.

19th Century

Industrialisation had a direct impact on fashion, and new technologies altered the way it was produced. The 19th century saw an even bigger leap in technology with the introduction of flexible steel and dyeing techniques, which had a colossal effect on the fashion and structure of the garments, people were wearing at that time. The main example being the production of the 'crinoline' which was a steel framed dress support made up of several layers of petticoats. It was a fashion that became more popular than could ever have been predicted. Most probably because it was the first real trend and advancement the fashion industry had seen, with its creator being Charles Worth, who has been described as 'the first great fashion dictator' (De Marly, 1980). The invention of the crinoline steel framed dress accounted for 1/7th of the out put of steel in Sheffield, each one used 65 yards of steel. It was responsible for changing the female silhouette in the 19th century as women wanted to follow the fashion, this lead to consumerism, Breward (1995, p.158) states 'The recent application of this metal to crinoline has no doubt given great impetus to the trade'. This really did change the face of the fashion industry at this time, and as noted by De Marly (1980), the crinoline "was a true child of the industrial revolution, for it could not have taken place without it". This shows an acceptance of modernity and the changes it was bringing.

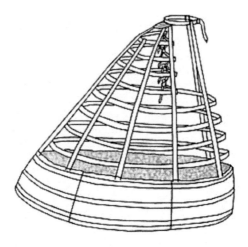

Crinoline Cage 1865

The invention of aniline dyes also meant that fashion could be made more individual through colours and prints. Industrialisation was seen as a novelty that created progress and change. Because of the level of consumerism the industry began overpowering its creators, factory owners were experiencing new levels of wealth through capital and merchandise and as a result a new capitalist class emerged fighting 'less with sword than through symbols' (Entwistle 2000, p.106) showing the importance of clothing at that time.

Suggesting capitalism encouraged this level of modernity as well as consumerism fuelling it. The Lancashire cotton famine (1861-65) saw the industry collapse as a result of Linclon blocking all cotton leaving the USA during the American civil war sending the British economy into recession, however, this period also brought greed and capitalism as cotton had become rare it was kept unspun for as long as possible so as to increase its value.

Individualism also lead to modernity through social changes and gender. A women's world was private associated with consumption and leisure and a man's was public associated with production and work. The ideal femininity, influenced by gender roles was shown through dress portraying the female lifestyle as leisurely.

Urbanisation brought great change socially through the development of big cities enticing people to publicly display their clothing as the city became a stage for modern life (Steele, 1988) and encouraged the continuous consumption of clothing and fashion through the new concept of department stores, A. T. Stewarts, New York opened in 1846 the environment made it a place women wanted to frequent in and shopping had become an activity.

The birth of the factory during the 19th century also bought a change in social roles, with the formation of workers unions. This caused major uproar when Lancashire was hit by the cotton famine between 1861 and 1866. It was the first time the UK had experienced a recession and an unstable state of economy and so workers began rioting due to the injustice they felt of an industry that had given them a proper way of life. Lancashire's cotton trade had hit its first problems and from here it was set to end as between 1866 and 1896, the 'Victorian Golden Age', the UK sold the rights to their machines to the Far East, who were becoming too much competition as they could offer much lower labour prices.

The industrial revolution had in effect, born and died with Lancashire's cotton.

Postmodernity

Postmodernism represents a clear break from the previous era-Modernity. 'In post modern society, people have more opportunity to construct their own identities and have more options to choose from' (Pilkington et al 2005; 195). Gender dichotomy emerged during the 19th century. Hebdige states 'the object is split, janw-like into the two opposed aspects: his and hers. His: functional, scientific, useful. Hers: decorative, aesthetic, gratifying.' (Hebdige 1988; 86). Social changes particularly in gender roles impacted on what both men and women wore at the time. Now a Postmodern women can choose her; sexuality, be single, a working mother, or business women, and a member of any political party she chooses and subsequently her life style and buying patterns can reflect her own identity. Brand names such as Gucci and Prada can be used as statements of herself.

However in a postmodern world these identities evolve from a media saturated society and the line between image and reality is unfocused. And these blurred media images are open to differing interpretations people interpret them in a variety of ways (Strinati 1992).

An early study by Tuchman in the 1970's showed stereotypical television portrayal where stresses were on women in roles such as mothers and house wives. Similar research in 1994 (Van Zoonen) revealed depressing similarities in research into media portrayals of women. In contradiction in Post-modernistic contemporary terms, media images do not conform to the stereotypical portrayals. For example most if not all of the popular cookery programs are presented by male chefs. So the social construction of women doing familycooking is not carried through to the images on television.

Despite the highlighting of the portrayal of stereotypical roles for men and women in past research, the programs are still peppered with negative representations of females and positive ones of males. 'Media fiction continues to perpetuate myths about human behaviour, history and present day society and its institutions, especially in relation to the nation, sexuality, gender, war and crime' (Stephens. P; 468)

In reaction to these perceived imposed social constructs theorists such as Delamont (2003) believe that the researchers own voice should be heard and this is termed the reflexive voice. This means 'The text will reproduce the actors own perspective and experiences. This may include extended biographical and autobiographical accounts, extended dialogues between the researcher and informants, and other documents of life.' (Pilkington A, 2005; 145)

However reality TV may give the impression that it represents reality, but in truth it does not as it is merely the portrayals and representations that participants want us to see. 'Constructing an identity' in terms of modernity is all related to the idea that function is beauty. Appearance and fashion should have a set structure and purposeful design. This contradicts greatly with the post modern theories, which suggest that identity can be constructed through fashion, with the idea of it being a subjective Dadaism. Wilson (1992) rationalises this view stating that 'post modernity questions the belief in continuous progress, evolution and dominancc of scientific rationality.'

When theorising 'identity' we must go back to the 18th and 19th century to consider the feminist views of how women should not be objectified by men, with their appearance and identity being dictated to by the other sex. They fought for the return of functional modes of dress, instead of garments like the restricting corsets, which became popular back in the 16th century.

Although the feminists were against the 19th century views of restrictive clothing, they still differ in contrast to post modern theorists who believe that it is the ability to construct an identity that is liberating, unlike the feminist view of the natural body and functional dress being liberating.

The post modern theories are very much centred on individuality and how everyone is capable of deciphering and expressing who they are through fashion. Malcolm Barnard (2001) believes that fashion reconstructs and reproduces existing class and gender identities'. This explains why during the 21st century, gender identities have become a lot more blurred in comparison to the 18th and 19th century. Although a person's sex is obviously scientifically decided, their gender is again an issue for them to resolve and discover, as these days it is much more common to see transsexuals or cross dressers.

Gender is a major component of constructing an identity and it is partly aided by fashion, which helps a person to distinguish themselves as more masculine or feminine. In recent times it is not just fashion that has been used as a tool in the construction of a person's identity, now it is becoming increasingly popular for people to permanently alter their physical appearance through cosmetic surgery. Imitation is a big factor of people undergoing such drastic procedures as they see their favourite celebrities doing it and that may be who they aspire to be. Also there are a number of television programmes now, which are dedicated to helping a person find or express their identity. There are huge variances in these as well though, which proves that 'constructing an identity' to some maybe a more emotional process whereas others take the physical route. For instance Gok Wan's show 'how to look good naked' takes inspiration from the feminists as it is all related to finding your identity through gratifying and accepting your own individual bodyand taking liberation from it, just the way it is. In comparison the show '10 years younger' takes a different concept, focusing on altering the body in a physical way through cosmetic surgery as well as fashion to create an individual's desired identity. It is the actual practice of construction in this case, which is shown to be liberating, very much like the views of post modern theorists.

The reconstruction of the women's identity is to become more attractive and appeal to the opposite sex. However, there are other aims to constructing an identity, supported by the reality TV show '10 Years Younger' which promotes drastic measures such as plastic surgery and teeth veneers to disguise the age of older women feeling the need to compete with the younger generation.

This idea of constructing a stereo typical female identity is promoted further by the media, fashion and celebrity magazines pressure women to strive for the perfection that they see on the air brushed pages. The fashion industry promotes being very thin as fashionable and as the accepted female image, the idolisation of celebrities in the magazines and models on the catwalks inspire women to diet to achieve this body image. Size zero models have been blamed for anorexia in young women, however, Wilson (1992) regards these views as over simplistic, as body discipline was present in the 19th century through the constraints of corsets and believes the mental attitude to exercise and diet is as psychologically constraining. Feminist theorists argue for the return of the natural body before either of these idealist constructions of identity. Whereas post modern theorist such as view constructing an identity as liberating to women. Madonna is constantlyreconstructing her identity through fashion, hair and make up, she veered away from theconventional female image in the late 1970's when she had short spiky hair and often took a masculine approach to clothing choosing black blazers as a signature look. She changed her image in the 1980's and adopted the punk to appeal to the mass market and adapt herself to popular culture, similarly at present she has created a new feminine identity with her long blonde hair and slim figure to comply with the current trend of femininity.

Subcultures

Subcultures are a formation of post modernity, Wilson (1992) believes modernity gave minorities the opportunity to create their own identity. A subculture is a group of people that rebel against popular culture through their image and dress, as well as social behaviour. Subcultures first appeared after World War 2 and emerged quickly in the boom of the 1950's. Subcultures are distinctive in their dress, and often in their social behaviour and activities, and are usually formed for aesthetic, religious, political or sexual reasons.

Cohen (1955) was the first writer to evolve the theory of sub-cultural crime in the working classes. Essentially he identified that groups of young working class males become alienated from the requirements of mainstream culture. They are subsequently then given low status and seen as the 'losers' in society. These 'deviants' then join together with others they view as the same as them selves and form a sub-culture. These sub-culture then form there own norms and values which differ from those of mainstream society.

American sociologist Cloward and Ohlin (1961) provide an explanation as to why subcultures form and there distinctive natures. They argue that varied social environments provide differing opportunities for deviant behaviour, which in term allows the development of varying sub-culture. The writer identifies three types of these sub-cultures. The first is a criminal sub-culture where there are adult role models and opportunities for criminal behaviour. Second the conflict sub-culture which leads to gang war fare. And the third is the retreative sub-culture where there is neither the means for criminal nor conflict behaviour and groups of illegal drug users or drunken behaviour will result.

Winlow (2001) however feels that Cloward and Ohlin ignore the overlaps between their stated subcultures, and many groups can have elements are all three aspects in therebehaviour.

A current example of a subculture is 'Football Hooligans' their formation was prompted through aesthetics, sporting interests and the desire to show unity. The first football hooligans appeared in the 1960's when their defining fashion items were Doc Martin boots. In more recent times particular brands were associated with certain teams supporters, Fred Perry was linked with Manchester United supporters and Lacoste with Liverpool FC. The modern day Football hooligans are typically white middle class males, they define themselves primarily through dress and their thug attitude, socially they are renowned for socialising in pubs and causing trouble at football matches. Subcultures unify themselves through dress to demonstrate their belongingness to the group. Football hooligans achieve this identity through certain brands such as Adidas, which now have connotations to this subculture. This can be very damaging to the brands who do not target this particular market. An example of this is Burberry, which became their signature brand in the 1990's, the famous Burberry check was instantly associated with football hooligans and the 'chav' culture that they represented. As a result of this Burberry discontinued much of its check branded merchandise including the infamous peaked cap to disassociate themselves from the subculture as the association was damaging to the brand. However, there are many other brands such as Stone Island and CP Company that do want to be associated with this subculture shown through their compliance to have their clothes featured in films such as Football Factory. This subculture of Football hooligans did not primarily set out to rebel against the mainstream cultures so as they have been more widely adopted they appear not to have lost the power of subversion but created masscustomisation for many of the brands they wear (Vignali 2006).

The Punks were one subculture that gathered momentum in both America and Britain in the 1970's. Punk coincided with the end of the era of the post war consensus to politics and the political rise of Thatcherism, with nearly all the British punk band expressing an attitude of angry social alienation. The original Punk sub-cultures were actually formed at different times in different areas due to different circumstances, some succeed and influenced others and some failed and diminished. The Punk culture was influenced by Bands at the time such as The Rolling Stones and Velvet underground. A British designer such as Vivienne Westwood incorporated the Punk look into her style and was known for being outrageous with her designs.

Punk fashion culture evolved in reaction to the Thatcherite materialistic ideology, particularly in areas of society that could participate in the upsurge of designer label fashion. Therefore members of this subculture would utilise second hand clothes held together with pins, full of holes. So the adoptions of designers such as Vivienne Westwood of this mode of dress the antithesis of the conceptualisation of the Punk movement. Thus bringing it out of the sub-culture to the main stream fashion design labels and so the Punks join the Thatcherite revolution.

What makes subcultures distinctive is their common aim to deviate their identities from the majority. They do this through representing their outward appearance in terms of dress, attitude and behaviour in an almost rebellious way. With factors such as age, race, class, gender, music tastes being crucial characteristics that can define them as a particular subculture.

Hip-hop is a strong example of a subculture, starting as an American musical genre. Its followers are distinctive in that the majority tend to be African American, around early teens up to late 20's/30's from working class backgrounds. Hip-hop became extremely popular during the 70's, with it being an actual way of life. It consists of four main interpretations which are; Mcing/rapping, graffiti art and break dancing. All three of which, are mainly trying to convey a political and /or social response to the injustices in the world that they can personally relate to. Over the years hip-hop as a culture has grown, with it now having its own dialect almost, as there are certain slang words that can be depicted in origin directly from hip-hop.

The popularity of hip-hop as a sub culture has been aided, as with most subcultures, by the media. Rap music was originally only likely to be played on channel BET, but it now appears on much more mainstream channels such as VH1, MTV and MTV Base, showing that it is a lot more socially accepted now. The 90's saw the release of many 'Hood films' as audience appreciation grew and also the release of related magazines.

Hip-hop suddenly came to be on a global scale, interweaving its influence with the everyday lives of those who followed it. People idolized their favourite rappers, wanting to be more like them and so this is where aesthetics become the immediate imitation, with followers copying tattoos, hairstyles and dress-code, which tended to be baggy jeans, sneakers, oversized sporting jerseys and 'bling' jewellery.

The brands most closely related to hip-hop today and the ones most likely to be sported by its followers now are 'Baby-Phat', 'Apple Bottoms', 'G-Unit', 'Ecko' and 'Timbaland.'

When looking at the beliefs of different subcultures, the majority seem to be adamant on being individuals and different to the majority. With this mindset being common between subcultures and them growing on such a globalised scale over the past century, it has to be considered whether they will loose their meaning of subversion and with a few more years these subcultures may all become undistinguishable amongst each other.

CHAPTER 2: FASHION IMAGES AND BRAND POSITIONING

IHN HEE CHUNG

Introduction

This chapter focuses on the theme of fashion image and its application to brand positioning. The term image is one of the essential concepts in understanding the consumption of fashion products. Consumers would select a branded product reflecting their own self-images (could be either actual self-images or ideal ones) on the basis of the perceived brand image of the product. At the individual product level, every fashion product has its unique image as an intrinsic attribute, which could be referred as clothing image or fashion image. Actually many research topics of fashion marketing field have been introduced various types of image: self-image, brand image, clothing or fashion image, store image, advertising image, etc. Fashion image is the most essential idea among them for the fashion marketing research and business, because every other types of image are connected with that by any means. This chapter discusses four interesting fashion image-related issues: (a) how fashion images are evaluated by consumers, (b) what kind of images do consumers seek when they purchase fashion items, (c) how fashion images function for product complementarities, and (d) how fashion images can be utilized in brand positioning.

Dimensions of Fashion Images

First of all, we need to know what image is. Yoo and Jin (2001) suggests that the image is a broadly defined concept covering both a visible object (such as Bilt or Gestalt in the German language, and picture, pattern, or frame in English) and the reflection of an unrealistic, virtual, even not existent one. With the development of information technology (IT), we can frequently encounter the word image where the word is synonymous with icon or any visible symbol. On the other hand, in the long tradition of philosophy, aesthetics, psychology, and other disciplines of art and human science, the abstract feature of the image has been the main subject of interest. The concept of image goes beyond the simple description of external visible feature of objects, so image is closely related with the human mind and mentality. It is a useful tool to understand consumers as human beings. Also, it enables us to understand from the individual decision making of fashion consumers, to the collective behaviors of social organizations.

The most basic classification scheme of fashion images is drawing a line between the feminine and the masculine image (Chung & Rhee, 1992). The ancient Chinese had an idea of the Yin-Yang (moon and sun; female and male) principle. According to this principle, every object in the world, whether it is from nature or of man-made, could be divided into Yin or Yang. The latter represents firmness, strength, endurance, and the masculine qualities found in the bright sun and the sturdy oak tree, while the former represents the opposite: gentleness, daintiness, sensitivity, and the feminine qualities found in the softness of the moonlight and the dependence of a clinging vine (McJimsey, 1973). This principle could be applied to a variety of matters, including, intellectual and physical properties.

McJimsey (1973) distinguished six types of style from the extreme Yang to the extreme Yin step by step: dramatic, natural, classic, romantic, gamin, and ingénue. Dramatic and natural styles belong to the Yang range; classic and romantic styles are in the area where Yang and Yin combine; and gamin and ingénue styles belong to the Yin range. These six style types are applicable for different types of people and dresses, alike. According to McJimsey (1973), the style of any person is determined by height, build, posture, face contour, face features, hairstyle, hair color, skin color, manner, voice, gait and gesture, and age. For the dress, the style is determined by silhouette, type and direction of line, scale and post of area or details, color, texture, balance, emphasis, and rhythm. For example, the characteristics of dramatic yang people are tall, slender figure, dark skin, and angular lines. The lines of the face and figure of the natural yang are rather square than angular. The typical classic types have oval shape and restrained curve in the features, facial contours, and hairstyle. The romantic type is distinguished by her unusual beauty and feminine appeal. The quality of gamin and ingénue is essentially youthful. In contrast to the sturdy little boy look of the gamin, the ingénue portrays perfectly the dainty little girl look.

Even though the most prominent criterion in distinguishing fashion images or styles is the masculine-feminine dimension, we need additional criteria to capture the personalized consumers in their fashion taste and the diversified whimsical fashion market. Chung and Rhee (1992) conducted multi-dimensional scaling (MDS) to identify representative criteria in distinguishing fashion images, and proposed three criteria on the basis of the consumers' responses to the image-words for the presented fashion stimuli. They are masculine-feminine, simple-decorative, and pastoral-urbane. Later these will be discussed in detail.

MDS is a statistical technique to identify the position of measured objectives in the consumer's mind space . The results of MDS are presented in the form of a map, which could be utilized widely in planning marketing campaigns. For example, MDS generates a brand positioning map based on the consumers' evaluations of a number of brands. It is possible to find out more or less competitive markets in the brand positioning map. In addition, MDS helps to compare the positions where target consumers are located in relation to the current location of the brand and to give guidance for the re-positioning of the brand.

The MDS is applicable for producing useful criteria to explain seemingly complex fashion images. With MDS, the relative position of each image-word in the mind of people can be identified; and, in addition, the dimensions which summarize the neighboring image-words can be found. The spatial distances among image-words give us insights on the similarities and the differences among them.

The validity of using MDS for the fashion image researches is based on the fact that fashion images occupy consumers' mind space. Fashion image is regarded as the holistic impression that clothing worn on the human body conveys, and can be measured by one's response when one senses the clothing. Normally, the response is represented in adjectival form i.e., "That dress is lovely!"

Semantic differential scaling has been the most widely used tool to measure the fashion images in many preceding studies (for example, Hong, 1988; Kahng & Koh, 1991) using a set of bi-polar adjective pairs; however, this approach has some limitations. Certain images may not have suitable opposites, while others may have multiple opposites. Thus, it is more reasonable to use a single, polar measurement presenting one adjective. Chung and Rhee (1992) used this measuring technique.

In their study, three hundred and eight Korean women aged from their mid-twenties to mid-thirties were asked to evaluate eight fashion stimuli using 53 image-words with a four point Likert-type scale (1-neutral, 2- a little bit agree, 3- agree, 4- strongly agree). These evaluations were used as input data for MDS. The analysis produced three dimensions for fashion image evaluation and/or classification: masculine vs. feminine image, simple vs. decorative image, and pastoral vs. urbane image. Since there are three dimensions, it is difficult to adequately represent them on a two-dimensional space. Thus, it is necessary to draw three maps to understand the relationship between the image words: dimension 1 × dimension 2, dimension 1 × dimension 3, and dimension 2 × dimension 3. A map showing dimension 1 × dimension 2 for the 53 image-words is showed in Figure 1.

From the three maps constructed to understand the relationships of image-words, we can find the result as follows. The first, and most significant, criterion resulting from MDS was the dimension of masculine-feminine, which coincides with the Yin-Yang principle. "Masculine" is in close proximity with sporty, casual, straight, active, etc. In opposition, "feminine" is in close proximity with shapely, slender, mature, curved, etc. The second is the simple-decorative dimension. "Simple" is in close proximity with easy, sober, modest, tidy, etc. In opposition, "decorative" is found to be in close proximity with daring, gorgeous, powerful, dressy, unique, etc. In the last dimension, pastoral-urbane, "pastoral" shows close proximity with oriental, classic, etc., whereas "urbane" is in close proximity with young, modern, western, etc. These three dimensions function as the classification criteria of fashion styles. Thus, these dimensions could act as tools to describe and judge fashion styles. One style may carry masculine, simple, and modern impressions; while, another may carry feminine, decorative, and modern impressions. A total of eight (2 × 2 × 2) combinations to constitute fashion styles are obtained as shown in Figure 2.

Figure 1. Evaluation map of fashion images: masculine – feminine vs. simple – decorative.

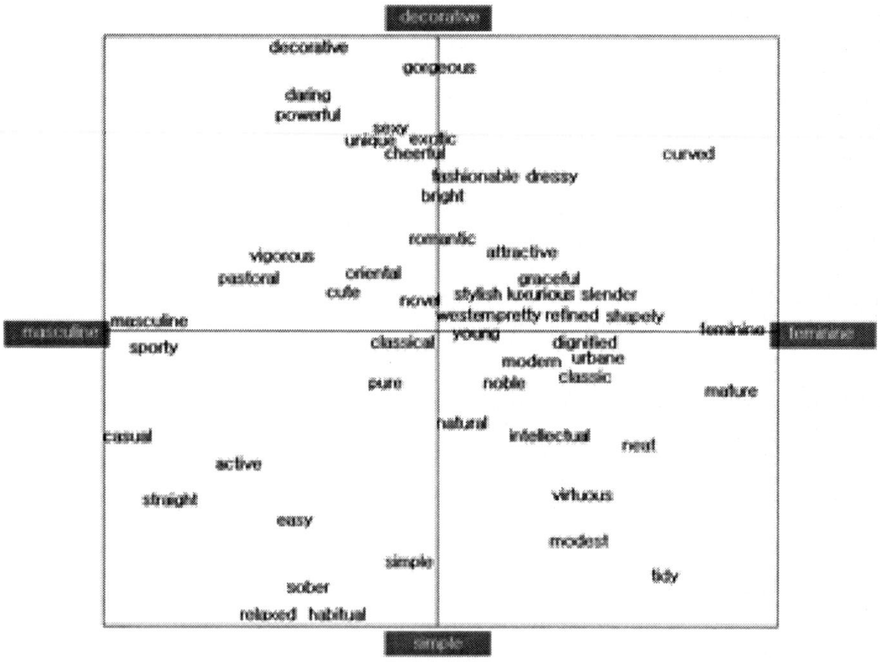

(Chung & Rhee, 1992, p. 387)

Figure 2. Eight fashion styles derived from the combination of three fashion image dimensions.

Desired Self-Image

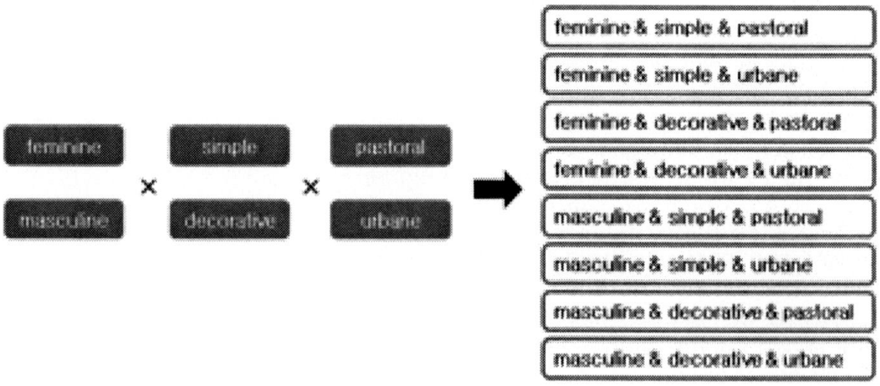

Desired Self-Image

Every person wants to have a beautiful and attractive body and to convey good impressions to others. To be presentable in the most ideal condition one may want to conceal or complement one's physical weakness, or emphasize certain parts of the body. Fashion items are very useful helpers here.

A desired self-image is the image that people want to display to others utilizing fashion items through complementing and emphasizing the image itself, and is influenced by context (Chung, 2001). Two dimensions constructing the self-image – actual vs. ideal and intrinsic vs. phenomenal – are suggested as shown in Figure 3 (Chung and Rhee, 1996). This 2×2 frame of the concept results in 4 categories of self-image. According to this conception, desired self-image belongs to the realm of ideal and phenomenal image, which is rather ideal than actual, and depends on the context or occasion. Therefore, the desired self-image is not the stable and universal feature of a person but the one repeatedly changing according to the context.

Figure 3. Two dimensions to measure self-images.

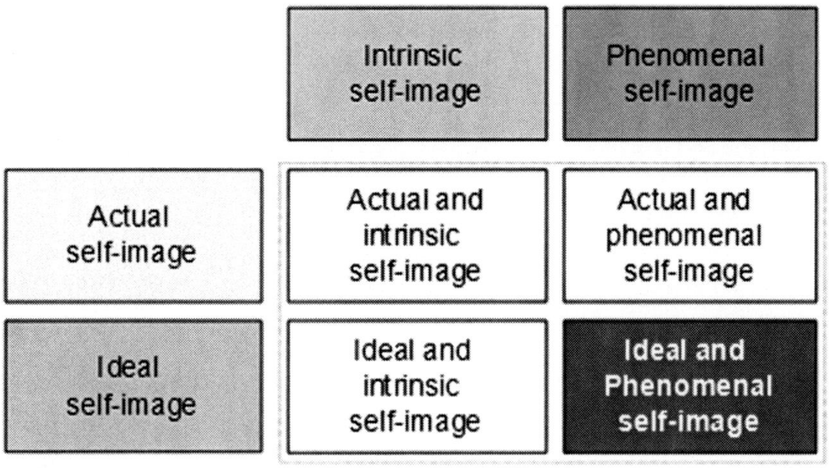

	Intrinsic self-image	Phenomenal self-image
Actual self-image	Actual and intrinsic self-image	Actual and phenomenal self-image
Ideal self-image	Ideal and intrinsic self-image	Ideal and Phenomenal self-image

(source: Chung & Rhee, 1996, p.214)

A series of study to investigate the desired self-image of Korean young people were conducted by Chung and her colleagues (Bae & Chung, 2006; Chung, 2001, 2004; Chung, Bae, & Choo, 2007). According to the results, young Koreans seem to seek for neat, natural, and refined image in the school context in general. They may have different desired self-images in different occasions. Hence, a young man seeking a natural image in everyday life may want to convey a sporty image during workouts, or give an intelligent impression in the interview for the graduate school admission.

Now, we should consider the possibility that one same image-word could be perceived differently by females and males. Chung (2004) found that certain image-words were differently perceived by male and female college students while other image-words had similar meaning schema. Figure 4 presents the perceptual differences between male and female samples. For example, the image-words of neat, natural, refined, vigorous, fashionable, modest, pure, and cute are similarly perceived by male and female students. However, the intellectual image means graceful to female students, and is interpreted as sporty by male students. The masculine image is perceived as a sporty image to female students, while male students feel it represents to a mature image. The feminine image is another image presenting a considerable gap between female and male perceivers. To females, the feminine image is associated with modest, pure, and cute images, while males associate it with sexy and graceful images. Fashion marketers should consider this gender bias when proposing product and promotion strategies. When developing unisex casual clothing lines targeting college students who want to display an intellectual image, it is necessary to add a sporty image to the product assortment for young men, and a graceful image for young women's.

Figure 4. The differentiation of image-word perceptions between male and female samples.

Male Samples		Female Samples
sexy and graceful	feminine	modest, pure and cute
mature	masculine	sporty
intelligent	sporty	masculine
masculine	mature	sober
(sober itself)	sober	mature
feminine and graceful	sexy	(sexy itself)
feminine and sexy	graceful	intelligent
sporty	intelligent	graceful

(Chung, 2004, p. 206)

Fashion Product Unity

Fashion product unity is a significant application of desired self-image. Holbrook and Dixon (1985) defined fashion as, "public consumption through which people communicate to others the image they wish to project," and emphasized the complementarity of fashion products. Fashion pertains not just to one product exclusively, but rather to a number of products fitting together consistently to form a mutually reinforcing representation of the image one wishes to convey (Holbrook & Dixon, 1985). Even though they belong to different product categories, several fashion items help each other to enhance the expression of consumers' preferences. The concept of a complementarity of fashion items should be a useful tool in building efficient fashion marketing strategies: product mix, advertising, promotion, and retail management.

On the consumers' side, they tend to purchase product constellations, that is, complementary products that are symbolically associated to reinforce self-image. We can call a group of goods that complement, harmonize, and unify each other product complements, or Diderot unities. Actually, the notion of Diderot unity came from the essay of Diderot, who was an important contributor to the codification and advancement of knowledge in eighteenth-century France. The summary of the essay entitled "Regrets on Parting with My Old Dressing Gown" was given by McCracken as follows.

This essay begins with Diderot sitting in his study bemused and melancholic. Somehow this study has undergone a transformation. It was once crowded, humble, chaotic, and happy. It is now elegant, organized, beautifully appointed, and a little grim. Diderot suspects the cause of the transformation is his new dressing gown.

This transformation, Diderot tell us, took place gradually and by stages. First, the dressing gown arrived, a gift from a friend. Delighted with his new possession, Diderot allowed it to displace his "ragged, humble, comfortable old wrapper." This proved the first step in a complicated and distressing process. A week or two after the arrival of the dressing gown, Diderot began to think that his desk was not quite

28

up to standard and he replaced it. Then the tapestry on the study wall seemed a little threadbare, and a new one had to be found. Gradually, the entire study, including its chairs, engravings, bookshelf and clock were judged, found wanting, and replaced.

All of this, Diderot concludes, is the work of an "imperious scarlet robe (which) forced everything else to confirm with its own elegant tone." Diderot looks back with fondness and regret to his old dressing gown, and its "perfect accord with the rest of poor bric-a-brac that filled my room." He has lost his dressing gown, the bric-a-brac, and, most important, the accord itself. "Now the harmony is destroyed. Now there is no more consistency, no more unity, and no more beauty." This unhappy revelation constitutes what is likely the first formal recognition of a cultural phenomenon here called the "Diderot unity" and the "Diderot effect." (McCracken, 1988, pp. 118-119)

As the specific terminology for fashion items, fashion product unity could be used instead of Diderot unity. This fashion product unity reflects the desired self-images and depends on the social settings. Bae and Chung (2006) found out Korean male students' desired self-images and fashion product unities for four occasions: school, dates, ceremonies, and workouts. For example, in the school setting, the most frequently desired self-image of male students was a simple image: A round shirt, jeans, running shoes, a bag, and a watch were selected as the fashion product unity for that image. They desired a natural image the most for the setting of dates, and they made up the fashion product unities with the combination of aloha shirt/knitted shirt/V-neck shirt, cotton pants/jeans/semi-formal pants, formal shoes/running shoes, and a watch. Figure 5 shows the illustrations of fashion product unities.

Figure 5. Examples of fashion product unity: for school setting and meeting girlfriends.

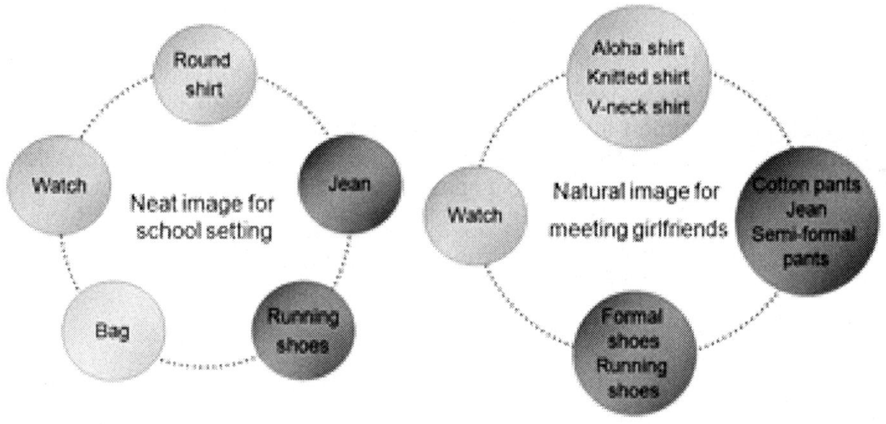

(Bae & Chung, 2006, p. 1143)

The introduction of the fashion product unity concept certainly should contribute to the whole fashion merchandising process, from manufacturing to retailing. With the knowledge of fashion product unity, it is possible to predict the fashion items that consumers will consider purchasing next, on the basis of their purchasing patterns. Fashion product unity theory proposes consumers would have potential needs to reinforce the images of the current possessions with new products if the images are desirable (Bae & Chung, 2006; McCracken, 1988). The concept warns that the perception of the target market for the current merchandise should be considered in product development, line extension, and any expanding strategy. Any image gap, the consumers feel, with their possessions should be monitored in a careful manner. Also fashion retailers are able to utilize this information for assortment planning, merchandise arrangement, and visual display, so as to promote cross-selling. They can stock and display the merchandise, that convey similar images while belong to different product type, together. Moreover, they can select their store location near to the ones selling their complements. Usually, a brand is positioned associated with its image in the consumers' mind and in the marketplaces; therefore, fashion marketers and retailers are able to utilize the declared brand positioning to capture the counterparts' brand image.

Fashion Brand Positioning

Today's marketing practice aims to offer the right product to a target segment rather than to sell everything to the whole market. In other words, STP (segmentation, targeting, and positioning) marketing replaced mass marketing and product-variety marketing. In spite of the recent attentions to mass-customization by some researchers and marketing staffs, STP marketing is still the most common and popular marketing concept. The first step of STP marketing is the segmentation of the market. The market is segmented based on the buyers' characteristics: residential region; demographic variables such as age, gender, family size, family life cycle, income, occupation, education, religion, race, and nationality; psychographic variables such as social class, lifestyle, and personality; buying attitudes and practices including usage occasions, benefits, user status, usage rate, loyalty status, readiness stage, and attitude toward product (Kotler, 1994). At the stage of targeting, any one segment or combination of segments is selected as the target market through the process of segment evaluation. This evaluation is conducted in terms of segment size and growth, segment structural attractiveness, and company objectives and resources. Lastly, the positioning stage follows.

Brand positioning is regarded as a process to occupy a certain location in the target consumers' mind, and the location of the brand is relatively determined by comparing competing brands (Ries & Trout, 1981). Therefore, in the perspective of a product developer, it is important to know the criteria with which consumers recognize and evaluate the product, and determine the appealing points for positioning. Appealing points for product positioning can be categorized by attributes or benefits; price or quality; use application or usage occasion; product user, product class, and competitors (Aaker and Shansby, 1982; Kotler, 1994; Reibstein, 1985).

In fashion markets, there is too much merchandise to construct a concise positioning map. Hence, brand positioning is more common than product positioning. An example of a brand positioning map for a women's prestige fashion market is given in Figure 6. To develop a brand positioning map, two positioning axes are required. In this example, one axis is simple-romantic image, and the other is young-mature image.

Figure 6. An example of brand positioning map.

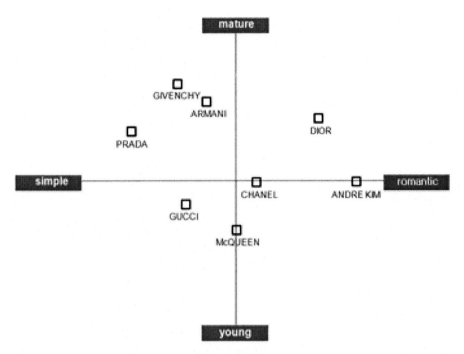

The most popular positioning axis in fashion brand poisoning maps is age: Price and quality follow. In addition to these three axes, many image-words are used as positioning axes. As we noticed, there are three main criteria of fashion images: masculine vs. feminine image, simple vs. decorative image, and pastoral vs. urbane image, which could be valuable brand positioning axes.

Previously, we discussed the limitation of semantic differential scaling. We can find similar problems in multiple opposing images for one image in many fashion companies' brand positioning maps. For example, the opposing images of casual have been suggested to be formal, classic, and elegant; and the opposing images of classic are often country, modern or casual images. So, how can we validate the existence of multiple opposing images for one?

To give a flexible answer to this question, Chung and Rhee (1993) conducted a cluster analysis to reveal the hierarchy of fashion images. As a result of clustering 53 adjectives, a dendrogram was obtained. This dendrogram presents the whole procedure of adjectives grouping, from the individual 53 to a single group. Figure 7 shows a portion of the grouping procedure. Here, 11 images are grouped and regrouped. Based on this hierarchy, we can select any two images not belonging to the same group in any distance point. Thus, the graceful image can be the opposite of the masculine image, active image, sober image, etc.

The benefit of this hierarchy solution is its flexibility and relativity. The opponent is never determined in advance. Two images that are assigned to different groups in the lower portion of the hierarchy, although they belong to the same group in the higher portion, could be opposed to each other, and therefore be used as two polar images in a brand positioning map. Marketers have a lot of discretion in selecting fashion image-words for making up brand poisoning maps.

Figure 7. The hierarchy of fashion images for women's fashion.

(Chung & Rhee, 1993, p. 534)

Fashion images are a serviceable concept for helping each brand to establish its positioning, and thereby to construct a brand positioning map. From many commercial brand positioning maps, multiple opponents for one image word are observed. To give a clear explanation to this confused condition, cluster analysis, a statistical technique, is applied. The image hierarchy, as the result of a clustering process using dendrogram, can be utilized broadly by the fashion marketers who want to build a brand positioning map.

In today's diversified market, the image is gaining more attention, because it provides valuable insights and helps to satisfy consumers' diverse tastes. Understanding the worth of fashion image and developing its application for fashion marketing strategies will be helpful to survive in the severely competitive fashion market. Especially three important concepts relating to fashion image (desired self-image, fashion product unity, and brand positioning) will give the marketers meaningful insight predicting fashion consumers' selection.

Figure 9. The hierarchy of fashion images for women's fashion.

(Chung & Rhee, 1993, p. 534)

CHAPTER 3:THE SOCIAL DIMENSION OF BUYING: OPPORTUNITIES RESULTING FROM NEW RETAILING FORMS

ALFONSO SIANO, MARIA GIOVANNA CONFETTO, GIANPAOLO BASILE & GIANPAOLO VIGNALI

Postmodernism: various schools of thought

This section aims to provide a contribution with regard to the evolution of marketing and communication studies in general, and to the relationship between brand and consumer. The study focuses particular attention on the role of social actor which brands increasingly have to impose in order to create, maintain or strengthen their links with the individual/consumer.

To this end the work is based on a presupposed concept borrowed from a social psychology principle, according to which the individual, by nature, tends to develop both their own "self" (concept, image, identity) and their "social identification" in the ambit of social groups (Turker, 1957; Turner, 1982; Schlenker, 1986; Brewer and Gardner, 1996). Social psychology studies have contributed a great deal to clarifying the changing social processes recorded throughout the last fifty years, caused by the passage from industrialised society by way of modernism to postmodernism. These changes have involved every form of society, from political to philosophical, from sociological to marketing, evolving the role in society both of the individual and of institutions in general, and in particular of the business. From a social point of view the individual has evolved its role, passing from the constant search for individual differentiation and extreme utilitarian relationships, elements which characterise modernistic society, to the search for rational and unconditional individualism – that is, to a condition of constant search for the self with the outcome of making oneself noticed and distinguishing oneself from others. The postmodern individual seeks to behave towards activating a large number of autonomous choices, with the result of producing and demonstrating their own existence and their differences in respect to others. This trend, in the last twenty years, has become the basis of an important reference point on the part of marketing researchers and practitioners, relative to concepts such as extreme individualism, social mobility of the individual, the difficulty in homologation of the individual into clusters, the fragmentation of ever more ephemeral consumerism and social links chosen rather than imposed, based on the sharing of emotions derived from the symbol/brand.

The evolutionary cycle between individualism and social links has revealed the emergence of two different streams of study in the phenomenon of postmodern consumerism, one North European and the other Latin/Mediterranean. The North European School is characterised by the definition of consuming as an act of self-definition by the consumer (Firat and Venkatesh, 1993; Firat and Shultz II, 1997). This stream of study sustains that postmodernism is the era in which the individual can and must put personal actions in place to customize and demonstrate themselves (their own existence) and their differences (Elliott, 1997). The North European School considers tribes, specific social groups, as alternative social enclaves on the outskirts of society (Firat and Dholakia, 1998). These considerations have caused two important aspects to emerge from postmodernism: (1) the individual evolves as sovereign subject at the centre of marketing activities, participating in the personalization of its world, of its image (its symbolic system), providing input, living direct experiences and expressing fragmented modes of being; (2) consuming, from a natural economic transaction, becomes the principle form of language by which the individual communicates their own identity to themselves and to others. In this respect Firat sustains that:

> *"The postmodern consumer recognizes that they are not just a consumer, but a customizer and a producer of (self-)images at each consumptive moment" (Firat et al., 1995).*

These aspects clearly show the emergence of the new figure of the consumer which no longer represents a segment/destined target of products and services, fruit of an unnatural correspondence with the firm/brand, but evolves and becomes a co-producer of experiences, of symbolic significance in the creation of fragmented and fluid self-image. These changes weaken the validity of traditional marketing concepts and tools, such as segmentation and analysis of positioning (Blattberg and Deighton, 1991). They make it necessary to carry out more active/participative analysis (interaction based), conducted with tools like ethno-sociology and/or network analysis.

The new trends favour marketing behaviour that offers contexts to the consumer in which the individual can live out experiences and experiment with their own self-image diverse from their role in society. Lately businesses, aware of these social trends of the individual, tend towards stimulation of search for the "self", seeking to suggest their own products/ brands as ideal partners in reaching the individual's social objective. Businesses actually seek to stimulate this dyadic relationship with the individual, in support of the expression of "I", by means of communication activities. One is reminded of the claim "Just do it" by Nike, or Apple's insertion of the "I" prefix in their products such as the I-pod and the Iphone.

In contrast to the North European School, the Latin/Mediterranean School considers the phase of individualism as the conclusive part of the modern period, marked by the freedom of the individual from socially-imposed links (for example, social class). For scholars following this thought, consumerism represents an inversion of social trends, so as to allow creation or maintenance of links between individuals (Maffesoli, 1996; Bauman, 1990).

From this perspective new technologies, which have always been considered a cause of social isolation, have become the means and the places in which re-socialization of the individual can be fulfilled. One thinks of the spreading of social networks and themed blogs, or of the stimulus given to customers and web-site visitors by businesses in order to create communities. These social dynamics are often represented by a multitude of experiences and emotions which are born from the behaviour of the individual and culminate in a demonstration of tribalism, or spontaneous social aggregation founded on the sharing of experiences, emotions and passions between individuals.

The Latin/Mediterranean School pays particular attention to the role of the tribe, and sustains that every individual, however socially mobile, is a component of tribes and plays a different role in each tribe. This train of thought emphasises the constant search for multisensory experiences both as spectator and protagonist, which lead the individual towards new forms of social aggregation in tribes and in neo-communities, characterised by increased involvement but resulting in being provided with links. The tribe, understood as the dynamic and flexible positioning of the individual, tends in this way to substitute concepts of social class and segmentation which are themselves representative of socially static positioning.

The view of the Latin/Mediterranean School changes the outcome of marketing, which functions as a "vector of tribal and social links" by which products and services permit and support social interaction between individuals. This evolution, induced both by new trends and by the constant search for the self and for social relationships on the part of the individual, is modifying the application of traditional marketing mix variables, especially in respect to communications and distribution. These effects drive businesses to radically modify their behaviour in marketing, passing from a general broadcasting approach aimed at a mass of predefined individuals to a narrow or net-casting approach as a result of which businesses express awareness of the constant search for individuality, even within groups, on the part of the consumer. This evolutionary trend drives businesses to modify their approach to the consumer, moving from a unidirectional "from-to" relationship to "between"-type networking.

The identification of the individual in a group, therefore, expresses the degree of selfperception, both individually and as a member of a group in relationship with other members and with the business/brand. This level of perception is developed based on sharing specific attributes of the product/brand – functional and above all symbolic - with other members (Dutton and Celia, 1994). The condition of identification by the individual satisfies the double need for developing the concept of self and identification with belonging to social groups (Mael and Ashforth, 1992). The achievement of this condition is demonstrated by the creation of a sense of belonging by the member both towards the group/community and the business/brand (McAlexander, Schouten, and Koenig, 2002; Muniz, O'Guinn, 2001).

Individuals do not seek out new products and/or services or places from which to buy in order to be more free, but rather to experience emotions which can link them to other individuals. Businesses emerge from this effect with a new social role, first through the products and/or services/brands and then through the creation of links. The places forconsuming and acquiring, therefore, transform into places for actual self-concept and social identification – actual "containers" which, by effect of their spaces and variety, transform into places of identity, for socialization and aggregation (Cardinali, 2009; Codeluppi, 2000).

Businesses do not limit themselves to creation of products ad hoc, but they often stimulate or ask for commitment from the individual in co-production of products. This redefinition ofboundaries, on the part of businesses, has been nourished recently by the multiplication ofchannels, places and moments of contact, fruit of an ever-clearer consumer connectionstrategy. Businesses increasingly target their actions in order to co-involve the stimulatedindividual to immerge themselves in the value element of the brand.

Distributive formats favourable to vertical branding strategy The most significant efforts made towards creation of a strong bond between brand and consumer are found in distribution, a place of value and perception in which the individual can express their own identity and their social identification. The sales point thus becomes the place of realisation, of experience and emotions, as much as possible unique and unrepeatable. Management of the customer experience (Berry et. al., 2002; Haeckel et. al., 2003; Schmitt, 2003) becomes the key managerial function.

Not only franchising but also, and above all, the recent concept stores, flagship stores and temporary shops, represent distribution formats in which the individual can immerge themselves in the value of the brand and create relationships with other consumers attracted to the brand value. These formats allow companies to activate vertical branding strategies (Richardson, 1996; Ravazzoni and Petruzzellis, 2004), fruit of the integration between production and retail. The focus on the social dimension of buying allows identification of vertical branding strategy and the characterization of two different strategic options: corporate vertical branding and cooperative vertical branding. Cooperative vertical branding brings about creation of contractual vertical marketing systems (Kotler, 1991), through affiliation, of which franchising is the most significant expression.

Corporate vertical branding, however, the system of vertical branding by companies (Kotler, 1991), is realised in the opening of single-brand stores managed directly by the producers. This is also the case with concept stores, flagship stores and temporary shops.

Franchising

In order to examine the franchising concept, it is necessary to investigate what is meant by the term franchising and how this method of doing business came about, the variations that exist, and the advantages and disadvantages to both the franchiser and the franchisee.

The Dictionary of Retailing defines the term, "franchise," as: •

"An authorisation granted to one person (the franchisee) to use the franchiser's trade name, trade marks and business system in return for an initial payment and further regular payments."

The term franchise covers a wide variety of arrangements under which the owner of a product, a process, a service or even just a name having a certain significance, for example that of a sportsman, permits another to make or use something in exchange for some form of payment. This can either be direct, for example a fee and/or royalty, or indirect in the form of an obligation to buy a service or product in which the license holder has some kind of business interest. It is unclear when franchising as a business concept, started, but its origins can be traced back at least to the 19th century. The first recognisable franchises were launched by Coca-Cola and the US car industry about a century ago. Many variations exist today. Some franchisers sell their products and techniques as a combination whereas other franchisers supply only the modus operandi and ancillary services of the business system. A classic example of the first type is Coca-Cola, which franchises bottlers in nearly every part of the world. The parent company sells its syrup, which is made to a secret formula. It provides franchisees or bottlers with manuals that define (and demand compliance with) the size and shape of bottles, advertising programmes, marketing techniques, and standardised systems of every aspect of the business.

The combination of one central organisation developing the entire, "package," and leasing it out to the franchisees is so effective that billions of dollars in profit have been generated for companies like Coca-Cola and Benetton, and billions of satisfied customers have been created world-wide.

Those franchisers that supply the modus operandi and subsidiary services of the business system sell only their knowledge, operation manuals, and marketing methods. This is paid for in various ways such as a franchise fee, and often includes an on-going percentage of profit or turnover as royalties, or a fixed-fee royalty.

The business format franchising has been responsible for the rapid growth in the franchised marketing method. It involves the use not only of goods and services identified by trademarks, and/or service marks, but also the preparation of a, "blueprint," of a successful way of operating all aspects of a business.

The seller of the, "blueprint," (the franchiser) will have prepared and smoothed the way for the franchisee to open up a business of his or her own in the predetermined established format. The franchisee will also have the backing of the franchiser organisation. Analysis of the work of Hall and Dixon (1989) and Golzen, Barrow and Severn (1985) and sustained by others, indicates that the main features of business format franchising are as follows:

1. It is a licence for a special period of time to trade in a defined geographic area under the franchiser's name and to use any associated trade mark or logo.

2. What is franchised is an activity, usually some form of service, which has already been tried and tested to produce a formula of operating that has been found to work elsewhere.

3. The franchiser provides the entire business concept of that formula (the blueprint) for the conduct of operations which the franchisee must follow.

4. The franchiser educates the franchisee in how to conduct the business according to the method laid down in the blueprint.

5. The franchiser provides back-up services in order to ensure that he franchise operates successfully.

6. In the exchange for the business blueprint and the services that the franchiser provides, the franchisee is expected to make an initial investment in the business and to pay a royalty to the franchiser thereafter, based on turnover or profits. There may also be an obligation on the franchisee to buy some or all goods and equipment from sources nominated by the franchiser.

7. The participation of the franchiser in setting up the business does not mean that s/he owns it. It belongs to the franchisee and s/he is free to dispose of it, though s/he will probably have to give the franchiser first refusal. Benetton is a good example of a company using business format franchising. It operates in the clothing market world-wide from its base in Italy.

In Field 1 of Nicosia's Model the company's attributes lead to a message which in turn tempers the consumer's attributes. In our case and especially as Business Format Franchising is the key, the company's attributes become the organisations attributes andcan thus be further explained by the diagram below:-

The Nicosia model focuses not on the act of purchasing itself, but the processes which proceed and follow the act. "The act of purchasing is only one component of a complex ongoing process – a process of many interactions amongst many variables." The firms attribute leads to a message being sent out to the consumer who in turn translates the message based on their own attributes and needs.

Hence the company's behaviour affects the consumer and the consumers reaction in turn affects the behaviour of the company. Nicosia conceptualises consumer behaviour itself as a decision process, rather than as a result of a decision process. Nicosia's emphasis on decision making as an ongoing process is paramount. When a buyer is beginning to purchase a product, s/he lacks experience. S/he lacks knowledge of choice criteria, as such elements of the retail marketing mix, or knowledge of the brand and its potential.

The general models of consumer behaviour do not provide a basis for predicting outcomes as they stand. They do not provide a clear picture of the types of factors that may be said to impinge on such behaviour, though in each case such a picture is partial. Broadly, each model contains variables that may be connected with the individual consumers characteristics, purchase situation characteristics and product characteristics. Each model includes a number of characteristics in each variable group, which militates against their straightforward extension (as flow models, inclusion of partly additional factors requires considerable revision). However, the Nicosia model offers greater scope for amendment/ extension for two chief reasons: -

1. The group of variables associated with, "company," impacts on consumer is not fleshed out;

2. The model groups together variables within sub-fields, thus allowing modification/extension without compromising its original integrity. For these reasons the Nicosia model appears to allow for as great a scope for proactive behaviour.

Concept stores and temporary shops

The function of thematic sales points renders the concept store the place where the consumer can not only buy products but also come into close contact with the "world" proposed by the brand, immersing themselves into the "business philosophy", into the spirit and history of the brand, into a memorable shopping experience. One of the first examples of concept store took place in 1986 in New York, where the stylist Ralph Lauren inaugurated his first concept store. He chose "American-style" as his theme, the store was constructed as a film set that suggested an American atmosphere, an ideal and luxurious style of life. In Italy in the 1980s, the stylist Elio Fiorucci united the sale of fashion, technology and articles for the home in one unique space, paying great attention to atmosphere and to the shopping experience. Recently the well-known car producer Ferrari has inaugurated its own concept store in Regent Street, London's famous shopping street.

The temporary shop, which appeared early in the 2000s, expressed a new retail concept, strongly innovative with respect to the traditional distributive formula. It was an attempt to transform the shop into an event and, therefore, as a branding instrument, to get near to consumers, to promote an active dialogue with them and to develop a relationship with them through the customer experience. There are many diverse cases of temporary store (Nivea, Lagostina, Saeco, Barilla, Breil, Chanel, Durex, Fiat, Gabetti, Lancôme, Levi's, L'Oreal, Nike, Philips,Veuve Clicquot) both in Italy and abroad.

This new format aims:

1. to arouse curiosity, to attract attention and to give visitors unique experiences and to feed their emotions by way of being an unrepeatable happening, destined to be exhausted in a short space of time;

2. to experiment with the effectiveness of brand extension projects (Aaker & Keller, 1990; Park et. al., 1991, 1996; Smith, 1992; Keller & Aaker, 1992, 1998; Sullivan, 1992; Rao & Ruekert, 1994; Choi, 1998) with reference to new segments of consumerism in contrast to those which traditionally presided. Durex implemented this strategy in their clothing line, and Nivea in their hair care category;

3. to launch new exclusive product lines (for limited periods), destined to personalize goods on offer;

4. to test new products (exploration of customers' tastes) before definite launch on a large scale;

5. to develop the relationship with the client and to acquire immediate informative feedback (awareness of the target, with respect to their needs, orientation and behaviour).

Temporary shops are located in large urban metropolitan centres, in zones which are particularly representative, in famous and prestigious streets and squares, in places exclusive to fashion and dedicated to shopping.

The search for locations attractive to visitors can also present the choice of places linked to culture (museums and art galleries). For example, Louis Vuitton designed an exclusive temporary shop inside the Brooklyn Museum in New York. Previously unknown places can also become the location of temporary shops, by way of the fact that these can feed curiosity and be spread by word of mouth by the public. Target has opened a temporary shop on a boat that sails along the Hudson River in New York.

The setting up of temporary shops and concept stores (Kotler, 1973; Donovan & Rossiter, 1982) plays a fundamental role in their success, these spaces being perceived in a strongly innovative and attractive manner. Visitors are offered spaces in which to relax, with multisensory visual marketing stimuli and experiences (Langrehr, 1991; Botti & Castaldo, 2001). Inside these spaces, visitors can take advantage of experiential shopping or, if they like, emotional shopping and hedonistic consumption (Hirschman & Holbrook, 1982; Holbrook & Hirshmann, 1982; Botti et. al., 1999; Pine & Gilmore, 1999; Schmitt, 1999; Codeluppi, 2001; Vescovi & Checchinato, 2004; Carpenter et. al., 2005). The uniqueness of the acquisition experience is often combined with the uniqueness of the products on offer (exclusive product lines, produced in limited edition, not on sale in the general market). The temporary shop avails itself of promotional support and information by various means of communication, above all by digital technology (company web-sites, mini-sites and blogs created for the occasion) in order to activate the process of viral marketing (Godin, 2000).

The temporary store and the concept store converge in the thematic temporary store, which can respond to diverse needs. Primarily, temporary shops can be dedicated to a target aimed for by consumers, as was done by United Colors of Benetton when they inaugurated their first temporary store in Milan, dedicated exclusively to children, in June 2008. The thematic temporary store can also provide the emblem of a specific theme that recalls the concept of basic brand positioning, expressed through the company claim/ slogan. This in theory aims on focussing competitive positioning on starting points (van Riel, 1995), that is to say, on the distinctive value of the elements on which the difference of the brand is founded and the promise it makes to the customer (Keller, 1998; Aaker, 2004). For example, Philips dedicated a temporary shop to the theme of "simplicity". In fact, the claim/slogan was "Sense and Simplicity", through which Philips expressed its brand promise. This included the intention of the company to create advanced easy-touse products and solutions to satisfy the needs of consumers all over the world. Philips opened the thematic temporary store in mid-December 2008 (closing in mid-January 2009) in Milan, which offered visitors the opportunity to personally experiment with Philips' "simple technology". Fiat also opened a themed temporary store in Milan, entirely dedicated to the new Fiat 500, to its values and to all those passionate about this model which made history for the Turin company.

Flagship stores

The flagship store has for many years represented an important opportunity to add value to strong brands (Kozinets et. al., 2002; Moore & Doherty, 2007). This particular distributive format is considered above all as a channel of communication. The pre-requisite for a single-brand flagship store is the possession of an already well-established brand (Aaker & Joachimsthaler, 2000). The "Epicentro" flagship stores, opened by Prada in New York and Tokyo, represent examples emblematic of the communicative force of these distributive formats supported by the existence of a previously well-established brand identity.

The communicative value, more than the distributive value, attributes particular relevance to the elements of entertainment in the flagship store, most of all in the ambit of the fashion system and the luxury sector – so much as to induce various authors to speak of making sales points into "theaters" (Pine & Gilmore, 1999; Wolf, 1999), and of the "show" of merchandise (Codeluppi, 2000). In consequence, the furnishings and structure exposed in this type of sales point are considered scenic elements of a theatre (Grove & Fisk, 1992).

The various theatrical elements in a flagship store (symbols, colours, music etc) represent by definition the many elements expressed in the world of the brand (Semprini, 2003), elements to make the acquiring experience unforgettable and always new (Aaker & Joachimsthaler, 2000).

To give an idea of the complex function carried out by the flagship store, the metaphor "laboratory" has also been suggested. The term "laboratory" indicates a place in which certain activities are carried out, the participants being actively involved and interacting both between themselves and with the equipment put at their disposition. From this perspective, the flagship store can be seen as a container that allows experimentation with new solutions, the discovery of solutions appreciated by customers and the reapplication of these solutions (Aaker & Joachimsthaler, 2000). Experimentation is linked in this way to the idea of the laboratory, which expresses a platform for relationships and the durable links of learning between the company (brand) and the consumer (Pellegrini, 2001). The idea of the sales point which goes beyond being the mere traditional meeting point between production and consumer to becoming transformed into a laboratory allows us to recognize it as a space where the company-customer relationship becomes a point for mutual learning (Pine & Gilmore, 1999).

The metaphor of the theatre, and more accurately, that of the laboratory, allows us to understand the reason why the flagship store is associated with the phenomenon of the shopping experience and the brand, and has also been attributed with the function of experience provider (Schmitt, 1999) inside the store.

Although the temporary store and the flagship store share the elements of theatre and experiential shopping, they present differences that can be taken back to a fundamental factor: time, or rather the use which is made of it. For the temporary store, the brevity of the life cycle makes this distributive formula a store-event; in the case of the flagship store the duration of the structure allows it to be stationed in specific places, so as to permit it to carry out its activities until its function is fulfilled. As a matter of fact, once created, the space that represents the best expression and the symbol of excellence of a company's brand cannot be seen to cease to exist but, on the contrary, must last through the course of time to confirm and consolidate its presence and to give its customers the possibility to visit at any time and to find there the valued stimuli of the brand. On closer inspection the duration, for which the flagship store is naturally suitable, also justifies the heavy investment in material and technology that companies sustain in order to guarantee a strong sense of theatre and experience for the customer.

This diverse use of the time factor, which constitutes one of the major differences between temporary stores and flagship stores, does not exclude the possibility that there could be a complementary relationship between the two formats. For example, Nike has experimented with the opening of a temporary shop even though it was one of the first brands to have opened flagship stores (Nike Town). Inside their flagship stores, besides promoting new product lines Nike also offers a series of activities and experiential and emotional spaces: personalization of products, fitness, music clubs and multimedia parks.

To be excluded, therefore, is an alternate use to these two formats that appear, above all, as complementary elements, insofar as they pursue the same ends of branding, even though using different methods.

Conclusion

The concept store, the temporary store and the flagship store represent, through their characteristics, the latest expression of the evolution of vertical branding and branded retail. In particular, the advent of the temporary store is overturning the traditional way of understanding the point of sale, anchored to the idea of a store for which limited duration in time is the qualifying element.

This idea is compared to the approach of vertical branding it contemplates a lasting and stable structure of retailing, as the franchising networks. Franchising envisages the creation of a network of retailer, which by its nature is intended to last over time to justify the investment for the creation and maintenance.

The classic ideas linked to the sales point are being emptied of meaning and importance: the geographic catchment area, spatial proximity, customer fidelity and commercial goodwill. The short or very short duration of the temporary shop sweeps away these old ideas, substituting them with the concept of the spatial event and the place of unique and unrepeatable experiences under the symbol of the brand of the producer.

The most direct and immediate consequence from this evolution in the understanding and management of the store is the loss of, or major reorganization of, the connotations of a selling space in favour of those of a place for experiential shopping and hedonistic consumption, in which the brand displays and speaks for itself and its values in order to develop a strong relationship with the consumer. The latter, constantly searching his/her self and social identification, can discover the world of the brand and its system of values.

In the meantime, branding opportunities on the part of the company are considerably increased with the spread of this new format, with respect to the flagship store which, in its most significant expression, seems to be in reach of only the strongest firm/brands that have much financial resources. The temporary store also assures a branding function - that is, allowing the direct management of the brand and its relationship with the consumer. The temporary store, nevertheless, does not require fixed costs for the amortization of its selling space in a building or for the renting of this space for many years, as is required for the flagship store. Besides, for symbolic significance, dimension and duration, the flagship store renders onerous investment necessary for the setting up of its internal spaces (using multisensory stimulation tools and solutions of visual merchandising in order to heighten the excitement of the show).

If the temporary store truly constitutes a more accessible distributive formula for branding, we can conclude that its arrival could generate similar effects to those that the internet has been producing for some time, allowing small and medium-sized businesses to bring and add value to their own brands, in order to increase their visibility and fame.

CHAPTER 4: MARKETING & CONSUMER BEHAVIOUR

CLAUDIO VIGNALI, GIANPAOLO VIGNALI & JURICA PAVICIC

The survival of fashion, its constant changes, development and decline, its connection with all historical events (wars, revolutions, scientific discoveries, change of customs, flourishing of art) indicate its importance.

Although there are many definitions of fashion, it generally refers to new, frequently perishable, ways of life in all areas of human activity in a determined time period such as science, politics, art, behaviour, entertainment and similar. Fashion is only one of the most important social and economic manifestations of our time. It also indicates and serves as a measure of psychological and socio-economical motivations of the humankind, and in a way the indicator of human ambitions and wish to compete.

The fashion began when the mankind left the savage ages – when the fulfilment of only existential needs and needs for security is left behind, when the esthetical needs appeared, often resulting from an additional need to be different, and later on from psychological and social motives to show social status. Decoration of body is visible already in the cavemen ages, when the so called fashion event was motivated by sexual needs and in this sense it still has existential importance for the natural, biological motive for the survival of the species. The decoration of caves with painted surfaces may also be characterized as fashion, although the true motivation for such an activity had existential character describing fight against natural disasters or good hunt and protection of hunters.

The researchers show that today's notion of fashion originated from higher social classes from the ancient times until the middle ages, which were shaped by strong inner hierarchy (Laver, 1996. p. 25). In these societies individuals and groups were entering the competition, temporarily excluding the lower classes from the competition. Therefore only higher classes followed the fashion, while lower classes had only a national garb. Luxury and splendour in fashion belong to the most prominent status symbols of the past until the middle of the eighteen-century. Luxury dresses worn in castles, public, religious and political ceremonies of all times witness to it.

The real fashion, or what we call fashion these days, has existed from the time of Enlightenment, the breakthrough of bourgeoisie. Only with the breakthrough of bourgeoisie, the fashion, at least partially, ceased to be only the expression of the social status of an individual, although numerous varieties still provided differentiation between the individuals, but this difference had socio-economic not caste or class character any more.

The governing classes always dictated the fashion trends in the past and there were no authentic fashion of the common people, whose clothes were mainly national garbs. This relation could and had to be more direct in the periods when each civilization was locked within its territorial borders of one nation, when exchanges between nations were difficult and very rare. Nowadays national fashion is declining (except what is left of folklore and regional customs), as well as the fashion of artistic and artisan's works bearing national characteristics, while internationalization and universalization of clothing fashion, decoration and internal design happens more often.

Three large periods can be defined since the fifties. In the fifties the fashion existed, it was important to wear fashionable clothes, live in modern furnished apartment i.e. belong to certain model in order to be accepted. The sixties meant the separation between the values of the youth and the established values, and in the seventies everybody was finally free to wear what he wanted.

Today, however, the situation has changed: the deciding role of middle classes in the economical sense and the growing importance of the fashion of the youth gave them the opportunity to dictate the rules of new fashion and has brought democratization of the system. Although stimulated by the appearance of new social classes, so called economic elite that is no longer neither as cultural nor as sociable as they were in the past, the fashion today increasingly depends on the economical-commercial point of view, or on the purchasing power of individuals.

Modern times are best explained by Yves Saint Laurent's statement that 'it is no longer fashionable to be fashionable' (Dorfles, 1997, p. 113). Today people who want to be fashionable must create their own image, and must not accept the influences from the ☐above☐. We can assume that in the near future the fashion phenomena will cease to be necessary equivalent to social constitution, but it will become only esthetical choice. The basic direction of the fashion will be that it will become more personal, more connected to the wants and taste of individuals and it will adjust to the wants of individuals for their differentiation within the community based on their taste.

The fashion is most frequently connected with the presentation of a person through his clothes. The level of technical modernization of the textile and clothes manufactories and constant stimulation of needs to buy clothes made the fashion into a big and very profitable business. Clothes present material made primarily to protect the human body. The shape of the clothes and kind of material, from early beginnings, primarily depended on the climate of the area where it developed and the level of technological development for its production. In the efforts to improve living conditions men has been constantly refining the materials and developing the shapes of clothes in order to be more and more comfortable and better protect the body.

With time clothes ceased to have only protective function and more and more esthetical elements were entering the clothes design. For example, clothes were coloured and more harmonious relations between colours and design were sought. Here we see the esthetical function of clothes besides the original protective one. This function has been loosing and gaining importance depending on the social and ethical conflicts. In the societies that showed conflicts at all levels, the fashion was loosing importance, and in those where there were established sets of values, clothes and fashion dominated as an indicator of economical and social values, driver of a whole industry sector as well as characterizing nations as dominant drivers of certain fashion styles.

Besides the protective and esthetical functions, since the earliest times the clothes has had also an important religious character. Event today there is an obvious connection between religious rituals and clothes in the uniforms of religious groups, as symbol of expressing mourning, or important religious events such as wedding, Communion and similar. Clothes are used to cover certain physical defaults or point out some physical characteristics, having certain sexual-esthetical function, as it has had through the human history.

Special clothes express belonging to certain social group; therefore one of the functions is to express social status. With bigger and various offer on one hand, and ideologization of life on the other hand, the clothes nowadays become deliberate communication media. This communicative function of clothes is expressed by the choice of clothes from a variety of offers and the way it is placed in the context of mens chosen or imposed environment.

In this communicative function clothes often clearly express social roles. Based on their clothes we can recognise men and women, the rich and the poor, an introvert and an extrovert, supporters of traditional and alternative cultural forms or followers of various ideologies, homosexuals, whores, fetishists, artists, solicitors and similar. These communicative signs shall not be taken for granted, but there shall always be a possibility of a favourable impression, which a person with his clothes wants to give to the surroundings. Regarding economy and development, the production and sales of clothes is important for each national economy. (Drvar, 1996, p. 170). Clothes consumption can satisfy human needs (protective, esthetical-communicative and other previously mentioned) or these needs may be artificially created by the fashion phenomena and all its characteristics.

Changes of fashion trends with the production of fashion clothes stimulate production of new and different kinds of fabrics, various additional material, shops and new school programs for education of professionals for textiles and designers. With continuous development and changes in production of clothes also develop the techniques of its sales. With the aim to create needs for always new and fashionable clothes, there are numerous magazines having function to establish certain fashion trends and awareness, fashion designer as profession is established, which today has a status of an artist and many other activities are established relating to changes of clothes, fashion itself, but also other activities relating to changes of fashion.

The fashion industry itself has been market oriented and directed to end consumption; therefore, marketing is inevitable for a successful business operation in accordance with the needs and market trends. The basic role of marketing in the fashion industry is to:

1. Investigate needs for textile and clothes

2. Offer products that various consumers need and want

3. Facilitate the choice of goods and affordable purchase through the best sales channels

4. Give sufficient information in constant communication with the customers in order to facilitate their choice of goods and final decision

The basic task of marketing in the fashion industry is to connect the production and consumption of clothes in the way that the suppliers achieve positive business results and get customers' satisfaction in the consumption of these products.

As the UK clothing economy is in growth, the UK has an attractive clothing market for retailers. The fashion industry is continuing to grow at an enormous rate, while the large retailers are leading the way for the ever-changing styles and trends. Therefore, we believe that many who read this book will find a lot of useful information on the fashion market in the UK, many fashion clothing retailers and methods of solving their future problems.

Benetton & Consumer behaviour

Whilst there is an abundance of work in the marketing literature referring to theoretical models notably in texts (Chisnall 1993; Cohen 1981; Howard & Sheth 1968; Loudon 1988 etc.), little reference is made to the practical use of such models. This is particularly the case in journal articles. In reviewing the applicability of models in consumer buying behaviour to the fashion retail sector, it is important to consider them not only in terms of the accepted psychology of human behaviour theory, but in terms of variables applicable to such buying behaviour. With this in mind, multi-variable models will be developed and applied to the Benetton consumer purchasing experience.

Literature On Consumer Behaviour

Consumer behaviour plays an important influence upon the policies and daily operations of organisations. We highlight the need for greater understanding of this behaviour as a need to:

> "....dig deeper into the underlying factors affecting behaviour in general, and to attempt to relate these findings to particular market situations."

Organisations can be regarded as, "entities," with a personality acquired as a result of their past behaviour and the messages that they have presented to customers and employees. Past, present and potential customers, may form opinions about an organisation which will subsequently guide their buying behaviour. By considering the viewpoint of the customer, and understanding the relationship between the marketing function and consumer buying behaviour, fashion retailers could control costs incurred through, for example, advertising, new product development and public relations, in a more efficient manner, thus sales through satisfied customers. Theories in the field of psychology determine that external influences form, "cognitions," in the individuals mind, and subsequently affect the way that the individual, "perceives," the surrounding world. In referring to the, "the complex pattern of buying influence," we suggest that the three main external influences on individuals behaviour are the cultural, sociological and economic aspects of the surrounding environment. Purchasing habits, being part of the overall consumer's behaviour, are deeply affected by the prevailing cultures of the society in which they live. Cognition encompasses the mental process s of knowing, perceiving and judging, which enable the individual to interpret the world around them. Cognition is therefore the systematic way in which the individual can interpret information in a meaningful manner from the surrounding environment and form subsequent opinions, attitudes and reactions. The individual, from past experiences, will form a cognitive, "map," in their mind which affects the way that they react to all future experiences. The

cognitive map of the individual is therefore a personal reflection of all the past experiences of that individual. We outline three main systematic characteristics of cognition, these being:

MULTIPLEXITY

CONSONANCE

INTERCONNECTEDNESS

"Multiplicity," refers to the degree of complexity of a cognitive system, for example, in considering retail fashion items, the individual may place importance upon a large number of criteria such as style, colour, pattern, shape and size. The way in which the individual achieves an acceptable balance between these criteria defines his cognitive, "consonance," i.e. the way in which the individual establishes a, "happy medium," between product attributes, for example, quality and price. The third characteristic, "interconnectedness," refers to the way in which the criteria fit within the consumers existing cognitive map and expectations. These three characteristics merely illustrate how dependent opinions are with respect to previous experiences.

How Perceptions Relate to Consumer Behaviour

"Behind every act of perceiving is the individuals past history of experience. Previous experience has built up a relatively stable cognitive organisation within the individual which determines the meaning of a particular percept." Perception then, is subjective, and is dependant upon how the individual interprets information which s/he from the external world, compared to the internal thought processes and attitudes. We define two key sets of factors that determine what will be perceived and how it will be perceived, these being:

Stimulus characteristics

Consumer characteristics

The sensory receptors, for example, seeing, taste, touch, etc. are stimulated by objects or events in the external environment (these occurrences are known as stimuli.) By using these sensory inputs, interpretation of the signals sent to the brain can be transformed into perceptions. The way inn which an individual perceives would depend upon the nature of, and the interpretation of any such stimuli, these being the, "stimulus characteristics".

The Gestalt School of psychology, which began 75 years ago in Germany (the German term, "Gesalt," is translated to mean, "whole,") found that an individual perceives objects and patterns in their entirety as opposed to its components, i.e. the sweater rather than the wool, dye and stitching. Therefore perception is not consideration of a single characteristic, but a subconscious evaluation of the stimuli within the whole; however that may be relatively defined.

The School also argues that individuals view stimuli which are close together in space as one unit. For example, by folding leggings and displaying them in a similar manner next to sweaters, consumers may perceive the leggings to be sweaters. Consumers will therefore ignore the product if other attributes are not desirable, or become disappointed with their analysis once they have discovered their, "mistake."

Colour blocking may also deter the customer from investigating the differing merchandise further, since the colour scheme may imply that all products are similar in nature.

The most basic lesson from Gestalt psychology is that consumers wish to organise their perceptions into meaningful, "wholes." They will favour simplicity, familiarity, consistency, and stimuli that have meaning to them. They will employ perceptual, "sets," that will help to guide the meaning that is given to external stimuli in the consumer environment. Retailers that apply consistency with regard to store format, merchandise, layout and design, are likely to reinforce the consumer's perceptions reassuring them of the familiarity of the company's outlets globally. Conscious inferences refer to conscious decisions made by the individual, for example, s/he tries to ascertain whether or not the quality of a product is of the standard required.

Unconscious inferences are those where the individual makes the decisions based upon their personal values, for example, "Does this sweater suit me?" Certain characteristics of stimuli, for example, colour, may attract the individuals attention. Previous experience or related stimuli characteristics may result in an association, for example, between the colour and the previous experience, thus that stimuli characteristic acts as a "sensory cue."

The physical characteristics relating to a product, for example, size, shape and packaging, will affect the consumers perceptual inference. The price of a given product is an important sensory cue for the consumer, since it does not represent a direct benefit; it is a measure of how much the consumer must give up in order receiving certain benefits. As with all aspects of a product marketing mix, pricing may be used as an external cue with which to judge the quality and availability of the product. We argue that consumers do infer product quality from the price charged for a product. They are more likely to rely on the price cue when other information to help with the quality inference is not available. It is also important that the language and visual elements relating to products with a brand name fundamentally stimulate consumer inferences. Consumer inferences from stimuli (for example, store layout, merchandise and displays, customer service and general store policies) within shops have become increasingly important.

What is a Brand?

"A brand is a name, term or symbol, design or a combination of these that identifies a seller's products and differentiates them from competitive products." Brands consist of tangible and intangible properties, which allow the consumer to differentiate one suppliers product from those of another, e.g. store layout, merchandise, quality and colours. The functional benefits of a brand satisfy consumer needs and demands whilst the intangible elements reinforce the overall image of the brand.

Combined, these properties create and promote a collection of perceptions in the mind of the consumer. We recognise the complexity of a brand, believing that any product with a successful brand develops a personality. However to distinguish between the product and the brand you have to see them as being exclusive of one another. We differentiate between the "process brand", which relates to the service encounter and the "product brand", refers to the functional and more tangible elements and we suggest that brands are measured against five criteria:

1. Coherence

2. appropriateness

3. distinctiveness

4. protects ability

5. appeal

Hence: "The ingredients in and a brand constitutes the product itself, the packaging, the brand name, the promotion, the advertising and the overall presentation.... .....the brand is therefore a synthesis of all elements, physical, aesthetic, rational and emotional....the end result must be not only appropriate, but differentiated from the brands of the competitors – the consumer has to have a reason to choose one brand over all the others."

We also identify four key characteristics that strong international brands should possess: the same brand name in all countries; common pack design; a broadly similar target market in all the countries, and a similar function.

Benetton's Position

Benetton's global success may be attributed to its compatibility with all these criteria. Regional variations in tastes, attitudes and preferences must be considered for a brand to be internationally successful. Although Benetton do adapt their range to suit particular nations, adaptation may be limited; Benetton has not altered their sizing to satisfy the UK consumer. Brands are more likely to appeal to consumers internationally due to a number of factors: improved communication, increased travel, and greater language tuition. We believe that "power brands" exist, and are those brands which are "well adopted to the environment." The skill of producing such power brands involves the successful selection of the elements in the marketing mix; the blending of these elements and then their presentation to the consumer.

In the overall retailing operation of Benetton brands, the company distinguishes between branded; none branded and other product lines. This was explained through an informal interview with Marco Tossi, the Northern Regional Agent of Benetton UK. Branded products are those with a clear and concise Benetton logo. Non branded products are those associated with Benetton according to colour and style but not displaying the Benetton logo and other represent any other item in the Benetton range.

We recognise the advantage this brings to the company, in that, "brands have an asset value, to their owners as part of the companys stock of goodwill." He suggests that the market value of the brand is higher than the value of both the plant and machinery used to produce them.

In Business Format Franchising, and Benetton in particular, the brand is more than the merchandise or stock and as the literature indicates it is also the retail outlet. The Benetton retail marketing mix directly affects the consumers perception of the Benetton brand. The marketing strategies implemented by the franchiser are communicated to the franchisees throughout the company and will ultimately affect its consumers buying behaviour.

The service sector revolution has resulted in an extension of the original marketing mix of product, price, promotion and place, to further include service, quality, fashion, atmospherics, location and branding. This mix provides a marketing tool in which a company can sustain a competitive advantage by differentiating itself in a highly competitive market place.

When referring to the product we identify the "timeless" style and high quality of Benetton merchandise. It is noted that Benetton sweaters were perceived as being "moderately priced" and acknowledges Benetton's promotional activities as having:

"Established the Benetton service package and brand name in the minds of millions of consumers around the world."

Physical evidence is fundamental to the service encountered at Benetton, incorporates the visual elements such as colour, the familiar Benetton frontage, store interiors and the level of consumer service provided.

"Customers cannot only buy the physical product, but they also experience the service package."

Brands can thus be seen to add value to consumers by increasing product choice enabling the consumer to reject, repurchase or recommend the product.

There are two types of non-functional needs that can be related to branding and subsequently fulfilled: symbolic needs, whereby the brand is related to the individuals ego and self-image needs and experimental needs, whereby the brand is used as a basis for variety and sensory pleasure needs. "Any given name may represent a wealth of meanings whether reverential, symbolic, associative or a combination of these."

Further to this we assert that consumers shop in outlets which they believe to be the most congruent with their self image. It is acknowledged that the value of a brand in the eyes of the consumer is a "guarantee of homogeneity and quality." The consumer receives additional benefits, which are added values, for example, past consumer experience of the product and its presentations in additional to the functional benefits. The brand value is measured in terms of the following: Extensiveness – how many people have feelings about the brand; Comprehensiveness – how generalised these feelings are; Intensiveness – how strong these feelings are.

We describe brands as "enduring assets" providing they are well maintained and continue to meet consumer requirements. The asset value of a brand helps to attract sales and implies that consumers will reject those alternatives which do not possess all these values.

Benetton The Retailer as a Brand

As a brand, the retailer must ensure that the merchandise offered and store ambience is distinctive and distinguishable from its competitors. Benetton has achieved this by offering its consumers a standardised format with a consistent store ambience. This differentiates Benetton from other high street retailers.

We define corporate identity as a brand thus: "....the brand and packaging of an entire company.....a way of communicating the corporate ingredients to target groups and market." and continue to explain that such a corporate identity for example, store layout, merchandise and displays, customer service and general store policies projects the unique personality of a company, positioning it within the market place and thus differentiating it in a memorable way. The programme is a "carefully defined system of al the visual elements which serve as points of public contract."

The logo and corporate name are key elements in this system, but are not the only factors. In order to reinforce a total impression on the consumers memory, as well integrated visual communications system must be applied using repetition of design or elements of colour, texture and line. This system is referred to as the "secondary format."

CHAPTER 5: FACTORS THAT INFLUENCE THE CLOTHES' BUYING DECISION

SUSANA AZEVEDO, MADALENA PEREIRA, JOÃO FERREIRA & RUI MIGUEL

Consumer behaviour research is the scientific study of the processes consumers use to select, secure, use and dispose of products and services that satisfy their needs. Firms can satisfy those needs only to the extent that they understand their customers. The main objective of this chapter is to study the sex differences and the valorisation of clothes attributes by Portuguese consumers when they go shopping. That is, we intend to study the consumer buying behaviour in a context of fashion with a special highlighting on the differences among male and female consumers and also on the clothes attributes valorisation. To attain this objective a survey was developed and administered across Portugal. The findings confirm the differences between women and men especially in terms of What, Where, When, and How they buy.

The relationship between dressing and the idea of individual expression is complex. It may be perceived in people's daily life through recurrent use of the same clothing colours, brands, fashion tendencies etc. Many people use contrasts and colours that express feelings according to their state of mind. Thus, the products' properties, like design, comfort, individuality, have a decisive role on apparel's buying behaviour, which may vary depending on a set of factors, mainly on sex (Fischer and Arnold, 1994).

There is a widespread recognition that consumer buying behaviour is the key to contemporary marketing success. In this way, the field of consumer buying behaviour has been characterized by a diversity of viewpoints and based on an interdisciplinary science. In this context, the understanding of consumer buying behaviour could appeals to a set of different areas of knowledge, such as psychological, cultural social psychological, physio-pyschological, genetics anthropology. The main objective of this chapter is to study the sex differences in consumer buying behaviour of a Portuguese population when they go shopping to buy apparel products. To attain this objective a survey was developed and administered across Portugal. The findings confirm the differences between women and men especially in terms of What, Where, When, and How they buy.

Fashion moves along with clothing and time, integrating the simple day to day wearing in a broad context such as political and social, among others. It comprises several styles which may be influenced by the most diversified aspects. It is an ephemeral manner easily changeable of behaviour and especially through wearing. Fashion is a socio-cultural phenomenon that, at a given moment, expresses values of society – uses, habits and practices. According to Lipovetsky (1987), fashion is actually a phenomenon of modern societies, also associated to values and socialising ways.

Fashion became an object of study in several areas which before were not at all awaked for it. Areas such as anthropology, sociology and history started using fashion as a way of understanding society (Lancioni, 1973). In media and society in general, fashion also has turned out to be a matter of interest, even being understood in many different ways, since in this environment fashion is mainly associated to glamour, to novelty, to consumption and to the definition of an individual through their appearance (Pesendorfer, 1995).

These factors are very important to understand what fashion really is, although this goes much further, it is a language through which society is related and communicates ones habits, practices and its culture (Cappetta, Cillo, and Ponti, 2006). Fashion contains meanings that go behind the continuous changes of collections, whose explanations are in the context of society, deserving study and reflection. Transformations that have taken place in the social structure and organization throughout time, coming from historical movements, wars, revolutions, technological developments and artistic manifestations, confirms the importance of the human research environment. In order to disclose movements which are on the basis of fashion phenomenon and constitute the reason of apparel style changes (Lipovetsky, 1987).

Clothes are undoubtedly the strongest way of representing fashion concept, although these being present in the most different of areas, such as music and art, amongst many others too. By definition, fashion can mean change and also goes much deeper and behind the actual apparel. It also provides an illusion, contributing to our well being, feeding our insecurities and increasing our confidence (Jones and Mair, 2005). According to Thrassou et al. (2008), fashion is temporary and a new fashion starts with the refusal of what is old and, often, through the impatient adoption of what previously was taken as ugly; consequently, it subtly denies its statement that the last fashion is, in a certain way, a definite solution for the appearance problem. However, according to Tuncay and Otnes (2008), fashion is a harmonious whole more or less indissoluble. It fits to social structure, accentuating separation between classes; it conciliates the conflict between the individualising impulse of each one of us (need of affirmation as a person) and the socialising one (need of affirmation as a member of a group); it expresses ideas and feelings, since it is a language that is translated into artistic terms". Not only are the aesthetical elements important to characterize fashion as it must be placed in the moment and time. Fashion reflects society and the time of living (Liu et al., 2009).

Nowadays, the society where fashion system has been installed is driven by consumption, by the change and by the individualizing desire, in opposition to societies ruled by habits and tradition. According to Barnard (2002), garments claim a position including respectability and outrageousness (sexual appeal), economic and social value (status), individualistic look, political symbol, religious rituals and pleasure.

Women play a better role perceiving garments communicative language, also being more engaged in fashion giving importance to garments and fashion when defining their identity (Bakewell et al., 2006).

Fashion marketing must answer to several questions, such as:

1. what product lines must be created in the different seasons?

2. which is the market segment?

3. how much product to be produced?

4. at what price?

5. which needs and preferences of consumers?

6. which distribution channels must be used to sell the product?

7. how to organize and control sales?

In other words, fashion marketing has the main objective to act as a guide for the different processes of creation, production, distribution, communication, promotion, commercialization, planning and control. However, since this sector is quite dynamic and differentiating, fashion marketing must adapt to each specific fashion market.

Fashion marketing starts and ends at the consumer. Thus, according to Arriaga (2005), the action must be focused on them, this is, it is necessary to identify the way how he dresses themselves, the product must be produced according to their needs and expectations, as well as produced in a short period of time, since the fashion cycle is becoming shorter and shorter. In other words, companies must study:

i) the consumer needs;

ii) the most adequate consumer segment and how approach it;

iii) the ideal positioning to reach this segment;

iv) the design level, colours, quality that the target segment requires;

v) the price to establish;

vi) the channel distribution demands;

vii) the marketing strategies and policies that best suit the market segment.

This means, in order to a company to be able to give the best answer to the market, it must have the best answers to this question

Consumer buying behaviour

There are several factors found in literature to justify the buying behaviour of consumers. Among them, may be highlighted: organisation's corporate values (Cambra-Fierro et al., 2007), perceived quantity and quality of information (Pelsmacker and Janssens 2007), cultural and environmental factors (Dewan and Dewan, 2007), culture, societal communicating factors (Grant and Spephen, 2005).

According to Arriaga (2005) and Kotler (2003) the main factors influencing the buying behaviour of consumers are the following: physiological factors, socio-cultural factors, personal factors, psychological factors, rational factors. For example, the physiological factors relate to physical protection, commodity, among others. The socio-cultural ones comprise family, friends, work, the social groups with which the consumer identifies himself and that influences the purchasing behaviour and the looking for a garment type. Family causes a strong influence on the choice of children garments or, for example, when a wife chooses a gift for her husband. Friends also play a certain influence on a consumer, as he will try to follow the tendencies of his group. A consumer pertaining to a given country, geographical region or a given social class will also end up determining the consumption options. Consumers coming from different cultures have different preferences respecting to some brands and garment products (Chang, 2005; Lukosius, 2004).

The purchase decision is also influenced by personal factors, namely age, consumer's life cycle stage, occupation, economical level, way of life and personality. Concerning age and life cycle stage as a function of marital status, consumers have specific needs. For example, children, as they are in the process of growing up, they need garments suitable to their age and physical development (McNeal and Yeh, 1996). Respecting young persons, usually follow their fashion mind leaders. In respect to the third age, these are less demanding when choosing their clothes, more lasting, most of the times, although this tendency had changed in the last few years and, at the moment, they are being considered as a target market (Capon et al., 2001). Occupation also influences garment purchasing decision, as an executive will choose buying more formal garments, while an unqualified worker will buy more practical ones.

The financial capacity is evidently a factor that influences the purchasing process, as the higher it is, the higher the acquisition power and garment consumption. In other words, demographic factors, age, monthly income, living place, marital status, professional situation all make an individual to choose certain brands or stores, instead of others (Paulins and Geisteld, 2003).

The way of life is another factor that influences the consumer buying behaviour, as a given garment is intended to a given life style. Consumers frequently choose certain kinds of products, services and activities since these are associated to a certain life style. Thus the fashion industry must pay more and more attention to life style tendencies.

Personality is another personal factor that influences purchasing, since every consumer has a different personality. Factors such as self-confidence, domain of himself, good fellowship and autonomy, define the individuals personality and, consequently, different purchasing processes.

Concerning psychological factors, these play a strong influence on consumers, as some of them choose a product simply by reliance, sympathy or even designer friendship. To these, motivations like personality attraction and interest of a consumer for a given fashion product can also be joined (Mittelstaedt, 1990). Psychological factors also influence the decision of buying products, despite its price. Often, a high cost is a determing factor leading to acquisition of one product and not of a cheaper one, since this may be regarded as to increase self-confidence of whom is wearing it. Among several factors, the psychological ones are those that bear more attention to companies, although many of these do not have professionals capable to best understand them.

The rational factors are the most visible ones, they are based on the rational consumer's behaviour, his way of thinking and decision making, on a reasoning manner. There are several individual and collective factors that interfere on the purchasing decision, such as the brand of a given fashion product as many consumers make purchases by influence of a designer or company brand. Quality is another factor to which consumers pay more attention (Acharya and Elliot, 2003; Hanf and Wersebe, 1994). The design is an important motivation for purchasing and consumption of fashion, since, in a garment, consumers give more and more relevance to aesthetical appearance, like the line and look, among many others. The characteristics or attributes of fashion products also influence purchasing, since they interfere on the value, style and quality of product. (Hong et al.,2002; Wickliffe and Psysarchik, 2001).

Product comfort is a important attribute, as consumers wish comfortable products to satisfy certain specific needs. The usefulness is also a factor that consumers have in mind when buying garments, because, for example, if they buy a garment that combines with those of their wardrobes, and they make their choices also considering aspects such as durability and easy care. The product novelty is a factor that fashion followers have into consideration, in each season they renew their wardrobes, and they look for innovation in their wearing way.

Price is a rational factor that influences a lot the purchase of a product since consumers consider a better product the one with better price (Hanf and Wersebe, 1994). The acceptance of a product is reached when there is equilibrium between value and price that the consumer is willing to pay for it. In general, the consumer considers a low price product the one that is outdated or with low quality.

The results reached by Dutton (2006) shows that the products' attributes of styling, brand, price, place, production and fiber content have a significant effect on the buyer intention of the consumers with a range age between 15- to 25-years old. May-Plumlee (2006) found that there are thirteen universal evaluative criteria used when evaluating an apparel product. These criteria include brand/label, price, color/pattern, style/design/uniqueness, fabrication, fashionability, appearance/attractiveness, care, construction, durability, fit/sizing, quality, and comfort. Pereira et al. (2009) used the same attributes of Dutton to study the valorisation of the apparel attributes according to the influence level of the advertising on the buying behaviour.

Attributes for garment evaluation

- Concrete

- Attributes (product features)

- Abstract Attributes (attitude-based)

- Intrinsic (hedonic)

- Extrinsic

- Aesthetics

- Price

- Brand

- Fun

- Style

- Color

- Country of origin

- Entertainment

- Pattern

- Fabric /fiber

- Salesperson's evaluation

- Enjoyment

- Appearance

- Approval of others

- Need

- Fashionability

- Coordination with wardrobe.

- Function

- Utilitarian

- Durability

- Comfort

- Quality

- Fit

- Care

Source: Dutton (2006)

Often, companies think that price is the most important factor in the purchasing process, but consumers also consider important other kind of factors, such as attendance, general environment, shop-windows, catalogues, store merchandising, product quality and service. Concerning store environment, according to Paulins and Geisteld (2003), it influences the choice of a brand or store by the consumer, as well as the purchasing decision. This means, fashion companies need to constantly improve space decoration, as well as their product turnover.

Consumers' reactions to a product are influenced by their evaluations of its advertising, over and above their feelings about the product itself. The evaluation of a product can be determined mainly by the appraisal of how it is depicted in marketing communications – consumers do not hesitate to form attitudes toward products not seed neither used. Advertising in fashion is relatively less explored than in other consumer. Normally the communication channels used are Fashion Magazines, newspapers and its supplements outdoor advertising, special fashion' events, television adds, sales promotion, radio advertising, internet pop ups and so on (Solomom and Robolt, 2004; Easey, 2009)

Fashion is based on emotions, as being aesthetically beautiful, conquering others, the emotional factors being on the basis of consumer's feelings and emotions. The wish to be involved with fashion is an emotional factor that leads consumers to buy fashion clothes, as they want them to be modern and novel. Often, the purchase of fashion clothes is not done by need, but for pleasure.

According to Tay (2008), the behaviour of the modern consumer lies on looking for pleasure with the consumption experience itself. Frequently, he looks for new stimuli, new sensations and, as pleasure is subjective and personal, consumption is thus oriented by the individual himself.

Products or services purchasing process goes through several stages (McEnally and Chernatony, 1999; Kotler and Keller, 2005): First appears the acknowledgement of the need, after the consumer does an information search, making than an evaluation of alternatives and, at last, the purchase decision and evaluation. For these authors, the acknowledgment of a need may take place throughout internal stimuli (if one is hungry, thursty, tired or has personal interests) or external ones (generally commercial, incited by other persons, etc.). Also, according to McEnally and de Chernatony (1999), internal stimuli or impulses to the individual are known of motivation. The Maslow motivation theory is referred by many authors as one that helps to understand the consumer buying behaviour (Kotler and Keller, 2005; McEnally and de Chernatony, 1999, De Brouwer 2009, Guillen-Royo, 2008). To these authors, the knowledge of this theory is a need for the marketing professional, for a better understanding of determinant psychological factors to human behaviour and, thus, of consumers buying behaviour. Kotler and Keller (2005) say that the Maslow theory helps the marketing professional to understand how several products fit in plans, objectives and life of consumers. This theory is of fundamental importance to understand factors that motivate behaviour and stimulate an individual to act. The motivation theory allows understanding, mainly the first stage of the purchasing behaviour already mentioned: the acknowledgment of a need.

The understanding of fashion consumer buying behaviour is required to best answer to needs and demands of consumers and to satisfy them in an innovative and original manner as, according to Arriaga (2005), fashion starts and ends at the consumer. This is because, either considering an haute-couture, prêt-à-porter or mass market product, companies must always bear in mind the consumer's satisfaction, considering loyalty as the major goal.

Consumer Buying Behaviour Approaches

Consumer behaviour research is the scientific study of the processes consumers use to select, secure, use and dispose of products and services that satisfy their needs. Knowledge of consumer behaviour directly affects marketing strategy (Anderson et al., 2005). This is because of the marketing concept, i. e., the idea that firms exist to satisfy customer needs (Winer, 2000). Firms can satisfy those needs only to the extent that they understand their customers. For this reason, marketing strategies must incorporate knowledge of consumer behaviour into every facet of a strategic marketing plan (Solomon, 2002).

The human behaviour is complex, replete with controversies and contradictions and comes as no surprise to marketing academicians as well as professionals. There is a widespread recognition that consumer behaviour is the key to contemporary marketing success (Hawkins et al., 2003). Consumer behaviour has been legitimized in marketing for it provides the conceptual framework and strategic thinking for carrying out successful segmentation of markets (Schiffman and Kanuk, 2000).

There have been a number of debates between positivistic and interpretive consumer researchers (Hudson and Ozanne, 1988). In this way, the field of consumer behaviour has been characterized by diversity of viewpoints; as a result, the entire field now is based on an interdisciplinary science (Kassarjian, 1995). The understanding of consumer behaviour appeals to a set of different areas of knowledge/factors: psychological, cultural social psychological, physio-pyschological, genetics anthropology. One of them is the psychology since consumer behaviour deals with emotions, beliefs and attitudes. Research on emotions within marketing has evolved three approaches: the categories approach, the dimensions approach and the cognitive appraisals approach (Watson and Spence, 2007). The categories approach groups emotions around exemplars and considers their different effects on consumption related behaviour.

The dimensions approach uses the affective dimensions of valence and level of arousal to distinguish between emotions and the effects they have on consumer behaviour. the cognitive appraisals approach has used emotions' underlying motivational and evaluative roots to explain their influences on consumption related behaviours. This approach supposes that underlying evaluations of a situation (e.g. its desirability, certainty, etc.) combine to elicit specific emotions. This approach may be used to explain how an extensive range of emotions, including those with similar valence and arousal levels, are elicited and how they lead to different behavioural responses. The cognitive approach has been considered relevant for understanding the emotional responses of consumers in the marketplace (Johnson and Stewart, 2005). Bagozzi et al. (1999) propose that the cognitive appraisals approach offers a more complete explanation of consumers' behavioural responses to emotions than other one. What is apparent from the new learning, however, is that we potentially miss those beliefs and attitudes held at the unconscious or implicit level that can be crucial to determining consumer behaviour. Also the memory that people hold on their consumer experiences will drive both aversion and preference towards products. Aversion behaviour is our avoidance of certain things (brands or marketing offers) made to us as consumers.

The importance of the implicit memory in terms of its capacity to process and store information cannot be understated. The implicit memory registers vast amounts of input from our surrounding environment as we move through life. Millions of experiences that we have had throughout our entire lives are stored away in a particular part of our memory system and can be instantly accessed to help us develop an intuitive 'feeling' about what we should, or should not do. The critical issue, however, is that most of the associations that drive intuition reside in the unconscious part of our brain. They are brought into play automatically, and are not the subject of conscious awareness. We can't normally articulate the basis of our intuitions. So consumers often make brand choices intuitively, and cannot tell why they made that choice.

Fishbein's (1967) attitudinal model has also been widely used in the marketing context (Lilien et al., 1992), and this paradigm provides researchers with a useful lens for examining the factors explaining consumer purchasing intention and adoption. According to this model, behaviour is predominantly determined by intention. Other factors like attitudes, subjective norms, and perceived behavioural control also are shown to be related to an appropriate set of salient behavioural, normative, and control beliefs about the behaviour. However, Fishbein's model stops at the adoption level and does not capture other important factors that explain and predict consumer continuance behaviour (repurchase). The expectation-confirmation model (Oliver, 1980), on the other hand, focuses on the post-purchase behaviour. It is a widely used model in the consumer behaviour literature, particularly in explaining consumer satisfaction and repeat purchase. Satisfaction is the central notion of this model, which is formed by the gap between expectation and perceived performance. The expectation-confirmation theory suggests that if the perceived performance meets one's expectation, confirmation is formed, and consumers are satisfied. Bhattacherjee (2001) stated that satisfied users are more likely to continue purchasing the same products.

As regards cultural it is the main external factors that shape human behaviour. It represents living style, which came into being after adjustments to the environment, people, and things through generations. The effect of culture on people's life is so great that it will even affect the motives and choices when consuming or shopping (Chang, 2005).

Otts (1989) defined culture as "All technologies, beliefs, knowledge and fruits that people share and transfer to next generations. Taylor (1958) believed that culture was everything that an individual learns in society. It is a combination of knowledge, beliefs, arts, morals, laws, customs, and any other capabilities and customs. Culture is one of the main factors to determine behaviour. The two external factors (culture and physical environment) and two internal factors (physiological and psychological factors) interact and form the basic factors to determine human behaviour. Culture also includes three parts, namely culture, subculture, and social class. Culture is the most basic deciding factor of human desire and behaviour. Everyone is included in many smaller subculture groups, which provide a clearer sense of identification and social process. Basically, subculture can be divided into four types: nationality groups, religious groups, racial groups, and geographical regions. Many subcultures can form some important market segments, and provide the decision reference on product designs and marketing campaigns for marketing personnel to serve the demands of consumers (Jen, 1990).

Through the interactions of the group, different people's experience and individual characteristics were combined. During the combination process, individuals would seek someone highly matched to himself in order to form a subgroup or small group together. Schein (1985) believed the subgroup could form a common history through a certain time development, by sharing experiences, attitudes, communication methods, and individual personalities, and, in doing so, give birth to subculture. The individual life style is affected by the interaction of internal factors such as value and personality characteristics, and external factors such as society and culture, and also reflects on daily life activities.

According to the paradox of personality in marketing, we all have a personality, but we do not know how it is systematically related to our consumer behaviour (Albanese, 1989). Social psychology is another knowledge field that helps to understand consumer behaviour. The social psychology focus on the understanding of individual's behaviour in the presence of other individuals or groups. Concepts such as social perceptions, social influence, social rewards, peer pressure, social cues, social sanctions, etc. all shed light on the mysteries of consumer behaviour. Approaches to understanding consumer behaviour have emphasized external influences on consumption-related acts. The whole idea behind this reasoning is that consumer behaviour takes place within the context of groups and other individuals' presence which influences consumer's processing of information and decision making (Engel et al., 1968).

Another area of knowledge that has been used to a better understanding of consumer behaviour is the physiopyschological one. Physiological psychology is the study of the interaction of the body with the mind. It is the study of the extent to which behaviour is caused by physical and chemical phenomena in the body (Morris 1996). Kroeber-Riel (1980) pointed out that cognitive and psychological processes originate from physiological ones. This field holds many promises for explaining consumer behaviour. For instance, the hypothalamus is that center of the brain which mainly controls consumption (Zimbardo and Gerrig, 1996). The chemical changes due to the use/eat of the first product results in a blood borne input to the brain to activate further consumption. Thus, the individual would order one more product to use/eat. Such behaviour is explained based on the research findings on the functions of the hypothalamus and other related areas of the brain (Valenstein et al., 1970; Zhang et al., 1994). Physio-psychology provides fascinating ways to help understand consumer behaviour without looking into the consumer's "black box" for hypothetically based variable explanations.

According to genetics approach our genes direct our consumption behaviour. Perhaps humans are all programmed to act in certain ways in their consumptive and consumer-related behaviour. Is the presence of certain genes that compel us to consume certain kind of products? Genetic science may very well come up with definite findings to explain consumer behaviour and thus we may strike a vein of truth in finding explanations and laws of consumer behaviour (Feder, 1977).

Business anthropology and its implementation in consumer behaviour studies have demonstrated to the business world that anthropological approach as new perspective will bring a new era for the consumer science. The applied anthropologists will become the hottest candidates for business related research jobs given the fact that anthropological methods are becoming more widely acceptable in the business world in general and in consumer studies particular (Demirdjian and Senguder, 2004).

CHAPTER 6: THE INTERNATIONALISATION OF FASHION RETAILERS

EMAAD MUHANNA

Chapter Objectives

The main objectives of this chapter is to provide an overview of the international of fashion retailers and in achieving this goal, the following is illustrated:

1. Gain a better understanding of the internationalisation process of fashion retailers;

2. Ascertain whether the international retailers have unique attributes that contribute to their success; and

3. Establish a theoretical framework for the internationalisation of fashion retailers;

Introduction

International retailing is not a new development in terms of cross border trading, but it is rather a new theme of research in the area of international business management. Increasingly more and more fashion retailers are engaging in cross-borders trading. International markets provide valuable growth opportunities and allow retailers to gain knowledge and experience about new markets and consumers. Akehurst & Alexander (1996) argue that the internationalisation of retailers and its pace is redefining channel relationships and the economics of distribution on a global scale.

The level of internationalisation can range from normal direct export to vertical integration into the foreign markets (Bohdanowicz & Clamp, 1994). The internationalisation of fashion retailers is unprecedented and primarily driven by a variety of factors, which contribute to international expansion. Some of such factors are related to branding such as Benetton, Gucci and H & M. such international brands are appealing to customers across border, satisfying customers' needs regardless of gender, culture or race. These international brands have enjoyed strong market position in the international market and are regarded to be among some of the most successful international companies. However with the globalisation of markets and the increasing speed with which industry and product life cycle occur, various methods may be needed in order to understand the contemporary behaviour of the fashion retailer's internationalisation (Fillis, 2001). Moore and Burt (2007) argue that it is difficult to identify the fashion retailers that operate internationally. They further state that this is due to some reasons; first, no single database that has tracked the international activities of fashion companies; second, if the database exists, its accuracy is questioned due to the fast changes of the fashion sector and that is due to the lower entry barriers to and from the fashion market. Moore and Burt (2007) further state that despite the difficulty in identifying exactly the international fashion retailers, it is possible to identify the categories of fashion retailers that are likely to engage in international activities.

In an attempt to understand the phenomenon of internationalisation, various studies have been conducted to explain the phenomenon of internationalisation as early as the 1970s (i.e. Johanson & Vahlne, 1977; Czinkota, 1982; Cavusgil, 1980; Welch & Luostarinen, 1988; Haahti el al., 1998). Fletcher (2001) maintains that for the most part, research has been devoted to factors causing internationalisation or to the process by which firms become increasingly involved in international activities. As a result a number of theories have been developed and applied, yet the research on detailed practices and activities that relate to strategic outcomes are still in the early development stage (Mughan & Lloyd, 2007). Previous research into internationalisation has viewed it as being an export-led phenomenon. Although this is a phenomenon that extends to other activities such as licensing and manufacture overseas, it is usually considered from an 'outward' perspective (Fletcher, 2001). Often, researchers use the traditional international management concepts as well as the traditional internationalisation theories to explain the phenomenon of fashion retailers' internationalisation (Wigley & Moore, 2005). However, the development of international retail operations in modern times impose challenges against the internationalisation theories due to the fact that the development and dynamics of the retail sector as well as the experience of retail organisations are often ignored (Akehurst & Alexander, 1996). Renko (2008) supports this view; Renko argues that there is a constant interaction between changes in retailing and the internationalisation of retailers. She further states that this is due to the large-scale volume and market-power of retailers as international retail chains have a significant potential to affect changes on the market in terms of the consumers' choices and suppliers production (Renko, 2008).

Globalisation of the Fashion Industry

As globalisation imposed mergers and acquisitions on a large scale, the fashion sector has also witnessed an extensive globalisation of fashion brands such as Gucci, Benetton, H&M and Gap. This produced major changes in the dynamics and consumption of the fashion products, which further created global fashion players, allowing the fashion industry to become a multi-national industry rather than a country or culture-specific products (Gilbert, 2000). Fashion companies, which have commitment to export make adaptations for different markets, producing country or culture-based products and the promotion and pricing will depend on the form of the form of distribution (Bohdanowicz & Clamp, 1994). According to De Burca el al. (2004) globalisation is:

The process by which firms operate on a global basis, organising their structure, capabilities, resources and people in such a way as to address the world as one market"

Governments worldwide have also realised the potential economic benefit from international retailers in terms of job creation, investment and foreign exchange earning. Therefore, many governments have eased their rules against foreign retailers allowing more and more international retailers to expand their operations globally. It is evident that international fashion retailers bring expertise and innovation, which may benefit local retailers (Treadgold, 1990; McGoldrick, 2002; Newman & Cullen, 2002).

The fashion industry relies heavily on manual methods of production, sometimes based on manufacturing techniques spanning several centuries; yet some of the fashion firms do internationalise rapidly by developing international networks, offering adapted and customised products and generally being much more flexible and faster in their approach to business than their larger competitors (Fillis, 2001). The process of operational involvement of fashion retailers in the international market has become the focus of debate among scholars, corporations as well as governments. Historically, internationalisation was associated only with large enterprises (Coviello & Munro, 1999). However, in modern times, small firms are also receiving more attention globally for their role in the international market at different levels through utilisation of resources and techniques such as innovation and technology transfer, to gain access to new markets (Antoncic & Hisrich, 2000; Jones, 2007). Theoretically, It has been argued that internationalisation is dependent, not only on domestic assets, which can be exploited abroad, but rather depends on the search for new resources as well as establishing of business relationships with the purpose of developing competitive advantage in their niche areas (Haahti el al., 1998; Alon & Lerner, 2007; Susman & Stites, 2007). Alon and Lerner (2007) argue that many studies in the field of international marketing with focus on motives for exporting and differences between passive and active exporters vis-à-vis non-exporters, and further exploration of market factors, which lead to export success.

When studying the fashion industry, we notice that the emergence of global fashion has transformed the way fashion is perceived in the contemporary world (Azuma & Fernie, 2003). Worldwide, internationalisation of fashion retailers is ever increasing, not many years ago one could find stores such as Gap, Gucci, Armani, and Benetton in only a few countries. Currently, stores that offer such international brands can be seen every where. However, internationalisation of fashion retailers can be experienced more in Europe, Far East and North America, where trade agreements provide opportunities for retailers to expand and offer their products in countries other than their origin despite cultural differences as well as consumer buying behaviours (Waarts & Van Everdingen, 2006).

Dawson (1993) as cited by Moore and Burt (2007) has identified five critical success factors to the international expansion of fashion retailers into foreign markets. He notes that the fashion industry enjoys relatively low market barriers in addition to a single brand may enable internationalisation. Various studies show that successful international retailers share common management attitudes, decision-making frameworks and personnel skills irrespective of their size, retail format and product segment. Moore and Fernie (2000) classified international fashion retailers as product specialists (narrow product range, clearly defined customer base), designer retailers (internationally recognised brand, exclusive positioning), general merchandise retailers (mix of fashion and non-fashion goods, large format stores) or general fashion retailers (broad range of products, accessible pricing). These retailers are positioned in international markets by virtue of marketing effort and product offering, which contributes to their overall brand appeal (Bridson & Jody, 2004).

Internationalisation of Fashion Retailers

The international expansion of fashion retailers has its roots back to the seventies; some have adopted a proactive approach in terms of international expansion to maximise opportunities, which are afforded by their merchandise expertise. However, internationalisation of fashion retailers is not always proactive, expansion to foreign markets can also be reactively, driven by foreign market demands for the companies products, other luxury fashion brands have expanded internationally due to the saturation of the domestic markets, other studies suggest that expansion was driven by the motivation to exploit the potential of distinctive brands and innovative product offerings within receptive markets (Moore & Burt, 2007).

The need for retailers to operate across border has no longer become optional. There is a number of push and pull factors that contribute to the internationalisation of fashion retailers such as searching for new customer, increase revenue, educe dependency on one market and most importantly achieve economies of scale. However, retailers respond differently to opportunities, some are proactive and some are reactive in their approach to expansion in foreign markets. Burt (2001) argues that internationalisation of retailers involves three broad categories of transfer; transfer of retail concepts; the transfer of retail operations and transfer of management functions. In addition, Burt maintains that cross-border trading as the case in Continental Europe creates what he calls consumer spending, where considerable amount of cross-border shopping takes place and retailers located in these areas may tailor their offerings to non-domestic consumers (Burt, 2001).

A number of studies focused on export behaviours, which they argue start with irregular foreign sales and as their involvement in foreign sales progresses, sales or business units are established abroad, which leads to a production unit outside the domestic market (Haahti el al., 1998). Other approaches analyse internationalisation as a rational process successively allocating resources to international operations (Acs el al., 1996; Haahti el al., 1998). When initiating an internationalisation strategy, fashion retailers reflect upon the congruence of their product ranges and brand images within the context of the prevalent cultural and trading conditions of foreign markets.

Westhead el al. (2007) argues that while the current understanding of internationalisation is shaped by integrating multiple theoretical perspectives, there is a need to incorporate an understanding of entrepreneurial behaviours into models of internationalisation. This view was similarly argued by O'Farrell el al. (1998), they suggest a flexible approach to explore internationalisation, whereby a theory should be developed to consider the strategic choices open to entrepreneurs and how the home region context may be linked to foreign market decisions. Furthermore, Johanson and Vahlne (1990) suggest that researchers of internationalisation should investigate how internationalisation is related and influenced by surrounding processes and how strategies are shaped by surrounding circumstances. Internationalisation has presented fashion retailers with major opportunities as one of the main sources of new customers, new technology and lower cost products and services (Burgel, 2004; Alon & Lerner, 2007). In addition, internationalisation has allowed fashion retailers to maintain control over their internal resources, which were the prime contributor to the retailers' success during the internationalisation process (Haahti el al., 1998; Susman & Stites, 2007). Internationalisation, however, is influenced by the size and resources as well as the sector in which the retailers operate (Griffiths el al., 2007).

The current literature on the internationalisation of fashion retailers provides a number of possible strategies; some studies argue that the process of internationalisation is driven by geographical and cultural proximity to their local market (Lualajainen, 1991). Yet other studies provide evidence that contradict the findings of Lualajainen in terms of mode of internationalisation and the market selection (Susman & Stites, 2007). Therefore, the internationalisation of fashion retailers can be better explained by studying the internationalisation process and the critical driving forces for successful transition into the international market. The internationalisation of fashion retailers has five dimensions. The first is linked to the retailer's position in the local business network, which determines the process of internationalisation as well as its ability to mobilise its resources within the network in order to use its business ties exploit opportunities provided by the network as well as using the knowledge base which has been acquired from the retailer's relationship with suppliers, customers, distributors and regulatory and public agencies well as other market actors (Egan, 1995; Susman & Stites, 2007). Coviello and Munro (1999) suggest that the network perspective goes beyond the models of incremental internationalisation, where strategy emerges as a pattern of behaviour influenced by the network relationships. This indicates that firms affect and are affected by the dynamics of the network. In light of this statement, Egan (1995) argues that the decision making process and international expansion affects not only the firm and its subsidiary, but rather affects the entire network.

Fashion retailers adopt different approaches to international expansion, in terms of market selection ,entry mode and product customisation; Fernie and Moore (2003) argue that fashion houses adopt a different approach in pursuing international engagement in terms of product standardisation in product characteristics, colours and specifications as the case in Benetton, which lasted for a long time, but until 2001 the company allowed 20% of its rages to be customised to meet the needs of specific country markets. Bohdanowicz and Clamp (1994) argue that there are two main types of multinational firms that dominate the fashion industry; first, the multi-domestic company, referred to as multinational; this type of firm operates across international boundaries with country independent operational structure and each country enjoys its own store formats and managed by local personnel such as the US brand Sears Holdings, which owns the fashion store Miss Selfridge in the UK market. Secondly the global company, this type of fashion companies integrates its operations in different countries and designs and markets its products for a single segment worldwide such as C&A and Laura Ashley (Bohdanowicz & Clamp, 1994). Bohdanowicz and Clamp further argue that international marketing depends on; (1) organisational objectives; (2) potential growth in the market; (3) size of the competition and (4) business environment risk.

International retailers can adopt different techniques to international expansion. First; the network-based approach, Ford (2002) argues that some of the exchange relationships in the domestic network may be connected to the existing or potential exchange network. Second, firm's resources; Ford argues that the firm can internationalise through resource-interdependence between the firms' own resources and the other firms' resources within the network. Third, Ford believes that the firm's network theory not only directs the strategic action towards specific efforts to influence resources and positions, but can also be communicated to other actors in the network. Johanson and Mattsson (1988) as cited by De Burca el al. (2004) describe the modes of entry using the network theory approach, in terms of firm's position in a network as: (1) international expansion, where the firm enters an new international network; (2) international penetration, which is capitalising on the firm's position in the international network; and (3) international integration, which is coordinating the positions occupied in networks in different countries.

The second dimension is related to the managerial know-how, which are associated with globalisation and puts the market knowledge at the centre of the internationalisation process. This means that the internationalisation process is a continued interaction between the "state" and "change" variables, where market commitment and market knowledge (state variables) influence commitment decisions and current activities (change variables), which in turn feedback to commitment and "foreign organising knowledge" (Johanson & Vahlne; 1977, 1990; Autio, 2005; Jones, 2007; Westhead el al., 2007; Mazzarol, 2007). Management attitudes can decide where retailers expand (Fillis, 2001; Treadgold & Mavondo, 2000). The concept of psychic distance, the degree of uncertainty a firm has about foreign markets, has been cited as critical in deciding the direction of a retailer's international expansion. However, research has shown that some retailers overcome psychological barriers because of their product characteristics and brand image. Retailers' international experience affects the attitudes of the key decision makers involved; on the other hand, the lack of knowledge and limitation of resources tend to prevent the retailer from growing (Fillis, 2001). Fillis further argues that as experience and knowledge increases, culturally distant export market, other markets will then be selected.

The third dimension is related to the retailer's resources; the availability of resources to the internationalising retailers and the degree of operational control play a vital role in the retailer's ability to internationalise and operate successfully in foreign markets. Resources referred to in the theory mainly address four critical attributes as described by Barney and Clark (2007) in the VRIO Framework; resources that are valuable, rare, inimitable and the way firms organise their resources to create economic value, in return create sustainable competitive advantage (Gottschalk, 2005). Therefore, internationalising retailers require adequate resources and competitive advantages and must possess unique attributes to ensure successful international transition. The resource-based approach advocates that competitive advantage comes from assets and capabilities that are valuable, rare, imperfectly inimitable, and non-substitutable (Griffiths el al., 2007; Alon & Lerner, 2007; Mughan & Lloyd-Reason, 2007). Gottschalk (2005) argues that sustainable competitive advantage is likely to be created from intangible resources rather than tangible resources. In order to achieve this consistency between resources and business must be maintained; through constant evaluation of resources against key success factors in each business. These advantages could include product, lifestyle, image and niche differentials, illustrated by internationally appealing brands and products or innovative retail formats facilitating international success. A strong brand has been identified as a factor assisting the international expansion of fashion retailers offering distinctive products in unique retail environments. There has been little investigation into the effect of corporate structure, company culture and management leadership with regard to fashion internationalisation [Moore & Fairhurst, 2003).

Gottschalk (2005) argues that resource-based strategy is concerned with mobilisation of resources as the basis for value-creation, where tangible and intangible resources, whether individual or organisational are recognised, combined and turned into activities. In analysing resources, Clarke (2005) had cited the model of Grant (1990, 1995); suggesting that the outcome of analysis is intended to give top decision makers a better understanding of their firm's relative strengths and weaknesses, which can be part of business process redesign. Clarke (2005) makes the point that analysis of resources has two main advantages; (1) it addresses the gap between the sock market valuation of a firm and the sell-off value of tangible assets; (2) the definition of capabilities is vital, yet tends to be descriptive.

Furthermore, Gottschalk proposes that despite the necessity to capitalise on rare, valuable non-substitutionable resources, firms should also compete on all other resources required to produce and deliver the product or service in each business. Barney and Clark (2007) described intangible resources as intangible assets such as knowledge, customers, market position, corporate culture and human capital. Moore and Burt (2007) present four types of international fashion retailers, namely:

1. The Product specialist fashion retailers: these are companies that focus upon a narrow and specific product range such as Nike, La Senza and Tie Rack, which has a defined target market and specific market segments.

2. The fashion designer retailers: Fernie el al. (1997) as cited by Moore and Burt (2007) defines this type as companies that have an international profile in the fashion industry and have been established in the fashion design sector. These firms retail merchandise through outlets bearing the designer's name within two or more countries such as Gucci, Valentino and Chanel.

3. The general merchandise retailers: the Corporate Intelligence Retailing (1997) as cited by Moore and Burt (2007) defines this type of companies as retailers that include a mix of fashion and non-fashion products within their merchandise offer such as Marks & Spencer, Harrods and Sogo.

4. The general fashion retailers: this type is defined by the Corporate Intelligence Retailing (1997) as cited by Moore and Burt (2007) as retailers that offer a wide range of merchandise either to a broad or defined target segment and is primarily characterised by low to mid-priced and located in city centres to allow maximum access.

Westhead el al. (2007) argues that while the current understanding of internationalisation is shaped by integrating multiple theoretical perspectives, there is a need to incorporate an understanding of entrepreneurial behaviours into models of internationalisation. This view was similarly argued by O'Farrell el al. (1998) as cited by Westhead el al. (2007), they suggest a flexible approach to explore internationalisation, whereby a theory should be developed to consider the strategic choices open to entrepreneurs and how the home region context may be linked to foreign market decisions. Furthermore, Johanson and Vahlne (1990) suggest that researchers of internationalisation should investigate how internationalisation is related and influenced by surrounding processes and how strategies are shaped by surrounding circumstances.

Factors influencing the internationalisation of fashion retailers

The factors influencing internationalisation of fashion retailers are common across countries; however they vary in the degree and extent to which they influence businesses. Fashion retailers seek growth (entrepreneurial factors), which cannot be achieved only in the home country (push factor), and this encourages retailers to pursue a strategy to internationalise through finding an opportunity (pull factor) that capitalises on the appropriate circumstances (chance factor), but a combination of such factors may lead retailers to internationalise in a rather passive or reactive way. Successful operations in the international market depends on understanding the business and cultural environments, which are summarised by Bohdanowicz and Clamp in; law, politics, technology, social organisation, aesthetics, education, values and attitudes, religion, language and economic status (Bohdanowicz & Clamp, 1994). Moore and Burt (2007) argue that the internationalisation of fashion retailers is driven by the need to import products and raw materials from markets (inward internationalisation). This pull factor is often influenced by the power of the country of origin, which influences consumers' perception of the quality, reliability and style. In addition, the brand perception, which has been created by superior brands such as Lacoste, DKNY and Gucci have forces retailers to stock products that perceived to be quality to meet consumer demands for such brands (Moore & Burt, 2007).

It has also been argued that retailers may experience challenges in the international market due to entry barriers, which can be natural, financial, legal or cultural, which creates risky ventures for retailers, and such barriers are higher for small retailers than for large ones (Acs el al., 1997). Jones (2006) argues that globalisation provides access to financing as a critical resource for entrepreneurship, through the increased integration of financial capital markets among countries. On this argument, Zimmerer & Scarborough (2002) believe that barriers to international trade can be a risk factor, particularly for small retailers to pursue global operations. They state that domestic factors such as attitude, information and financing can be higher barriers than the international ones such as tariffs and embargo. This is an additional to political, cultural and technological barriers. Herrmann (2007) adds to this view by stating that one of the major challenges facing businesses in trading globally is managing risks arising from uncertainty and complexity. In addition, there are the cultural and behavioural challenges faced by businesses (Palich & Bagby, 2007; Herrmann, 2007), these include:

- Difficulty locating prospects;

- Identifying reliable foreign representative;

- Lack of management expertise;

- High costs;

- Tariffs and non tariff barriers such as regulations and red tape

- Shifting currency values;

- General lack of information;

- Language and cultural barriers; and

- Finding qualified employees

Tordjman (1995) as cited by Moore and Burt (2007) provide a number of external and internal motivational factors that influence the fashion retailers' decision to engage in international activities. The external factors include emergence of homogenous consumer tastes, saturation of national markets, improvements in logistics and international information exchange; and the internal motivational factors include the exploitation of brand image, and corporate know-how over a wider range of markets.

Alexander (1997) as cited by Moore and Burt (2007) present a number of push and pull factors that influence the internationalisation of fashion retailers, as presented in the following table:

Table 1: Push and Pull Factors of Fashion Retail Internationalisation

Boundary	Push	Pull
Political	Unstable structure, restrictive regulatory environment, anti-business culture dominant, consumer credit restrictions	Stable structure, relaxed regulatory environment, pro-business culture dominant, relaxed consumer credit regulations
Economic	Poor economic conditions, low growth potential, high operating costs, mature markets, small domestic markets	Good economic conditions, high growth potential, low operating costs, large market, favourable exchange rats, depressed share prices
Social	Negative social environment, negative demographic trends, population stagnation	Positive social environment, positive demographic trends, population growth
Cultural	Unfamiliar cultural climate, heterogeneous cultural environment	Familiar cultural reference points, innovative business/retail culture, homogenous cultural environment
Retail Structure	Hostile environment, high concentration levels, format saturation, unfavourable operating environment	Niche opportunities, company owned facilities, favourable operating environment

Source: Alexander (1997) cited by Moore and Burt (2007)

Internationalisation Process of International Fashion Retailers

Many fashion retailers aim to constantly generate revenue in the international market. This process of fashion retailer internationalisation requires securing international competitiveness and innovation. In realising the importance of retailers' roles in the national economies, the European governments have developed policy measures aimed at both new and established retailers. The process of fashion retailer internationalisation has several strands; First; to encourage fashion retailers to trade internationally from the outset, Second; the encouragement of "export capable" and "inexperienced exporter" firms to sell their goods and services outside the domestic market (Griffith el al., 2007; Susman & Stites, 2007; Westhead el al., 2007).

Established fashion retailers often expand their operations into new foreign markets, benefiting from their exclusive brands and their innovative products, where their brand position plays a key role in their market development, which is attractive to retailers operating in niche markets such as high-end accessories or children's clothing (Portolese, 2003). Retail internationalisation has been studied, where a number of frameworks have been developed to explain the retailers' internationalisation process in terms of strategy, organisational structure and within the influence of the environmental factors, yet it is difficult to find common characteristics among all themes. Further studies focused on export behaviours, which they argue start with irregular foreign sales and as their involvement in foreign sales progresses, sales or business units are established abroad, which leads to a production unit outside the domestic market (Haahti el al., 1998). Other approaches analyse internationalisation as a rational process successively allocating resources to international operations (Acs el al., 1997; Haahti el al., 1998).

Phatak (1983) as cited by Haahti (1998), argues that the process is based on the mode of international operation; (1) foreign inquiry; (2) the export manager; (3) the export department and direct sales; (4) sales branches and subsidiaries; (5) assembly abroad; (6) production abroad [(a) contract manufacturing, (b) licensing, (c) investment in manufacturing]; and (7) integration of foreign affiliates (Haahti el al., 1998; Mazzarol, 2007) . However, Haahti el al. (1998) and Griffiths el al. (2007) argue that some firms do not necessarily operate according to the theoretical stage model of internationalisation; they rather use different operational approaches simultaneously. They favour a model developed by Luostarinen and Hellman (1993), which allows the researcher the flexibility to study the international operations on he firms' level. The model presents the following four stages: (1) domestic stage; (2) inward stage – technology transfer or import of raw materials; (3) outward stage – export, licensing, manufacturing; (4) cooperation stage – cooperation agreement on manufacturing and R&D) De Burca el al. (2004). Other critics confirms Haahti's view against the incremental, step-by-step character of the model since studies have found that it is possible for firms to skip some of the stages and achieve internationalisation rapidly rather than doing gradually (Chetty & Campbell, 2003; Griffiths el al., 2007).

Modes of Internationalisation

Fashion retailers often engage initially in international activities through exporting; however, other forms are also used such as joint venture, partnerships, informal alliances and establishment of sales offices offshore. Internationalising firms are obliged to select a mode of operation through which it engage in international activities such as exporting, direct investment, licensing, etc (Dawson, 1994; Haahti el al., 1998; Susman & Stites, 2007). Dana (2000) argues that the internationalisation process is influenced by four main environmental conditions; (1) characteristics of the domestic market; (2) characteristics of the foreign market; (3) market internationalisation and (4) industry in which small business is operating. De Burca el al. (2004) believe that the nature of the government support or involvements may influence the entry mode; they argue that initially governments are concerned with export and to a lesser extent on establishing joint ventures. Furthermore, incentives offered by the host governments can influence the shape and size of entry into market (i.e. if the incentive is attractive this may encourage firms t directly invest, or establish a joint venture. Dawson (1994) argues retailers pursue one of five market entry modes; internal expansion, merger or takeover, franchise agreement, joint venture or non-controlling interest. Each of these has advantages and disadvantages, is chosen by a retailer on the basis of its corporate confidence, product portfolio and brand image and has consequent set up cost and operational control implications.

It has also been argued that not all retailers internationalise pursuing the same mode. Although some modes are common such as exporting or licensing, fashion retailers often engage in traditional manufacturing and service activities or direct exporting and rarely pursue other modes such as joint venturing or partnership. Without a doubt each mode comes with associated risks, control and costs (Westhead el al., 2007). They further argue that modes of entry into foreign markets are likely to differ on key dimensions such as resources, risk, potential return on investment and degree of managerial control. Acs el al. (1997) suggest different perspective to modes of internationalisation; they argue that internationalisation can be through one of two forms; (1) direct international expansion, whereby the retailers directly expands its operations to the international market without use of any partners or mediators (Zimmerer & Scarborough, 2002); (2) firms may expand through using a mediator or established large firm that has its own international network and resources.

Some researchers and scholars argue that there is some disadvantage to the intermediated mode; they argue that firms would constantly be paying the intermediator, which may at some stage exceed the costs of expanding directly into the international market. However, in analysing the risk factor, the researcher believes that risks associated with direct expansion may be higher than risks associated with the intermediated mode. Boekholt and Thuriaux (1999), as cited by Aramburu el al (2009), believe that co-operation and networking with other firms can provide:

a.   More channels for learning and creating expertise;

b.   Economies of scale;

c.   Economies of scope; and

d.   Heightened flexibility and shared risk

Fashion retailers entering into foreign markets can pursue of the many approaches. Bohdanowicz and Clamp (1994) suggest a number of approaches, which are common for retail entry into foreign markets such as franchising, licensing, joint-venture, direct investment. Therefore, the process of internationalisation may involve:

1. Retailers may internationalise by means of an evolutionary strategy based on export and import (Susman & Stites, 2007);

2. Initial internationalisation usually involves close regions either geographically or culturally; and

3. Retailers may prefer an independent approach to internationalisation (Acs el al., 1997).

Market Selection

Market selection does not appear to be influenced by cost/benefit analysis, government initiatives, infrastructure or psychic distance; it is rather driven by location of consumers and network contacts (Coviello & Martin, 1999). However, the literature in other areas shows that the initial entry into the international market is based on two main factors; first, the regional markets that are considered to be geographically close, which maximises the ease of conducting business in these markets. Second, the cultural similarities play a vital role in market selection, which reduces the psychic distance unless the internationalisation is driven by strong network. Market selection for international fashion retailers is often influenced by established contact networks and institutions of particular cities such as London, Paris, Rome and New York (Gilbert, 2000).

Bohdanowicz and Clamp (1994) argue that fashion companies cannot penetrate all overseas markets simultaneously and therefore, it is necessary to select which markets that offer the company the greatest competitive advantage at the minimum risk. Bohdanowicz and Clamp point out that the three main areas of focus:

1. Business environment; this refers to demographic details, governmental/political philosophy; legal and political system, country infrastructure and the economic conditions.

2. Marketing factors; this refers to cost and availability of data, distribution channels, competition and government regulations on pricing; and

3. Financial factors; this refers to government fund for local manufacturers, taxation system, capital availability and ability to transfer funds

Once the above factors have been analysed, the fashion company can begin to select its strategy and its means of implementation (Bohdanowicz & Clamp, 1994).

Retail Operations

Fashion retailers may internationalise in a number of ways, some authors have identified a global standardisation approach to internationalisation as being critical to the success of fashion retailers. Success has been attributed to their brand image and innovative products, implementing aggressive marketing campaigns. Dawson (2000) defines international retail operations as the operations, by a firm or alliance, of shops or other forms of retail distribution, in more than one country. Hollander (1970) as cited by Moore and Burt (2007) found that internationalising fashion retailers tend to focus on capital cities such as Paris, London, Rome, and New York, opening flagship stores within the leading centres in order to create an allure and sophistication for the organisation.

Treadgold (1990) identifies four types of internationalised retailers; (1) Cautious internationalists, these retailers are characterised with limited international activities and very cautious in market selection and often pursue acquisition strategies; (2) Emboldened internationalist, these retailers are characterised by maintaining high level of control in geographically spread operations; (3) Aggressive internationalist, these retailers are characterised by high level of experience in the international market, have clear corporate goals and maintain high level of control over operations; (4) World powers, these retailers are fully experienced global firms that are able to expand their international operations in various markets in efficient operational manner.

Internationalising firms are obliged to select a mode of operation through which it engage in international activities such as exporting, direct investment, licensing, etc (Haahti el al., 1998; Susman & Stites, 2007). Dana (2000) argues that the internationalisation process is influenced by four main environmental conditions; (1) characteristics of the domestic market; (2) characteristics of the foreign market; (3) market internationalisation and (4) industry in which small business is operating. De Burca el al. (2004) believe that the nature of the government support or involvements in the small business sector may influence the entry mode; they argue that initially governments are concerned with export and to a lesser extent on establishing joint ventures. Furthermore, incentives offered by the host governments can influence the shape and size of entry into market (i.e. if the incentive is attractive this may encourage firms to directly invest, or establish a joint venture. However, modes of entry into foreign markets are likely to differ on key dimensions such as resources, risk, potential return on investment and degree of managerial control. Acs el al. (1997) suggest different perspective to modes of internationalisation; they argue that internationalisation can be through one of two forms; (1) direct international expansion, whereby the small business directly expands its operations to the international market without use of any partners or mediators (Zimmerer & Scarborough, 2002); (2) firms may expand through using a mediator or established large firm that has its own international network and resources.

Treadgold (1991) as cited by Moore and Burt identifies three strategic options for operations in foreign markets; first, high cost/high control strategy, which is adopted mainly by firms with limited foreign market experience; second, medium cost/medium control strategy, which is adopted in a form of joint venture agreement; third, low cost/low control strategy, which is achieved through a franchise arrangements. Some researchers and scholars argue that there is some disadvantage to the intermediated mode; they argue that small firms, particularly would constantly be paying the intermediator, which may at some stage exceed the costs of expanding directly into the international market. However, in analysing the risk factor, the researcher believes that risks associated with direct expansion may be higher than risks associated with the intermediated mode.

Salmon and Tordjman (1989) as cited by Moore and Burt (2007) identified three strategic approaches to retailer internationalisation, namely; international investment, global and multinational and suggest the strategic selection is dependant upon the firm's internal competencies as well as industry dynamics. Salmon and Tordjman argue that the international investment strategy involves the transfer of capital from one country to another. They believe that the global strategy is adopted on the basis that the retailer has access to consumer groups with shared lifestyle characteristics and purchase requirements independent of their place of residence. Multinational strategies determines the use of customised strategies that suit every markets own dynamics, conditions and the retailer's own market position and brand strength. However, management expertise and availability of resources are of importance in the internationalisation process. According to Boekholt and Thuriaux (1999), as cited by Aramburu el al (2009), believe that co-operation and networking with other firms can provide:

e.   More channels for learning and creating expertise;

f.   Economies of scale;

g.   Economies of scope; and

h.   Heightened flexibility and shared risk

On the matter of strategy selection; Barney (2001) as cited by Gottschalk (2005) suggest that resources are often connected to strategies pursued by the firm and once a firm realises that it possesses rare, valuable, inimitable and non-substitutionable economies of scale, cost leadership becomes apparent as a strategic direction. Gottschalk (2005) argues that strategic choice may not be obvious in certain circumstances; and so, the resource-based strategy has to determine when, where and how resources may be useful. Barney (2001) finally suggests that more empirical work needs to be done to help executives to embark on the right strategy.

Gottschalk (2005) argues that resource-based strategy is concerned with mobilisation of resources as the basis for value-creation, where tangible and intangible resources, whether individual or organisational are recognised, combined and turned into activities. In analysing resources, Clark (2005) had cited the model of Grant (1990, 1995); suggesting that the outcome of analysis is intended to give top decision makers a better understanding of their firm's relative strengths and weaknesses, which can be part of business process redesign. Clark (2005) makes the point that analysis of resources has two main advantages; (1) it addresses the gap between the sock market valuation of a firm and the sell-off value of tangible assets; (2) the definition of capabilities is vital, yet tends to be descriptive.

Conclusion

Fashion retailers' entry into foreign markets is influenced by a number of external factors such as economic, socio-cultural and political as well as the understanding of the market dynamics and consumer buying habits and preferences. The internationalisation of retailers is a complex process that requires unique and valuable resources. Internationalising fashion retailers face a number of challenges and constraints, which require adequate planning and strategising to ensure successful transition into the international market. Internationalisation can take various forms and shapes such as joint venture, direct and indirect exporting, franchising and direct investment.

Internationalisation of fashion retailers depends on the retailer's strategic network ties. These strategic issues pertaining to the network are related to: (1) corporate positioning; (2) product positioning; (3) marketing channels; (4) contracts and agreements; (5) integration; and (6) joint venture, mergers and internationalisation. This means that strategic investment must obtain, defend and develop a position in the network and as the retailer being part of a network, its strength depends on its network ties rather than on its own individual resources.

CHAPTER 7: THE MIX MAP METHOD

CLAUDIO VIGNALI & GIANPAOLO VIGNALI

Close co-operation with practitioners from a broad range of companies and discussions with management educators from a large number of institutions alerted the authors of this book to the apparent lack of practical application of basic marketing tools by management of leading companies. Even though there seems to be an understanding of the marketing mix and company objectives, practitioners appear to find it difficult to translate the theoretical frameworks into practical tactics which would help them achieve their goals.

This book re-visits the marketing literature and reviews present methods for the application of marketing concepts. This is to clarify where the stumbling blocks for practitioners lie. The conclusions from this review are used to propose a new framework for the congruent mapping of marketing mix elements and variables at both the strategic and tactical level. This text starts from a view of marketing as both the study and management of the initiation, continuation and termination of economically-determined, market-related, mutually beneficial exchange relationships that exist between individuals and/or organizations. Such relationships may be transitory or longer lasting, encompassing a series of transactions.

It was after the second world war (1948) that Culliton originated the notion of the marketing executive as a decider, an artist, a mixer of ingredients. Borden (1964) famously took up this idea to broaden it to include both a list of ingredients and a list of forces that bear on decisions in marketing management. Borden's list of the elements of the marketing mix of manufacturers (an important distinction to which we will return) was as follows:

- Product planning
- Pricing
- Branding
- Channels of Distribution
- Personal Selling
- Advertising
- Promotions
- Packaging
- Display
- Servicing
- Physical Handling
- Fact Finding and Analysis

This list of twelve factors was then condensed by McCarthy (1964) into the famous 4Ps formulation of:

- Product
- Price
- Promotion
- Place (Distribution)

More recently, others have once again increased the number of Ps to be included, resulting in a list not too different from Borden's original. In the service marketing literature in particular (Booms and Bitner, 1981) extended the marketing mix list, broadening the traditional four Ps into the 7 Ps of services by adding Physical Evidence, Participants and Process. By this they seek to include all those elements an organization can control in order to satisfy its target market.

The development of the marketing mix as a conceptual model provides the historical background for the development of a deeper understanding of the practical tactical implications of the use of this concept as a framework for strategic analysis and decisionmaking. STRATICS (bringing together strategy and tactics) addresses the question of how the marketing mix framework can be used to analyse the competitive standing of a business organisation and how the outcome of this analysis can then be translated into practical tactics which capitalise on the organisations strengths. The MIXMAP model, the key in STRATICS, was developed as a guide for making this transition from the strategic to the tactical level and is intended to serve as a means by which purists can become practitioners and finally use the Ps in their every day environment, thus developing further Cullotin's philosophy of Business by Practical Marketing.

As shown below, a cross axis map is developed for one of the factors under consideration.

The Mapping Quadrant

The operationalisation of High and Low levels of two variables relating to the factor is defined and they are held constant for the purposes of the strategic mapping exercise.

Many authors have used variations of this quadrant model as a technique to develop and explain many a marketing problem through a practical viewpoint:

a) The Boston Group Matrix/Share Matrix

b) The Ansoff Matrix

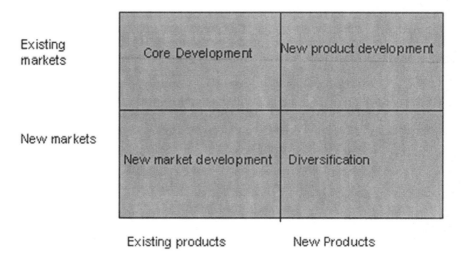

	Existing products	New Products
Existing markets	Core Development	New product development
New markets	New market development	Diversification

c) The MacDonald view on Porter's Competitive Strategy

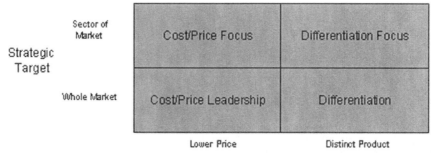

d) Kotler's Brand Perception, are but a few examples.

Whilst a variety of aspects of strategic analysis are covered; throughout the literature, there has been no consistent application of this type of quadrant model to its practical, tactical use in the marketing mix. This is largely due to a widespread confusion between mix variables and mix elements. Kotler (1997) defines mix variables as "A set of controllable factors that a firm can use to influence the buyers response". These are different from mix elements, which can be regarded as the traditional 4 Ps of McCarthy (plus S, for service). It is only when a company maps its elements using the quadrant model and the relevant, appropriate variables that it can effectively determine its tactics. These may in turn define the strategy it intends to adopt. Alternatively, it can take the strategy as the starting point from which to develop the tactics most likely to succeed in achieving company objectives. It is this mapping process which is facilitated by the MIXMAP model.

Tactics and strategy are not in question. The correct mapping of the marketing mix is. The lack of understanding of the distinction between mix variables and their constituent elements is the reason for confusion among practitioners. This confusion has resulted in practitioners sometimes questioning their own activities. Research carried out among UK companies highlights the extent of the problem. When companies are questioned about their approach to product development (a mix element), 90% claimed that the foremost considerations are price (a mix element) and brand (a product variable). In the course of evaluating a promotional idea, 85% of the companies questioned would take into consideration the service aspect of the idea (a mix element) and the likely spending on promotional channels (promotional variables). Almost all business decisions involve both marketing elements and variables.

This book advances the proposition that much of the confusion encountered by practitioners is due to confounding the mix elements and their constituent variables. This confounding then results in a lack of congruence in strategy and tactics. The cause of this is often found in an incorrect match of elements and variables, because of an absence of a consistent mapping framework. The use of which would ensure such congruence.

Below is a clear perspective to the distinction between mix elements and mix variables. It has been extended to include the additional mix elements.

Elements PRODUCT PRICE PROMOTION

Variables Brand

Quality

Style

Level

Discounts

Trade Ins

Credit

T.V.

Radio

Press

Personal

Selling

Elements PLACE PEOPLE SERVICE

Variables Outlet Type

Outlet Nos.

Location

Stocks

Politics

Age

Social Group

Quantity

Warranty

Freight

Insurance

The Extended Marketing Mix - Variables and Elements

This table can be used as the basis for the application of the quadrant mapping technique to both elements and variables, i.e. the MIXMAP approach and the use of STRATICS. Congruence between strategy and tactics is indicated where related elements and variables are consistently placed in the same quadrant. Furthermore, the quadrant would correspond to the quadrant the company is positioned in, if the mapping technique is applied using the strategic frameworks of the BCG Matrix, Ansoff and Product Life Cycle (PLC). It is proposed that such a match results in a consistent marketing message and is likely to enhance the probability of achieving strategic objectives. In contrast, a mismatch implies incongruence between the strategic and tactical level, resulting in a contradictory message to customers, with many of the marketing measures taken neutralising each other.

For purposes of tactical level mapping, the variables are operationalised by achieving a shared group understanding, amongst relevant decision makers. Following this, the Hi/Low axes remain constant throughout the application of the MIXMAP model. By using any combination of variables, the companies positions can be plotted.

The MIXMAP quadrant model for product positioning is shown below. In a theoretical example, the variables selected (by relevant decision makers) as most crucial were, Quality and Branding for the element Product.

In this example a company plans its product in the X quadrant, meaning high quality and branding.

Product MIXMAP

Likewise for Price, Place and Promotion once the crucial variables have been selected by the respective company the consistent approach is followed.

Price

Promotion

Place

Discount

Press

Stocks

Promotion and Place MIXMAP

The proposition of congruence between the Tactical and the Strategic position is a necessary condition of success.

Current

New

Products

Products

Relative Market Share

Time

Product Life Cycle (PLC)

	Development	Growth	Maturity	Decline
	1	2	3	4
Buyers	Few	Growing numbers: trialling product	Can rely on repeat business	Main buyers dropping off
Competitive conditions	Few	More competitors, trialling ideas, un-differentiated	Fight to maintain share; differentiate product; emphasise low costs	Competitors exit

It is proposed that when the above congruence exists companies are more successful and it is the tactical application and management of the above that develops the STRATICS in marketing. Thus the re-examination of the marketing mix, the establishment of the difference between mix elements and variables; plus the development of a proposition of the MIXMAP model which can be used as a tactical level planning tool in conjunction with established strategic level models such as the BCG Matrix, Ansoff and Product Life Cycle; the use of STRATICS has proved a great help to marketing practitioners. The MIXMAP approach enables them to revise their perceptions and to redefine their activities. The practicality of the models application has further been highlighted in the context of group discussions during short courses with marketing practitioners from a range of organisations, who as a result now view their operation differently. However, whilst the model clearly has a great deal of face validity and practical appeal, it should now be subjected to more rigorous testing. The first step towards this aim will be a more clearly defined operationalisation of the variables, drawing on the literature. This will allow a broader testing of the proposition that marketing success is linked to the congruence between strategic and tactical level positioning of a companys activities (as depicted via the BCG Matrix, Ansoff and PLC on one hand and the MIXMAP model on the other). In this the success of the companies marketing activities will be evaluated using a basket of criteria, including turnover growth, market share and a number of financial ratios.

The use of STRATICS must be developed within a planning process. Traditionalists on both sides of the Atlantic use a Marketing Plan approach to strategy. The authors in this text propose the following plan and name it the STRATIC Process, whereby the traditional marketing models and tools are used at specific times. There is a unification of strategy and tactics - STRATICS in the STRATIC Process.

MIX MAP CASE STUDY - GAP

Introduction

This case study will look at Gap's marketing strategies and whether it operates a push or pull strategy. The Mix Map model will be used to help determine whether the marketing strategies have been successful and what could be done to improve Gap's market position.

Gap was founded by Donald and Doris Fisher in 1969 in San Francisco, and named it Gap due to the generation gap. They opened the store because of their frustration of not being able to find well stocked jeans stores and began selling Levi Strauss jeans. This store was such a success that they opened a second and by 1983 there were 550 stores. The couple then decided to hire Mickey Drexler as the new president who helped create the Gap image and a $22.9bn global retailer (Vignali et al 2006a).

Advertising Strategy

Gap operates a pull strategy, which means they focus on "promotional activities (mainly advertising, and consumer promotion) at the end customers, with the aim of getting them to induce the retailer or other intermediary to stock the product. Advertising and promotion encourage customers to pull the product through the distribution chain by creating the demand" (Doyle, 2002). The main marketing tools being used by Gap are Television, billboards and the use of celebrity endorsement. When Madonna and Missy Elliot teamed up in 2003 to advertise the jean range, it turned out to be a huge success. Gap's use of music and celebrities in their adverts has helped to create the cool, laid-back image of Gap clothing. By featuring celebrities and musicians collaborating together, portrays Gap to be a very hip, stylish and fashionable store. This encourages consumers to shop there, as they too want to be considers stylish and cool, like the celebrities and musicians in the adverts.

Another successful global campaign was "for every generation" it included television, print, direct mail, web and in store marketing (Vignali et al 2006b). Gap's strong marketing campaigns, is the reason why it operates a pull strategy, to help create a demand for the brands products. By saying the products are for every generation is targeting the entire market, and as GAP has a wide range of products, this is true. Gap's clothes are quite simple and casual, and this means that a large share of the market can wear them.

However, to operate a pull strategy requires a lot of money, and while it is clear Gap's campaigns are very successful using the pull strategy, Gap is in a lot of financial trouble. This may not have been caused by their expensive advertisements and marketing, but this will affect Gap's marketing budget. Being in debt means they must minimise their expenditures and may mean in future advertisements, costs may have been cut, which could jeopardise sales, if the campaigns are not that successful, due to lack of budget.

Gap needs to manage its finances in order to keep producing strong marketing campaigns, using the pull strategy.

Mix Map Model

"The Mix Map Model was developed in 1994 by Vignali, Davies and Schmidt" (Vignali, 1997a). It is being used to determine whether GAP's marketing strategies are working and whether GAP is in its desired position on the market. It also looks at how the marketing mix is being used and how the outcomes of the analysis can be used to make strategic marketing decisions using the companies strengths. (Vignali, 1997b)

This model incorporates lots of different models including the Boston Matrix and Product life cycle to help determine the companys market position. The Mixmap approach enables a review of ideas and a redefining of activities connected to the market approach. During the conception and application, marketing prectians from many different types of businesses claimed that, after the discussion of the model, they began viewing their activities in a completely new light, both on the tactical and the strategic level, which was the desired affect." (Vranesevic, Vignali and Vrontis, 2006)

This model should help show the areas which Gap Inc needs to work on and which areas are working well with their marketing strategy in the present market climate. Product Life Cycle Model. The first model on the mix map is the product lifecycle (PLC), "The stages of the life cycles of the products in the industry offer useful insights about the industry environment." (Cravens and Piercy, 2006) The PLC shows Gap's position to be in the maturity stage, this is because Gap is already a well-established brand that has over 4200 stores worldwide (Vignali et al, 2006c), and is on every high street so it is quite hard for it to grow. Also due to Gap's financial situation of being in debt, stores have in fact had to close to try to reduce the debt by minimising expenditures.

Boston Consulting Group Matrix

The second model is the Boston Matrix (BCG Matrix) which, "developed in the early 1970's, probably became the most popular management technique ever." (Doyle, 2002) This showed Gap's growth rate to be quite high, this is due to the opening of stores in Israel and the expansion into Canada, showing an importance to Gap for new markets. "US clothing retail group Gap has opened its first Banana Republic Factory Store and Gap Factory Store in Canada. The openings are intended to target new value-conscious customers in the Canadian market and broaden the accessibility of Gap brands." (Mintel 2008) However, with Gap's financial situation, expanding further will be tricky as it can cause even more debt.

"US clothing retailer Gap has announced that sales in the three months to January 2009 dropped to $4.1 billion from $4.7 billion the year before, while profits dipped 8.3% year-onyear. The company said it would close around 100 stores to cuts costs." (Mintel, 2008) The closing of 100 stores will affect Gap's growth, and could start to move it out of the growth stage, which Gap does not want to happen. The opening of the factory stores and expansion into Israel will hopefully keep Gap in the growth stage, where they desire to be on the market.

Ansoff Model

The Ansoff Model "is useful in that it provides a convenient and easily understood framework within which marketing objectives and strategies can be readily developed." (Wilson and Gilligan, 1997a) Having this matrix as pat of the mix map model, will help provide a more thorough analysis of Gap's marketing strategies and their current position on the market. It can help suggest recommendations to improve their overall business strategy and also how they can develop their company to put them where they want to be on the PLC.

The Ansoff Model shows Gap to be in between stage three and four, for new products and percentage of new markets. This is due to Gap having a very basic range with merchandise seasonal not fast fashion like a lot of Gap's competitors on the high street.

Gap has started to enter new markets like Israel; "Expanding its worldwide network of franchise partners, Gap Inc. today announced an agreement with Elbit Trade & Retail Ltd. to bring Gap and Banana Republic stores to Israel. Under the franchise agreement with Elbit, the first Gap store in Israel will open this fall, featuring clothing for adults, kids and babies. Banana Republic, which will offer apparel for men and women, is expected to open in spring 2010". (Businesswire.com, 2009) This expansion is starting to portray Gap as a growing company, and could move it into the growth stage in the market.

Having stores in the USA and Europe and franchises in Russia, Oman, Kuwait, Singapore and the Philippines already, (businesswire.com, 2009) means there are not that many new countries for them to expand in. This means after a few more years, it will be much harder to keep Gap from reaching the Maturity stage.

Elements of the Marketing Mix

The elements part of the mix map model shows the 4Ps: Product, Price, Place and Promotion and uses these to gauge an idea of where they put Gap on the PLC by focusing on the two most important things to each element. (Wilson and Gilligan, 1997b)

Product

For product, simple design and quality are the two things being focused on; the model shows that they are on the borderline of growth and maturity. This is due to Gap having good quality products and always keeping the same simple design. The design needs to become more fashion forward for Gap to reach the growth stage fully. Consumers also believe this to be true "Gap's silhouettes are really strong but the colour palette is narrowit could have more pattern and print." (Brewster, 2008) Gaps simple design is keeping them in to maturity stage and the only way to increase sales and continue to grow is to have more complex designs and patterns introduced into ranges. This would change what is important to the product, but in a positive way, and as product is seen to be the most important element of the marketing mix, it should definitely be considered as it would attract a wider consumer base. (Wilson and Gilligan, 1997c)

Price

Price focuses on Gap's good value and how this then reflects the quality of the product. On the PLC, Gap is seen to be in the growth stage, this is down to Gap's simple price strategy. Gap has a medium value price plan and being on the high street means it must attract high street shoppers, so cannot be too expensive for the goods being sold. "Some of these looks pass for premium branded fashion and provide great value. Slim-fit Oxford shirts are strong at £29.50." (Mirza, 2008a) The fact that some of Gap's products can pass as premium branded products is one reason why Gap is successful, consumers can buy clothing that looks designer but at affordable prices.

Place

For the Place part of the marketing mix, a well laid out store and accessibility are used. This shows Gap to be in the growth stage once more; this is due to the fact that Gap has stores that are well merchandised. All the stock is easy to see and get to and well presented which entices the consumers into the store and to purchase the stock. "The glass-panelled twin storey fascia is an impressive statement and the collage of window mannequins in soft summer shades gives an aspirational image. At the top of the escalators is a white-walled menswear area, which has a lively shopfit featuring a grey tiled floor and mannequins showing complete looks."(Mirza, 2008b)

Promotion

Gap's use of Television advertisement and celebrity endorsements makes Gap in the growth stage of the PLC for the Promotion part of the marketing mix elements. Gap has strong advertising campaigns one in particular was the 2005 Favourites campaign. "From rock and rap to Motown and country, Gap has celebrated almost every genre of great music throughout its history. This August, Gap launches an integrated marketing campaign to celebrate this connection between jeans and music. The campaign will span two months, and focuses on "favorites" and how favorite jeans and favorite songs are individual expressions of personality and style. Each element of the campaign, from partnerships and promotions to television and print, will underscore this theme. The first element of Gap's fall 2005 marketing campaign features the iTunes Music Store (www.itunes.com) to help introduce three new denim fits for women (Curvy, Straight and Original) and one for men (Straight). Designed to fit an array of specific body types, these are the jeans that will become "favorites." (Gapinc.com, 2005) Having, well known celebrities as part of their campaign, wearing the products attracts consumers into the stores to buy the products. Celebrities are known for wearing high-end expensive clothes, and by seeing them in affordable high street clothes, enables the public to own something a celebrity has worn. This gives them a sense of pride, self-confidence and most importantly self-actualisation according to Maslow's Hierarchy of needs. (Easey, 2003). By having other well-established popular brands like iTunes linked to Gap, increases their cool brand image and they continue to aim their campaigns to their target market. This is because everyone always associates music and musicians with fashionable clothing and a desired way of life, and by having Gap's jeans associated with this, will surely make them best sellers.

This has helped establish Gap on the market as a fashionable retailer and the continued use of this marketing strategy, will continue to keep Gap on the market. The last model on the Mix Map model represents the final position of where Gap is on the market on the PLC. This takes into account all the models that Gap has had to be assessed on, and shows Gap to be between stages, two and three on the PLC (the growth and maturity stages). Considering that Gap is seen to be in the maturity stage by the public on the PLC, means that it must put some strategies into play in order to be in the growth stage and stay in the growth stage. Expanding into Israel is a great first step to achieve its place on the growth stage but more still needs to be done to stop Gap being seen in the maturity stage forever.

Analysis of Mix Map Model

Gap's use of the pull strategy has helped create a global brand, targeting young adults aged 20-35 years old and due to its diversification, Gap now targets mothers because of its Baby Gap and Maternity Range. The use of celebrities has been the main way to activate their pull strategy by creating a demand via their adverts. Celebrities are always having their looks studied and copied in magazines and if a Gap product is shown in the magazine then this also creates a demand for the product, so the reader can have the same look as the celebrity.

On the BCG model, Gap needs to continue its expansion, it is already expanding into Israel and this will keeps Gap in the growth stage. However, due to the debt that Gap is in, it may make this financially difficult, which means until Gap has got back onto track with its finances expansion may be harder and lead to more debt. However, this is something Gap is trying to do, by trying "to focus on cutting costs after predicting a tough retail climate for 2008". (Donati, 2008)

The Ansoff Model shows Gap is on the border of stage three, the maturity stage however, to overcome this Gap can start to introduce new products into its ranges, or even branch into a new range or section in the market. It has already branched into maternity and baby Gap, but another area Gap could focus in on would be to expand its footwear range, and have a big department area on the shop floor for it. At the moment, the footwear range is very limited, with just a few styles to choose from and they are not always presented well, usually just hung up on the accessories rail. This would certainly improve Gap's position and could even move into stage two.

To continue to keep Gap on the growth stage on the PLC, for the elements of the marketing mix, it needs to maintain its good value products and well laid out stores. However, it could make its design more complex or introduce a range of products that are more fast fashion orientated. This would try to make Gap appear as more of a fashionable, catwalk inspired brand than one people associate just with classic casual clothing to increase their share of the market. Gap's use of advertising and promotion helps put Gap into the growth stage, as its campaigns are always fresh, original and creative and are not gender or age targeted, making the brand accessible for everyone.

Recommendations

Considering Gaps financial problems, due to its quick expansion and desire to grow on the PLC, it has built itself up into millions pounds of debt, $2.9bn in 2002 (Vignali et al, 2006). However recently it has been getting back on track by shutting down unsuccessful stores and trying to refurbish tired looking stores. This reduces mass growth and instead Gap has been trying to focus solely on growth that will guarantee profit. Gap's recent expansion with Israel is proof of this, as Israel is a wealthy country with a rich cliental. The expansion for Gap Inc in Israel will help to transform Gap position on the PLC from maturity to the growth stage. After completing the Mix Map Model it is clear to see why Gap is a successful brand but also what can be done to make it more successful Recommendations: Make their products available online for the UK and the rest of Europe, so far it is only available in the US. This would prove to be a huge success as ecommerce is such a huge market and is increasing its share in the fashion industry. "The growth of ecommerce continues, with online spending forecast to grow by 32% this year according to retail research consultancy Verdict" (Drapers Record, 2008)

This shows that Gap Inc is missing out on a potential market sector in the UK and Europe that could help boost their sales and increase profit, without opening new stores. Being online in the US already, means that it would not be very difficult to make either the US site deliver to the Europe and the UK. Alternatively, a European and UK site could be set up separately, just using the US website as a template. This expansion would not require as much investment or time as opening a new store would, but will make Gap more accessible to a wider market, increasing profits and showing it as a growing company.

Expanding into the Far East is another way to help Gap be in the growth stage of the PLC, but first testing the market is necessary. Competitive shopping and market research needs to be carried out to see if their brand is wanted in the Far East markets and whether there is a demand for their product. Gap has expanded its sub brand Banana Republic into the UK, "Banana Republics Flagship Store is situated in a prime location on Regent Street, in the heart of London's west end" (BananaRepublic.eu, 2008) and has been a big success since it opened in August 2007. Gap could also expand its Old Navy brand into the UK following the success of Banana Republic. This would help increase Gap's share of the market and also increase its percentage of new products on the market, which would easily push Gap onto the growth stage on the PLC, where Gap wants to be situated.

Conclusion

Gap's marketing strategy has helped build up its brand awareness and create a large global group of loyal consumers. However, Gap wants to change its marketing strategy that has worked well over the years, which used celebrities and music to sell their products.

Gap is planning to change its marketing strategy by concentrating on "a mix of traditional and non-traditional tactics," and cutting TV advertising. Gap brand will not buy any more television ads for this year. Other clothing retailers owned by Gap will also adjust their plan of attack; Old Navy, Gap's worst performing unit, has hired Crispin Porter & Bogusky as its new marketing agent." (Mintel, 2008)

This change in Gap's marketing strategy will reduce gap's marketing budget, which may be why Gap has taken this direction, in order to minimise their debt. This strategy is different from the usual Gap adverts, but as Gap is a well-established global brand, it should not reduce sales due to their consumer loyalty. It will however, be more difficult to reach consumers by not using TV advertising, but this still can be done through billboards, magazines and in-store and local advertising.

Considering the Mix Map Model, and the fact that Gap wants to be in the growth stage of the PLC, the change in marketing strategy should not affect this, as Gap can still grow by carrying out the recommendations. Also by joining with a franchise company for a number of expansions internationally, means that Gap does not have to put up the capital to achieve the growth. This is a very clever strategy to achieve growth without the expense and need for capital investment.

The mix map model has successfully analysed Gap's strengths and weaknesses and has shown what could be done to achieve Gap's desired growth stage. However, by altering its tried and tested profitable marketing campaign, could affect Gap's progress on the market and not reach out to its target market.

CHAPTER 8: PORTERS 5 FORCES

GIANPAOLO VIGNALI & CLAUDIO VIGNALI

When discussing the microenvironment of a company, the questions of the competitive environment must be give special importance. Constant collection of information about the competition, through which the company can recognize their strengths and weaknesses, enables it to draw conclusions about their objectives, behavior, and responses to certain activities of the company. By knowing the marketing activities of the competition, their marketing budgets, a company can better prepare itself for the challenges of the competitive fight. This information is used to explain sudden activities of the competition and to predict how the competition will react to our activities.

Microenvironment is the public that surrounds a company — its employees, suppliers, owners (stockholders), and clients. It is very important how clients and the rest of the public perceive the company and its products and services. It is not good to have an uncoordinated image of the product and the company. Public perception enables (re)positioning of the company and the product, to coordinate the position to the expectations of the market segment. If the company views its product through the picture it casts on the market, and the target segment does not like this picture the marketing strategy is apparently not appropriate, and problems should be expected. The same holds for the employees perceptions of the company. A bad perception, image, means trouble, while a good one leads to success.

The way in which a company defines its environment is of crucial importance because the reasons for the biggest failures have to be looked for in the failures of the company to adapt to the changes in the environment. The environment must be viewed through all the forces which have influence over the company, including its products and services. To correctly build their knowledge of the market, companies must constantly monitor the environment, which will help them choose the correct strategy and positioning for the company, its products, and services.

The conditions analysis must also include an examination of the competitive position and the competition on the market. These elements are especially important for strategy development according to the famous Porter's five forces model. Porter (1980, p.44) is convinced that the "the essence of strategy formulation is coping with competition...In the fight for market share, competition is not manifested only in the other players. Rather, competition in an industry is rooted in its underlying economics, and competitive forces exist that go well beyond the established combatants in a particular industry." Furthermore, Porter claims that competition in an industry depends on five different forces. These forces are:

Porter's five forces model

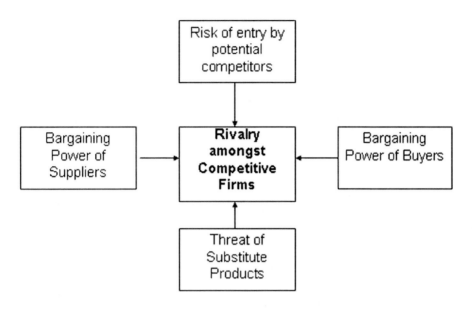

Source: Porter, M., Competitive Strategy: Techniques for Analyzing Industries and Competitors, Free Press, New York, 1908, p. 45.

Products

Porter's "five forces" model shows which potential threats can influence the process of market segmentation and competitive strategy determination for the target market. This can definitely be viewed as a great contribution to the understanding of the ways in which the environment determines the strategy. The entire model is based on the idea that the competitive match in an industry does not depend only on the players who take part in it, but also on the rules under which they are forced to play. The competitive match, in turn, influences the environment just as much. Porter stresses that the first determinant of the profitability of a company is the appeal of the industry of that company. This model draws attention to the analysis of present market conditions and can provide an important contribution to strategy formulation and implementation. What follows is a description of the basic characteristics of these models: the products life-cycle, the BCG growth-share matrix, and the McKinsey-portfolio multifactormatrix.

CASE STUDY USING THE 5 FORCES - LEVI'S

A Brief History

Levi Strauss & Co. was established in 1853 by "Bavarian immigrant Levi Strauss" (Vignali, Vranesevic, 2006; 91) and was first based in San Francisco, clothing the mass amount of workers that saturated the area at this time due to the California Gold Rush of 1849 (levistrauss, 2009) and with the help of Jacob Davis, Levi Strauss produced and patented the first "waist overalls (the old name for jeans)" (levistrauss, 2009) in 1873. Jeans quickly became the favourite choice of attire for many working tradesmen due to their strength and durability and eventually spread from the workplace to become an iconic fashion item, worn by "cowboys in westerns" and "James Dean in the 1955 movie rebel without a cause" (designboom, 2009). Levi's jeans, particularly their 501 style, was at the heart of this new product boom, jeans now being "the most popular wearing apparel on earth." (levistrauss, 2009).

Current Marketing Communication Strategy

Levi's uses, and always has used, a pull strategy. A pull strategy "...is aimed at encouraging customers to pull products through the channel network." (Fill, 2001; 286) and by directly sending the end message to the target customer through advertising and direct marketing, Levi's pull strategy will "generate increased levels of awareness...and ultimately provoke a motivation within the target group." (Fill, 2001; 286)

Levi's first television advertisement was aired in 1966 (levistrauss, 2009) and their campaigns can still be seen on TV today, with the added addition of also being online, and all are aimed at the young and fashionable. Levi's Live Unbuttoned campaign focuses on a care free, daring generation who like to live life to the full. This campaign features young, beautiful models participating in activities that are out going and care free, such as jumping off a pier into the sea, whilst adding sexual twists with the jeans unbuttoned and both male/female roles. This is done to generate situations that will create desire in the consumer, as the target customer of Levi's is late teens to early 30's, a generation that not only wants to believe they are care free and gregarious, but will also choose to use Levi jeans as "...not just pieces of clothing but symbols and ways...to express a certain lifestyle." (Evans, Moutinho, Raaij, 1996; 7) These advertisements pull the consumer into the brand and create a desire for that particular make. They associate the brand with their target customers generation, with the intension to build the belief that the brand understands what the customers want and expect from the products as the advertisements relate to their lifestyle. In theory this should create brand equity, where Levi's jeans are perceived to be the better choice over all other similar products/competitors but it has been suggested that in the 1990's other "Competitors such as Calvin Klein, Gap, French Connection etc, were able to role with the competition and offer equally competitive lines where as Levi's appeared to stand still and churn out standard 501s" (Vignali, Vranesevic, 2006; 92) and therefore brand equity has been affected by this added pressure from many competitors. Today Levi's still mainly produce the 501 range alongside only a few other styles, the suggestion that Levi's began to fall behind and stand out less as a market leader in the 1990's may still be true for today as competitors such as Diesel continue to be successful and have advertisement campaigns that follow similar lines to Levi's Live Unbuttoned, Diesel for example released a campaign in 2008 where the theme was live fast, a very similar campaign to the one Levi's is promoting today.

Diesel seem to be excelling in this market where Levi's could soon be entering, if not already experiencing the decline era of the product life cycle, with regards in particular, to their 501 style. Brand equity may be being lost to younger, stronger brands and therefore Levi's pull strategy is not working to its full potential and their status may be perceived as one that is a fashion follower, rather than the fashion forward brand they once were.

Innovation

To decipher whether Levi's are an innovative firm or not, their time through the product life cycle must first be reviewed. As the first producer of blue jeans, Levi's were, to begin with, during their time in the Introduction stage of the product life cycle, a very innovative firm, creating both product innovations and process innovations, not only were they the first to create blue jeans (a new product in the trouser sector) but also the process of producing this type of product was innovative to that of other methods of trouser production, "… putting metal rivet at point of strain: pocket corners, base of the button fly, etc." (levistrauss, 2009) created a stronger, improved type of trouser for the miners of San Francisco, "Within a very short time, all types of working men were buying up the innovative new clothing, and spreading the word." (levistrauss, 2009)

When Levi's and their 501 style jeans moved further into the Growth sector of the product life cycle during the 1950's they were still to be classed as innovative. More product based than process based now, as the process of producing jeans still remains almost the same today, with the exception on new machinery. At this time of growth "early adopters" (Evans, Moutinho, Raaij, 1996; 71) began to wear the jeans as innovative fashion items and the new trend hit it off.

Now slowly descending into the far end of maturity and touching on possible decline, the 501 jean is no longer innovative and Levi's products are on the same lines, no new innovations have been founded and processes, such as the pull strategy previously mentioned, have stayed the same for many years of Levi's maturity level. Levi's products are trusted and recognised worldwide for their quality and style, but with the market fast growing and competitors such as Diesel beginning to take over, new innovative processes, and possibly products, may soon be needed in order to maintain market shares, as the tried and tested "Smart advertising campaigns…why Levi's have been so successful." (Vignali, Vranesevic, 2006; 94) may no longer be strong enough to carry the brand forwards.

Porter's 5 Forces

Bargaining Power of Buyers

The bargaining power of buyers can have direct "effects in constraining the strategic freedom of an organisation and in influencing the margins." (Johnson, Scholes, Whittington, 2006; 84) The bargaining power of the buyer may be greater if the market if flooded with similar products and if the product was once but is "no longer considered to be exclusive". (Vignali, Vranesevic, 2006; 93)

Levi's is struggling with both of these factors and the bargaining power of their buyers is currently very high. Due to the high levels of similar products available at the same market level, Levi's key consumer can easily switch from one product to another and this move "involves little risk", (Johnson, Scholes, Whittington, 2006; 84) ultimately making it harder for Levi's to obtain and maintain sales as their buyers bargaining power increases with a growing choice of alternative products. Levi's has also seen a plunge in the exclusivity of it products, where the jeans have been bought by discount warehouses and sold "at a lower rate, often reducing the product by some 30%-50%." (Vignali, Vranesevic, 2006; 92 -93)

Asda was involved in this, selling Levi's jeans at massively reduced prices to a different type of consumer at a much lower market level and "Levi's feared that they would lose their core target market and hence their brand position." (Fill, 2001; 349) As a result Levi's buyers gained yet more bargaining power, and they may struggle to maintain margins at it has been suggested that Levi's "can no longer charge their recommended retail prices (between £40 - £60) for the product, as the consumer cannot rationalise paying that amount." (Vignali, Vranesevic, 2006; 93) When assessing these key factors it can be established that the bargaining power of Levi's buyer is high. The buyers have a wide choice of other products available and a hold on the cost at which Levi's products can be sold, together that means that Levi's must not only identify exactly what their target market wants but abide with their requirements and expectations of quality goods at lower than usual prices for the level of market that Levi's wishes to trade at. All of this together is having a negative effect on Levi's brand image.

Bargaining Power of Suppliers

In order for Levi's to ensure high quality products and good standards of production, "to this day many of the original suppliers and techniques are still used by the company" (Vignali, Vranesevic, 2006; 92). This is not an innovative way of working, and means that their suppliers have high bargaining power as they know that Levi's is tied up with them, trusting their work and have become dependant on their capability to turn out the right quality products. This means that the suppliers have higher bargaining power when it comes to price negotiation and, as with the bargaining power of buyers, directly "effects in constraining the strategic freedom of an organisation and in influencing the margins." (Johnson, Scholes, Whittington, 2006; 84) By having high bargaining power, Levi's suppliers are able to charge that bit more, ultimately reducing the final margins of the products. As a company with heritage at its heart, "Our past is a glimpse into the future" (levistrauss, 2009), Levi's has been "reluctant to move into larger scale overseas manufacturing…" (Vignali, Vranesevic, 2006; 92), this will also be increasing the bargaining power of their suppliers and yet again it ties Levi's down to a smaller number of suppliers. In order to reduce costs and free themselves from the power of suppliers, Levi's need to move forwards. They need to expand their supply base and show suppliers that are taking advantage of their power that they are not afraid or unable to move on.

The Threat of Substitute Products

"Substitution reduces demand for a particular class of products as customers switch to alternatives…" (Johnson, Scholes, Whittington, 2006; 84) and with this in mind Levi's not only has to contend with mass amounts of other jean products readily available at all levels of market, but also must consider the threat that jeans will experience a downfall in sales due to customers substituting them for another type of product all together. Today jeans are worn all over the world and could be seen as the most common item of clothing to own, back in 2007 it was estimated that "three pairs of jeans were sold every second, with annual sales rising year on year" (which, 2009) this figure will now be even higher. Jeans look to be a favourite that is here to stay so the threat of substitution is minimal. Fast fashion is now a way of culture, especially for western society, and with this comes the small threat of fast, but possibly furious, substitution, as quick fire trends may cause a slump in jeans sales if a new trend takes a strong hold. These trends will not last long enough, or be wide spread enough to make jeans obsolete, the Arabian Knights trend of today for example, may push buyers to purchase a different type of trouser for some time but as this fast fashion fades jeans will still be a core item of every consumers wardrobe.

These flashes of trend diversion are not a serious threat to the blue jean industry as jeans still rein supreme and "Jeans sales in the UK will rise by a further 38 per cent to hit £2.1 billion by 2012, Mintel predicts." (which, 2009) These slight dips in sales dues to fast fashion trends are not strong enough to have an effect on overall annual sales and will compare nothing like to the mid 1990's, when "Customers substituted jeans for a period... which affected the whole industry." (Vignali, Vranesevic, 2006; 93) Levi's has little to worry about in the way of substitution but should be aware that key fast fashion trends should not be ignored and if a change in style should occur in the jeans sector, Levi's should acknowledge it and do their best to provide for their target market's wish to be fashion forwards and on trend.

Rivalry Between Competitive Firms

Levi's was once the only manufacturer of blue jeans, protected by a patient set up in 1873 and "set the standard for many years..." after, (Vignali, Vranesevic, 2006; 92) but once the patient was lifted other competitors were able to form by producing similar products and now rivalry in the blue jean industry is fierce, the market is flooded with very similar products at competitive prices. Diesel, an Italian jeans retailer has taken off to become Levi's biggest competition. Whilst "Levi's failed in its attempt to move into quality mens clothing because the target market associated Levi and the Levi brand with the production of jeans." (Fill, 2001; 346), Diesel excelled in this product area, drawing more fashion conscious consumers towards its jeans ranges whilst Levi's missed out and lost potential sales. Rivalry between the two is strong as many of their core jean products are similar and whilst Levi's lags behind, Diesel is powering forwards with its fashionable ranges, gaining dominance over Levi. Diesel began to be a serious competitor in the 1990's, by which time Levi's jeans had reached the maturity stage. It has been summarised that once one competitor has reached maturity whilst the other is still undergoing growth, growth of the younger company "has to be achieved by taking market share from competitors." (Johnson, Scholes, Whittington, 2006; 85) This is what happened with Levi and Diesel. "Within two years of the mid-nineties Levi's market share had halved..." (Vignali, Vranesevic, 2006; 92) whilst Diesel experienced growth, alongside other competitors such as Tommy Hilfiger, Calvin Klein and GAP. Today Levi's still struggles to keep up with competition as other, more fashion forwards, brands stand to be very competitive rivals with higher market shares than Levi's. To avoid being lost in the crowd and forgotten Levi needs to bring themselves forward and re-establish themselves as a key brand. They need to re-market products and think about moving on from the standard 501 style into a more fashion conscious, fast reacting, product based company.

Risk of Entry by Potential Competitors

As there is not just one market leader in the blue jeans industry the threat of entry by potential competitors is possible, if buyers are willing to swap and change who they buy their jeans from then there may be room for more competitors to open up and gain a share of the market. Realistically, with the recession of today, it is unlikely that entirely new competitors will quickly appear and this threat is relatively low for Levi. On the other hand, it could be argued that, as Levi's current market level is debatable, between high fashion and high street that new competitors may appear if they develop into stronger brands.

Topshop, for example, now show at London Fashion Week and are consciously hitting the high fashion market with stylish, quality products at affordable prices. As this retailers denim range could soon be seen to be on the same market level as Levi's, they need to prepare for the risk that this new entry could potentially take sales from them. As Levi's is not at its strongest point and currently heading for decline, any risk of entry by potential competitors holds a serious threat for the brand. Slowly but surely Levi is disappearing and it wouldn't currently take much to push them out of the market all together. Levi must fight back and be prepared to compete with new entrants at any time if they are to succeed and maintain sales if or when this threat is to become a reality.

Competitive Strategies (Porter's 3 Generic Strategies, Based around overall price leadership, differentiation and focus.)

Levi's focus is the quality jeans segment of the clothing market. Within this segment their key target market is late teens to early 30's, a fashion conscious generation of today. From this focus Levi's previously used to try to compete by having differentiation at their core.

Denim jeans were new and innovative and this product first carried Levi's into success. Once blue denim jeans became a worldwide, saturated market Levi's lost their differentiation but did not move their focus on to overall price leadership, although offering good competitive prices, today's market offers cheaper alternatives at the same market level, and this has now found them stuck in the middle of a brimming market. Levi's need to concentrate their efforts into one of these two strategies, price leadership could be a the way to go for Levi's as differentiation will be hard to achieve in such a vast market where the chosen product segment has many alternatives styles/products already available. If Levi's could promote good quality, stylish products at a price low enough to achieve price leadership whilst still achieving good margins the brand could maintain, and possibly gain higher, market share.

Conclusion

In an opposing approach to the suggestions made above, where Levi's should go for a price leadership strategy, it could be suggested that in order to rebuild the brand name and ensure the right target market is catered for without lowering the brands status or identity, a differentiation strategy needs to be taken on board. Although a price leadership strategy is a safer option, in terms of sales, this approach may damage the brand name further and the target market may see the brand as a cheap, discounted alternative to high fashion designer wear. In order for Levi's to rebuild its brand name back to its former market leader self, and to improve its relationship with its key consumer, not only the marketing strategies but also the products need a revamp. Product development should be undertaken in order to produce a range that should be more exclusive and fashion conscious than current ranges. In order to make it desirable this range should be priced higher than current ranges, only made available in certain stores or areas with an air of luxury being created (Vignali, Vranesevic, 2006; 99). Promotion should be a key factor and Levi can learn from their competitors who "use methods such as posters, magazines and the sponsorship of club nights/events." (Vignali, Vranesevic, 2006; 97), also celebrity endorsements could get the right type of media attention and create desire in the target market. Making this range more difficult to get hold of "the more fashion conscious consumer would find them more appealing..." (Vignali, Vranesevic, 2006; 99) and would ensure that Levi's keeps their brand name and brand equity at the high end level of the market, rather than losing their status, which becoming a price leader runs the risk of doing. With a more fashion orientated, ready to react strategy, Levi's could rebuild themselves and regain their market leader position, if they continue along the lines they are on now they run the risk of becoming a dead brand. They need to take action and improve their marketing mix, products need to be not only high quality but stylish too, prices need to reflect the exclusivity and desirability of the new range, also reflected in where the product is sold, making it harder to get hold of, and finally the promotion should follow suit of successful competitors, ensuring the range relates to the right type of consumer. In doing so Levi's could still achieve higher market share and improve relationships with their key target consumer, putting Levi's back at the top.

CHAPTER 9: THE SWOT AND TOWS MATRICIES

GIANPAOLO VIGNALI & CLAUDIO VGNALI

The goal of auditing external and internal factors is to determine which factors could be threats and opportunities on the market, with a clear definition of the companys strengths and weaknesses. In other words, the audit should result in a SWOT analysis — an analysis of the companys strengths, weaknesses, opportunities, and threats. Only the key factors should be taken into account, so as no to create on over-saturation with unnecessary data. The next step, after completing the SWOT analysis is the process of ranking of each factor according to its importance or influence. Threats can, for example, be ranked according to the probability of happening and consequences on the company.

A different theoretical mode can now be used — the GE/McKinsey matrix, which enables us to identify the relationships between the internal abilities realized through an internal audit and external opportunities realized through an external audit. The analysis shows whether the company should invest into a product, support the current position, reap as much profit from a product as possible, or neglect the product and stop producing it. SWOT analysis also helps to determine the future strategy, by shedding light on the areas where the companys strengths meet the opportunities and where the companys weaknesses meet outside threats. The reverse is also true, of course. The information obtained by completing the SWOT analysis for the company and its products and services and representing them in a GE/McKinsey matrix can also be applied to the Ansoff's matrix to identify the most appropriate strategy for the future.

SWOT analysis

Strengths	Weaknessess
Market Share	Low market share
Product Range	Poor level of profitability
Access to distribution channels	Exposure in declining markets
Strength of corporate image	Product range limited
Levels of Brand Awareness/strength	Low levels of brand awareness
Ability to innovate	Limited differentiation
R & D Capability	Failure to successfully introduce new products
Manufacturing Capacity	R&D investment low
Financial Resources	Financially Susceptible
Cost Structures	Production processes obsolete
Utilisation of technology	Management attitudes old and entrenched
Organisational structure	Organisation not customer focussed
Management expertise	Limited Market intelligence
Strategic planning Culture	Poor internal marketing systems
Customer loyalty	Little or no strategic planning
Global Reach	Limited control over resources
	No vision for the future

Opportunities	Threats
New market sectors	Maturing and declining markets
Market growth	New competition
New product development	Advanced technology
Product range extensions	New rules of competing
Utilisation of new technology	Product Obsolescence
Develop a customer orientation	Changing customer tastes/attitudes
Reposition the organisation/products	Widely available substitutes
Reduce/neutralise competition	Differentiation eroded
Forward and backward integration	Political change
Acquisition, merger , joint venture	Legislation removing barriers; creating competition
New management approach	Forward/backward integration by suppliers and buyers
Increase investment in R&D	Supply side restrictions
Improve degree of strategic planning	

Regardless of what business the company is in (whether its profit or non-profit), to be successful it must implement a rational approach with which it will anticipate and prepare to take advantage of the future changes on the market.

Taking advantage of the opportunities from the outside environment must be carried out keeping in mind the available resources of the company. Internal strengths and weaknesses are numerous, but can usually be categorized as follows:

- management and organizational system

- daily business activities

- finances and other factors, like raw materials, inventory, machinery.

During the analysis of external factors, the PESTLE factors should be examined in relation to the present and possible future activities of the company, according to its mission and vision. SWOT analysis is the basic tool for comparing the opportunities and threats from the environment with the companys weaknesses and, especially, its strengths. This is all well-known and is no news to anyone. What can be considered news is that it is possible to attempt to identify the relationship between these factors and base strategies on these relationships.

SWOT strategic implications

Source: Hooley, G., Saunders, J., Piercy, F. N., Marketing Strategy and Competitive Positioning, FT Prentice Hall, 2004, p. 44.

SWOT analysis can be viewed in relation to the direction towards clients as well. The basic supposition here is that the assessment of strengths and weaknesses examines only those means and abilities that the companys clients will be able to asses and evaluate. This approach is important because it incites thinking, which is important for the company, since the customers are the companys biggest value and they are, in the end, the ones who give the company their trust, by buying products and services.

Customer-oriented SWOT analysis

Source: Piercy, F. N., Market-Led Strategic Change, Butterworth Heinemann, 2002, p. 542.

Piercy (2002) claims that the key limitation of SWOT analysis is that often the same occurrences can be viewed both as strengths and as weaknesses, and the question of which factors of the occurrence can be examined needs to be posed. The customerorientation of the company in general is understandable, especially in the circumstances when the need arises to build barriers of entry for the competition in order to preserve and keep ones customers. There are many objections to SWOT analysis; most frequently they refer to the superficial approach and unclear strategic implications of the results. This has brought about a modification and evolution of SWOT into TOWS analysis. TOWS analysis uses the same entry factors, but they are organized and examined in a different way.

Breaking down strengths and weaknesses

Source: Piercy, F. N., Market-Led Strategic Change, Butterworth Heinemann, 2002, p. 543.

The following example of the TOWS analysis illustrates the preparatory steps that VW used when drafting their strategy to improve the market position when the company was struggling on the market. The analysis covers the period of 1973—1975, a key period for the success of VW. External threats and opportunities refer mostly to the situation in the United States, a market on which VW had major problems at the time.

There were also certain indications that similar problems might occur on the European market as well. According to the TOWS analysis, the results of the situation analysis can be categorized into four groups of factors: factors of threat, opportunity, weakness, and strength. The analysis of opportunities and threats form the environment and the companys strengths and weaknesses encourages the managers creative processes in developing alternative solutions. As experienced managers know, various decisions can be made in all situations, and various alternative actions undertaken. One strategy can be to specialize or concentrate. In that case the company can use its energy and strength to satisfy one need, or can concentrate its efforts on only a few tasks. In this way, American Motors has, for example, for years preferred to concentrate its resources exclusively the production of small cars, rather than enter in direct competition with General Motors, Ford, or Chrysler, which were producing a whole range of cars, from relatively small to large, luxury vehicles.

The TOWS Matrix

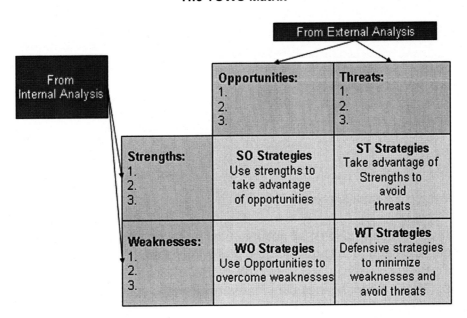

Preparatory steps for TOWS analysis

First step: Prepare a profile of the enterprise which embraces:

a) the type of business,

b) its geographic domain,

c) the competitive situation,

d) the preoccupations and culture of the senior management team.

Second step: Identify and evaluate the following factors:

a) economy,

b) society,

c) politics,

d) demographics,

e) production and techology,

f) market and competition.

Third step: Prepare a forecast, make predictions and asses the future.

Fourth step: Prepare a detailed strengths and weaknesses audit of:

a) the management and organization,

b) daily business activities & production,

c) finance,

d) marketing,

e) other areas deemed important.

Fifth step: Develop alternative solutions.

Sixth step: Show strategic options, all options must be taken into account, in accordance with activities undertaken and results gained during previous step.

Seventh step: Devise a contingency plan for every strategic option, depending on future movements.

Source: numerous sources — e.g. Gilligan, C., Wilson, M. S. R., Strategic Marketing Planning, Butterworth Heinemann, 2004, p. 101.

TOWS analysis point also to strategic options, where the results of SWOT analysis continue to be examined through appropriate strategies in order to take advantage of the opportunities and avoid threats.

CASE STUDY - ASDA (GEORGE)

Introduction

This case study will provide a brief analysis of company, George at Asda. The report will focus on looking at George clothing in depth. This case study analyses George's advertising campaigns, and discusses how these adverts link to their chosen segment.

This case study includes a discussion of Georges key target consumer, and includes suggestions to improve this relationship in developing future campaigns. Wal-mart took over Asda in July 1999, as mentioned by Vignali 2006. "Since being bought out by Wal-mart, Asda has steadily increased its market share to become the second largest retail chain in the UK" (Ebscohost, 2009). George clothing was launched in 1990 by George Davies and was the first supermarket to sell clothing in the UK. Vignali states "Georges strategy is based around price and convenience of purchase" (Vignali 2006:35).

With the recent credit crunch, this case study will analyse if there is anything else George can do to increase their market share and customer base.

Overview of current communication strategy (Push / Pull Strategy)

George uses two kinds of communication promotional strategy. These are push and pull and encourage customers to make a purchase which can be either a product or service. "A "push" promotional strategy makes use of a company's sales force and trade promotion activities to create consumer demand for a product. A "pull" selling strategy is one that requires high spending on advertising and consumer promotion to build up consumer demand for a product" (Bnet, 2009).

Their push strategy includes sales promotion in store. "The George range is also promoted in their monthly magazine and Asda leaflet which are both available free in store. In addition to these the range is also promoted in a summer pre-view catalogue" (Vignali, 2006;40). However their main communication strategy is a pull strategy. Vignali states "They have become a major corporate advertiser. The 2003 Mintel report showed that in 2001 they spent £25 million on advertising, £2.3 million of this was spent on the George range. It was aimed at raising awareness. The bulk of this was spent on television advertising, and the strategy behind the campaign was to show George as a modern and affordable brand for all the family." (Vignali, 2006;40).

George most recent pull strategy to build up consumer demand, was their recent advertising campaign in February 2009. "George clothing brand will take a dramatic departure from the fashion industry's current hunger for international models and celebrity faces by using everyday models. This radical strategy is designed to encourage customers to take a new look as the George fashion brand". (Just Style 2008). This was decided after a customer survey. "In a customer survey of 10,000 people, ASDA found that 72.3% of UK women would rather buy an outfit based on seeing it on a real person than on a celebrity" (Retail week 2008). "The ad campaign is "honest", according to Lambert, and appeals to Asda's core customers: Mums and families. This is part of Georges strategy to "Refocus the George brand on its core customers, family shoppers aged 25-45" (Talking Retail, 2008).

This chosen strategy creates brand equity as George has passed on the savings from not using celebrities to their customers. By passing on these savings it gives the customer confidence and satisfaction in purchase decision and George a competitive advantage. This enhances perceived qualities including price, value, quality and reasons to visit the store.

Brand associations include customer focused values associated with George, and increasing store loyalty by reducing marketing costs and attracting new customers. As part of the "pull" strategy the advertising campaign featuring real women featured in national newspapers, magazines and press releases.

This pull strategy encorporates the AIDA communication tool model of:

Awareness: George creates message of real women in advertising campaign.

Interest: Creates interest with George customers as they relate to models.

Desire – Creates a customer need to want garments modelled on real people.

Action – Purchases made and monitored by George.

Innovative Product / Process

George is a very innovative brand which currently has both innovative products and processes. "An innovation can be defined in a variety of ways, but most commonly accepted definitions is any idea or product perceived by the potential adopter to be new. It follows then that a product innovation is any product recently introduced to the market or perceived to be new when compared to existing products". (Blackwell, 2001:412). This theory relates to product launch of George's mid size jeans in February 2009. George understood this recognition need for demand innovation which relates to theory "Identifying a market segment with unsatisfied desires provides businesses with new sales opportunities" (Blackwell,2001:101).

George recognised the need for these jeans after conducting a study carried out by the University College London, and listening to its customers. "According to a study by the supermarket chain 62% of women consider themselves to be a mid size." (Daily mail, 2009). ASDA fashion label said "One of the most common complaints from our customers is that they are in-between sizes, we aim to solve this dilemma with our mid sized jeans" (Telegraph, 2009). These in-between sizes, use zone two relative innovation to "Build on existing products and services, taking products to new markets" (Vignali G, 09).

This new innovation gives George a competitive edge compared to its rivals. An example of their innovative processes if there recent advertising campaign. George previously used celebrities including Coleen Rooney, Jordan and Suzanne Shaw to promote their clothing but George realised the potential strategic innovation to use real models from the British public sector after a study.

"The study which was commissioned by Asda on the 1st of September 2008 asked whether you would buy an item of clothing if you have seen a celebrity wear it, 79.1 % of British women said they don't pay attention to what celebrities wear"(Asda, 2009). The new models which feature in the advertising campaign are real life women who are doctors and nurses and are supposed to reflect today's society.

Another example of George's basic innovation of their brand assets is their new logo which was launched this year. Brand Director Fiona Lambert stated that "The new logo reflects our brand values- modern and relaxed. It has an inclusive feeling and an element of fun" (Retail week, 2008).

Another example of George's concept innovation is the introduction of their transactional website, which was launched in February 2008 and allows UK customers to purchase George clothing online.

George Company Information

ASDA is Britain's second largest grocer in the UK. The George clothing range uses a low pricing strategy. Vignali states "From the position Asda is currently in, they would appear to be using a good-value strategy for the George clothing range. This involves providing a product that is of a reasonable quality but at a low price". (Vignali, 2006:38). George can stay competitive due to their massive buying power of volume sales. In 2009 George recently simplified their ranges and refocused on its core customer of families aged 25-45 years old. George is currently in the shakeout stage of the product life cycle which falls in line with the current climate.

Discussion of Swot and Tows in relation to George

Strengths:

- Growing market-share of 8.7 % to 16.94% in the last year. (Drapers, 2009)

- £2 Billion annual Global sales (Drapers, 2009)

- Have refocused on core customers (Mums with families) aged 25-45. (Talking Retail, 2009)

- Simplified and cut down product ranges to cover all ages. G21: Under 25's men andwomen, Boston Crew menswear 25+, Moda womens wear 45+. (Talking retail,2009)

- New modern logo

- George clothing available in 347 supermarkets, with a constant flow of customers 24:7. (Verdict,2009).

- Online website available to UK residents. (Talking retail, 2009)

- Keep up with innovation, including: in-between jean sizes and real life models. (Mediaweek, 2008). (Daily mail, 2009)

- Research and Development include studies by Universities, including body measurements taken by state of the art 3D scanners to gain a clearer understanding of their customers body shapes and needs. (Telegraph, 2009)

- New "real advertising campaign" appeals to core target market of mums and families as they can relate to real women rather than celebrities. (Retail week,2008)

- Ethical policies in-place including clothing made with Fair-trade cotton through the Fair-trade Foundation. (Fair-trade Foundation, 2009)

- Online website available to UK residents. (Talking retail, 2009)

- Strong management team. (Vignali, 2006:46)

- Strong Customer loyalty due to competitive prices, quality and savings passed from celebrity fees onto the customer. (Just Style, 2009)

Weaknesses:

- No presence in city centre retailing. (Telegraph, 2008)

- Some stores need re-vamping. (Vignali, 2006:46)

- Not seen as a key fashion retailer. (Vignali, 2006:46)

- Website only available in UK.

- Catwalk copies are not advertised.
- No student discounts available.
- No budget basic lines.
- No luxury sub-brand available, like the food line (Asda Extra Special).
- Not everyone is aware that George has a website.

Opportunities:

- To become the UK's leading clothing retailer by Volume by 2011. (Talking Retail, 2008).
- Revamp older stores to bring up to date.
- Launch website in Ireland and make it Euro compatible.
- Push for advertisements/features in fashion magazine for G:21 fashion conscious range, to create more demand.
- Advertise catwalk copies in magazines to increase demand.
- Create a basics range which has low price points for everyday essentials, as these are what customers are more likely to purchase during the credit crunch.
- Introduce student discounts to students aged 18-25 to boost G:21 range.
- Opportunity for luxury sub-brand, for customers with a higher disposable income, or customers who want to invest in luxury key pieces that will last them and save money in the long run.

Threats:

- Operating costs- property, wages and transport costs rising, making sales growth harder to achieve. (Vignail 2006:141)
- Tariffs to trade internationally are constantly changing and interest rates and exchange rates can be a threat when buying abroad. (Vignali, 2006:124)
- Increasing competition from Primark, Tesco, M & S. (Telegraph, 2008)
- Competitors Primark & M&S have advantage of high street locations.
- Employment levels could fall.
- Due to the credit crunch, customers have less disposable income compared to last year.
- Government restrictions on expansion. (Vignali,2006:46)

Tows Matrix

SO Strategies:

* New ranges simplified and cut down, can order more stock and to become UK leading clothing retailer by 2011 and increase market share.

* Management team, to create a basics, no frills range, aimed at core target market, Mums and families during the credit crunch.

* Create another "real ad" campaign using mums for new basics range to appeal to George's core target market of mums with families.

* Management team to create a luxury sub-brand to target customers who have more disposable income and are looking for investment pieces.

* R and D team to find out if there is a market to launch website in Ireland.

ST Strategies:

* Push advertising campaign that George use "real women" not models compared to competitors to create more demand from customers.

* Advertise new logo to let customers know George has changed, its ranges are now simplified and they use real women to model to try and appeal to new and existing customers.

* Management team to negotiate price points but not compromising on quality, to keep customer happy and returning to George.

* Signage instore to make customers aware that they can shop at George at convenient times (24:7 Monsat) giving them a competitive advantage to rival high street stores.

WO Strategies:

* Re-vamp older stores to make them more appealing to customers.

* Create demand for under 25 fashion conscious customers by featuring in fashion magazines.

* Offer student discount to under 25's to create demand on G:21 range, creating a competitive advantage on competitors.

* In-store POS to make customers aware they can now buy George clothing online.

WT Strategies:

* Do not employ any new staff at present.

* Use management teams to monitor operating costs and keep them to a minimum and pass savings onto customer.

* Management to keep up to date with interest rates and exchange rates and consider buying currency to hold back when it is a good rate.

* Keep up to date with Government restrictions on expansion.

The SWOT analysis tool has been used as it is as it is, "Probably the most popular tool used in strategic planning and organisational problem solving." (Trizjournal, 2009). It is also used today by many large companies including Tesco and Nike. Research shows that there are mixed opinions when it comes to using SWOT analysis. Duncan Haughey PMP, mentions advantages of SWOT include:

• Simple and only costs time

• Generates new ideas to help take advantage of an organisations strengths and defends against threats

• Awareness of political and environmental threats allows an organisation to have response plans prepared. (Projectsmart, 09).

Other advantages include "Swot analysis which is by far the most popular, can serve a dual function: it can be used for both internal and external environment scanning (Kheng- Hor and Munro-Smith, 1999) (Usca-edu 2009).

However theorists argue there are many criticisms of SWOT. Theorist Koch (2000) "Contends that most criticisms of SWOT analysis deal with its poor and inappropriate uses rather than inherit weakness of the method". (triz-journal 2009). In this journal by Dr. Rod Kuhn King is (President of Ideal-Solutions Management Consultancy) it also states that "Other limitations of SWOT analysis include the subjectivity, integrity and instability (over time) of listed strengths, weakness, opportunities and threats. Information contained in a swot matrix may be biased and not reflect consensus reality for the system". (triz-journal 2009).

Recommendations

In conclusion, this case study demonstrates that George's marketing strategies are reaching its main core target market successfully, which is shown in their recent market growth from 8.7% to 16.94%. This is an incredible achievement in the current financial climate. Having used analysis tools, SWOT and Tows Matrix, it has provided clear instructions on how George can improve and move the business further. Although there are many criticisms of SWOT it is used today by Tesco, Carlsberg, Nike and Toyota to name but a few. Kheng-Hor and Munro-Smith Supports this choice of model and it has provided instructions on how George can improve in the future. George clothing also relates to Michael Porters book "The Competitive advantage" the concept of the value chain. Porter states "suggested that activities within the organisation add value to the service and products that the organisation produces, and all these activities should be run at optimum level if the organisation is to gain any real competitive advantage. If they are run efficiently the value obtained should exceed the costs of running them i.e. customers should return to the organisation and transact freely and willingly" (Learn marketing, 2009).

This theory relates to George in relation to its competitive advantage of in-between jeans sizes, and "real" advertising campaign. Research shows that George's main key target consumer is Mothers with families. Improvements to this relationship in the future can be to continue to promote "real" advertising campaigns, using real women, as Georges customers can relate to these women. George could carry on the "real" advertising theme to its other departments, including childrenswear, Boston Crew menswear and Moda womenswear with George continuing to pass on these savings from hiring a celebrity onto its customers. No other retailer at present has switched from celebrity to "real" person, thus giving George a unique selling point and competitive advantage.

Plans to improve the relationship between George and its customer include developing a future advertising campaign, again using "real" people to promote its new no frills basics range. This will appeal to mums who are on a budget and want cheap, good quality essentials. The basics range will be extremely popular for mums especially with the current financial climate and customers having less disposable income. The Swot and Tows Matrix determined external factors that could affect George, but by using the Tows Matrix, strategies are now in place to control and protect these. The Swot has shown that there are opportunities to expand the George range giving it a competitive advantage and how to attract new market segments. These are listed below:

Short-term Recommendations:

• Implementing in-store POS to make customers aware that the George website is up and running.

116

• Implementing in-store POS to make customers aware that they can shop at George 24 hours a day.

• Create a new "real" advertising campaign to promote new no frills basics range, which mainly appeals to Georges core customers who are on a budget.

• Implementing in-store POS to make customers aware that George has a new logo and has changed with new simplified ranges.

Mid-term Recommendations:

• Research and Development team could create a Luxury sub brand like Asda food range "extra special", aimed at customers who have more disposable income and/or want to buy investment pieces.

• Research and Development team, analyse if there is a market to implement George website in Northern Ireland, and implement if there is a market, making it Euro compatible.

Long-term Recommendations:

• Advertising team could try to feature selected fashion items from the G:21 range to appear in fashion magazines for example, Look magazine to create more demand on Georges younger fashion conscious customers who the "real" advert doesn't necessarily appeal to.

• Offer students under 25 discount to increase sales on the G:21 range presentation of a valid student ID card.

• Invest profits in re-vamping older out of date stores, to make them more appealing for the George customer.

CHAPTER 10: THE PEST ANALYSIS

GIANPAOLO VIGNALI & CLAUDIO VIGNALI

Circumstances are determined not only by politics, economy, social, technological factors and development, but also by the awareness of the company of its own place in the market (the target market and the competitive environment) and its clients. All of this is important for an effective situation analysis of the company, and has a great deal of influence in the process of strategic decision-making. The level of understanding how much the environment influences strategy varies from company to company, depending on the development of the information system, the implementation of the market audit, the ability of the managers to recognize the influences, and, in the end, even on the company culture. The way a company recognizes this and views it through its own strengths and weaknesses shapes the strategic decisions and tactical activities of the company. Pass et al. (1995) define a company as a "business venture". At the same time, theydefine the organizational structure as a "business or administrative structure designed andconnected with a special purpose."

Companies can be viewed as profit or non-profit. A short look at the development of retail business offers a simple example of the different sizes and types of profit companies. Retail can be created on the basis of small corner stores, usually owned by private individuals or families, which sell groceries and some household goods. It can also be created on the basis of a small chain of stores, or on a larger chain, like Selfridges or Tesco. However, we can also view large supermarkets individually and/or as the chains they belong to (B & Q Warehouse, Asda, Wal-Mart, etc.). Each store sells numerous products (according to a rule with exceptions — the larger the store, the larger the selection), employs workers, and has its place and purpose on the market. Non-profit organizations include charities and volunteer organizations, like the Cancer League, Scouts, amateur sports clubs, etc. The public sector, for example, the health services and education, should also be viewed as non-profit organizations.

No companies or organizations conduct business under a glass bell. They all must take into account the circumstances on the market on which they do business. Kotler et al. (1996, p. 75) claim that marketing is "a social and managerial process by which individuals and groups achieve what they want and need through creating, offering, and exchanging values with others". They immediately go on to define external market conditions important for the company as "a place where the company must begin to seek opportunities and notice possible threats. These conditions include all the factors and powers that influence the company's ability to be effective in its target markets."

A somewhat more detailed definition is offered by Dibb et al. (1994, p. 32), when they define these conditions as "external powers that, directly or indirectly, influence the companys inputs and outputs. Inputs can include the employees, financial resources, materials, and information. Outputs can be information (e.g. advertising), packaging, goods, services, or ideas." The environment id comprised of forces that the company has absolutely no control or very limited control over. For example, a small corner store will be threatened if a new Asda or Sainsbury opens in the immediate vicinity. Equally, they will all be threatened should a large center like Makro or smaller Lidl open nearby. The environment of a certain company can include numerous aspects. Everything that influences or can influence a company is considered to be its environment. Kotler et al. (1996, p. 149) define external marketing environment as all the influences and forces that are outside the marketing management function, but still influence the possibility of a successful relationship with clients. Kotler's definition of the environment is well-known.

He emphasizes the fact that these are all factors that influence the function of marketing management, thus suggesting to people in charge of the marketing plans that business is under the influence of numerous factors. The process of planning and determining a strategy includes the audit of circumstances as a part of the general situation analysis, which is carried out before the development of a marketing approach. Kotler et al. (1996, p. 155) go on to suggest that, for audit purposes, circumstances are examined through their parts: the macroenvironment — which includes the social, legal, economic, political, and technological factors, as well as demographic movements environment protection issues, etc.; or the microenvironment — the relationships between the company and its suppliers, target markets, competition, and immediate public.

These areas must be examined separately, since the situation analysis provides the awareness of the forces that arise from these factors. In all that, we must keep in mind that these forces act together, and that they are not easily viewed or separated into certain categories.

The external audit is an important part of the marketing planning process. Since everything constantly changes, external factors should constantly be monitored, so that companies could undertake certain activities and react to the changes in the environment at the right time. Dibb et al. (1994, p. 37) suggest that "when marketing managers fail to recognize changes in the environment their companies are not ready to capitalize on market opportunities or deal with the threats such changes might cause." The marketing process has become extremely complicated lately, since the focus has changed from a price-based to a non-price-based direction of the competitive fight, i.e. from the physical characteristics to other characteristics of the product, as well as since the clients are better educated, have higher expectations, and increasingly more specific needs. The purpose of the marketing planning process and of the environment audit lies in the wish to utilize the company's resources to take advantage of the opportunities and the avoid threats. If we asses the various above mentioned forces, it becomes clear that companies must be sensitive to all changes in order to achieve or protect the desired position on the market.

Macroenvironment

Plans exist so that, with the help of the external environment analysis, consisting of numerous factors, we could take advantage of opportunities and avoid threats. Factors need to be analyzed and their changes in the near future, as well as not-so-near future, need to be predicted. These factors can be looked at as the macroenvironment factors. The most frequent model of representing the analysis of the external environment factors is the already mentioned PESTLE model, which point to the need for analyzing the following factors:

a) political,

b) economic,

c) socio-cultural,

d) technological,

e) legal (legislative), and

f) ecological / environmental.

Political forces overlap with legal ones in some aspects of the company politics, and sometimes can be viewed together. The governments politics influences the entire market through a number of regulatory measures carried out by state institutions (like in the UK, for example, DEFRA, the Office of Fair Trade, Health and Safety Institutions, etc.).

The decisions made and the rules enacted influence business in a number of ways — how should products be produced, how can they be sold, etc. The crisis caused by mad cow disease in the UK was in great part cause by the uncoordinated actions of DEFRA, the meat industry, and numerous other institutions. The failure to publish current and credible information caused enormous losses, among other reasons, due to the consumers fear of buying and eating beef and all meat products that include beef. An absurd example of the madness occurred when some customers refused to purchase shoes that had beef hide soles. This offers proof that numerous, not easily predictable circumstances can arise, and when they do, it is difficult to realize their effects, especially if the first signs of the problem are ignored. Regulations regarding health, transport, and education can influence the public opinion in regard to which products are considered good and which are not.

The External Environment

External Analysis - The Firms Environment

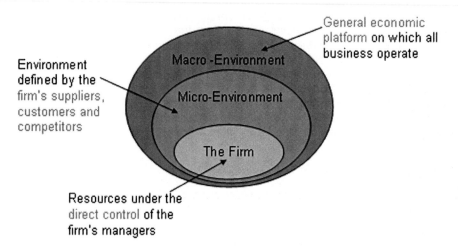

Economic trends, which are extremely important for business, as they influence the purchasing power, also depend greatly on the governments politics. During periods of prosperity, people will have more money to spend in general, and will be more likely to spend it on those goods that are not necessary for survival. In such times, customers become less sensitive to prices, which definitely influences the choice of marketing strategy.

An apparent instability of an economy gives more importance to short-term measures, such as sales promotions and special offers, while during positive changes in the economic climate we suggest more applicable approaches, like positioning.

Social factors cover numerous areas which have lately gained great interest of marketing experts. Social trends and consumer behavior must constantly be monitored. Changes in life-style and opinions influence the demand and the way of selling products. For example, the alcoholic beverages market must adapt to the increasing consumption in households as opposed to the consumption in public places, and the producers need to adapt their products to these changes. Marketers must be sensitive to the opinions of the clients, as an integral part of the changing environment. Clients are becoming more and more educated about marketing, and more and more critical. All businesses are operating under an ever growing eye of the public. With the increased usage of promotion, clients become more demanding and critical towards advertising and approaches used to increase publicity, so the companies must do everything in their power to make sure nothing goes wrong, while at the same time monitoring all the efforts of their competition.

In general, it is suggested that companies not only consider social responsibility, but that they, without compromise, maximize positive and minimize and negative influences on the society. Changes in the purchasing power are also under the influence of demographic trends. This is another area of the macroenvironment which should be carefully and regularly monitored. Kotler et al. (2003, pp. 160-167) identify 4 major areas of demography which bear influence on the marketing of a product. The analysis of population fluctuation can suggest to marketers which age groups might show the largest demand for a certain product.

A baby boom will bring about an increased demand for baby care products, followed by the toy industry, educational products, etc. the same process occurs with the increase in the number of elderly people, who also have special needs and desires. The lengthening of life expectancy and the increasingly better health of senior citizens makes tourism a very perspective industry. A new trend in the structure of the family is also on the rise — a traditional family with a mother, a father, and two children is declining. In the part addressing living accommodation needs, the 1995 Mintel Report shows that the decline of traditional families results with an increased number of smaller flats and houses, and with changes in the way these homes are furnished. These demographical changes affect such matters as packaging of food into smaller containers, because more and more people live alone. The next big change is expected in the number of employed women, who are becoming important consumers with their own sources of income. Companies must take all this into consideration and think about their products positions on the market.

The technological development which enables easy travel and communication leads to the situation in which people are more open to various influences, which causes their behavior and habits to change at a faster pace than ever. According to Shannon (1996), Europeaners have long become saturated with standard TV advertising. Promotion experts are beginning to understand that the decreased enthusiasm for accepting ads seems to be correlated with the fact that clients are beginning to perceive ads as merely an attempt to increase sales, and not as a process of informing the public. Mitchell (1997) predicted something along these lines: the more aware the public is that the company has information about them and is using this information for marketing purposes, the more the balance of power will shift to favor the clients over the companies. Furthermore, he suggested that data collection will be carried out in situations in which the clients will have the option to choose whether or not they will give or sell personal information when they accept or are offered products of their choosing. Although Mitchell's suggestions sometimes seem too drastic, today we are witnessing that people are less and less willing to give their personal information, express their opinions, suggestions, and ideas without some reward. Information technologies further empower the clients. A balanced two-sided communication between the company and its clients is no longer a problem. The reverse flow of information form the outside in, which is in part facilitated by information technology, leads to the assumption of acceptance of opinions and wishes of each individual client, which necessitates a completely new way of thinking about marketing.

Technological changes incessantly affect business and marketing. One example of this could be in-house correspondence: through e-mail or fax. Computer networking and connection to the Internet also influence the way of doing business. Computerized, automated production affects the need for educated workers, the costs, the way of communicating,and workers responsibilities. All this is reflected in the competitive environment, the competitive position. Companies invest into audit and development within their industry. Technology changes the marketing activities, by, for example, enabling the creation of data bases, advertising on line, and Internet sales. Internet marketing is a challenge — the World Wide Web is increasingly used as a promotional, but also a sales channel, although so far this has not been caused by the volume of sales, but by the desire of the company to be recognized by the clients as following the modern trends.

Legislative factors are also important for numerous businesses. They are changeable and differ from one market to another. Each market has its legal regulations for the opening of companies, competition, and marketing activities. Examples include the agencies for the protection of market competition, agencies for the protection of consumers, as well as regulations prohibiting advertising of certain products (cigarettes, alcoholic beverages, other than beer, prescription medicine, etc.), or laws forbidding large stores from opening on Sundays, while the smaller ones are allowed to open on a rotating schedule.

The need of many producers to adapt to the growing concern of the consumers towards ecology is well-known, which, in the end, is not only the problem of the producers, but of the general public. The Green movement is no longer a marginal aspect of politics and/or society, as it might have been when it first started, and as it might sometimes be seen in Europe. This leads to the increasing importance of the product being friendly towards the environment. Those companies that have accepted the importance of ecology have already started, or will start very soon, to capitalize on their efforts in this area. Other companies, which fail to respond to this growing concern, will have to invest much more in the future into defending or improving their market position.

Finally, above all others, the question of internationalization and globalization as elements of the macroenvironment must be answered. Although all of the above can be also viewed in an international context, most companies usually do business on domestic markets. In the conditions, however, of the omnipresent globalization process, the awareness of the international environment becomes crucial. Various trade groups and alliances can cause changes in pricing and quantities of raw materials and semi-manufactured products, which can influence many companies. Furthermore, political instability and political changes can affect the export into some countries. The Gulf War, for example, caused a lot of problems in the oil industry, automobile industry, and all the other industries connected with these. The consequences of the terrorist attacks on New York, or the war in Iraq that followed them, do not even need to be mentioned.

Using Doyle (2002, pp. 373-381) as a starting point, we can conclude that the dominant market trends are:

- intensive market faddishness, which causes changing and unpredictable demand

- breaking down of otherwise homogeneous markets and segments all the way to micromarkets and microsegments

- growth of the increasing expectations of consumers and clients in general

- increasingly faster technological changes

- intensifying of relationships with the competition

- market and business globalization

- constant expectations for superior services in relation to the market conditions and generally

- standardization of technical quality of products and services

- erosion of traditional strong and dominant brands

- increasingly intensive and complicated changes of political and legislative limitations and measures on certain markets in the conditions of globalization.

Examining the above mentioned trends, one can notice further complexity of competitive efforts for the achievement of long-term market success.

CASE STUDY - M&S MENSWEAR

This case study aims to scrutinize the current communication strategies employed by Marks and Spencer Menswear. Furthermore, it will analyse the retailer's market position, its key market consumer and how Marks and Spencer can develop future advertising campaigns to progress its relationship with its consumer. Additionally, the case study will investigate how the external environment has influenced its activities and abilities as a retailer.

The History of Marks and Spencer Menswear

Marks and Spencer (M&S) originated in the late 19th century as a market stall, implementing a simple pricing strategy of vending all their goods for a penny. After rapid and successful expansion, the company soon traded as a private limited company, and a short while later became a public company. By the 1970's Marks and Spencer had attained market governance within the UK, and was identified as "the number one group for menswear." (Vignali & Vranesevic, 2006, p. 132) The retailer then took the decision to expand and develop the brand internationally, through strategies such as organic growth and franchise.

Originally, M&S based its marketing strategy around the middle age, middle class male, targeting "men in their 30's working with family commitments but still cared about their appearance and needed smart reasonable priced clothing for work." (Vignali & Vranesevic, 2006, p.132)

Marks and Spencer Menswear Today

Today, Marks and Spencer prides itself on "quality, value, service, innovation and trust." (Marks and Spencer, 2009) Mintel note that the retailer is in "a good position as it has re-established its core values of quality at competitive prices, and across a broad price architecture, married with product innovation and increasingly attractive stores." (2007) Marks and Spencer's hastily growing market share in the menswear sector, in recent times, has been identified as owing, in part, to its "growing online business." (Marks and Spencer, 2009) M&S enlarged and protected its volume market share from "11.1% in 2007" to "13.1% in 2008." (Marks and Spencer's Annual Report, 2008) M&S Menswear has emerged as "the clear leading destination for men buying both formalwear and casualwear." (Mintel, 2007) It can be suggested that the target consumer for Marks and Spencer today is middle class males aged 40-60 years. The retailer's biggest challenge comes with broadening its appeal to attract younger men, such as those in their 30's.

The Nature of the External Environment: A PESTEL Analysis of Marks and Spencer Menswear

The PESTEL (Political, Economical, Social, Technological, Environmental, and Legal) analysis provides an overview of the different macroenvironmental factors that a company should take into consideration. It is a strategic tool for comprehending factors such as market growth or decline, business position, potential and direction for operations. Taking into account the UK's current economic climate, which in turn shapes many other aspects of the external environment, the PESTEL analysis is highly apt to perform for M&S Menswear.

Political

Interest Rates:

The government's decision to cut interest rates, in recent times, creates an abundance of marketing opportunities for M&S. The BBC notes that "the sharp downward trend in rates began during the second half of last year (2008)" (2009). The action of cutting interest rates is among the strategies available to the Bank of England, in its endeavour to enhance the UK's economy facing severe global recession. The table below indicates the decline in interest rates since October 2008.

For the consumers of Marks and Spencer Menswear, this means the cost of borrowing is lowered, favourably affecting them in terms of mortgage repayments. For M&S themselves, this could lead to an increase in spending.

Green Belt Land:

Government planning regulations impede developing on greenbelt sites. Newman and Cullen (2002) note that "in retailing, the use of greenbelt sites has become increasingly difficult to justify." Whilst this could hinder M&S expansion of its out of town portfolio, its presence on the high street and the strength of its internet business could counteract any negative impact.

Economical

Recession:

In late January 2009, the UK was announced to be in recession, the first time since 1991. At that time, the state of the economy triggered consumers to be more frugal with their spending habits and initiated "a partial rejection of fashions that require a total new look, causing a move towards more classic styles that will last beyond the season. " (Easey 2002, p.39) M&S, today, could take inspiration from this, and offer its male consumers more in terms of basic, timeless garments. Consumer confidence is likely to be dented by the recession, therefore it is vital that M&S continue with the sales promotion activities, as previously discussed.

Unemployment:

As displayed in the graphs below, the recession has had a direct impact on the levels of unemployment. In turn, people have less money to spend on non-essential items, such as fashion goods. This could direct M&S Menswear to increase its Outstanding Value line.

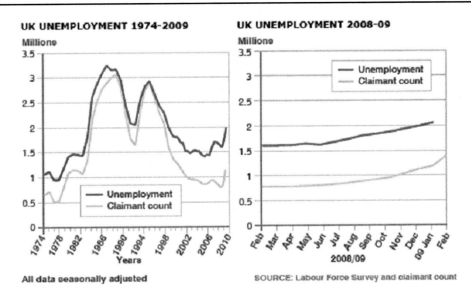

UK UNEMPLOYMENT 1974-2009

UK UNEMPLOYMENT 2008-09

All data seasonally adjusted

SOURCE: Labour Force Survey and claimant count

Credit Crunch:

"The housing market was the first area to be affected by the credit crunch." (BBC 2009) This has now led to a decrease in house prices (as displayed below) – another issue shaping consumer spending and confidence.

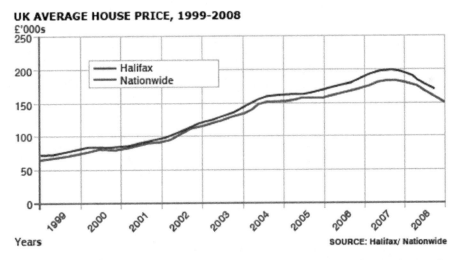

UK AVERAGE HOUSE PRICE, 1999-2008

SOURCE: Halifax/ Nationwide

Furthermore, spending on credit cards is likely to reduce. This could undoubtedly have a knock-on effect on sales using M&S own &More card, potentially having an adverse effect all areas of the business.

Social

Demographics:

Hines and Bruce observe that "social and cultural changes are major determinants of emerging fashions." (2001, p.129) Marks and Spencer Menswear could thus react to the following modifications, in order to enhance their relationship with their key consumer, and furthermore to interest new ones.

The UK has "begun to undergo a quite radical change in the make-up of its population." (Easey, 2002, p. 31) Notably, this can be identified through changes in age predicted for the future. The tables below depict how the UK's population is forecasted to alter.

There is going to be a clear increase in the number of potential customers in the over 65 age bracket. Whilst M&S Menswear are striving to appeal to a younger audience, they would be wise to maintain their relationship with the mature market. Adhering to their current strategy of producing quality, value for money garments should allow them to do so, as "most older groups...are not as interested in fashion as in comfort and quality of clothes." (Easey 2002, p.34)

Changes in Customer Size:

As widely reported upon in the media, the UK, along with many other countries, is experiencing a shift towards larger sized people. It is therefore essential that retailers act in response and offer a wide range of sizes. M&S Menswear have introduced a range for the larger gentleman, Big & Tall. It has been positively marketed by utilising a top sportsman, Martin Johnson, as its figurehead.

Family Changes:

In recent times, couples have shown an inclination to marry later. This, subsequently, has led to them possessing more disposable income when they are in their late 20s/early 30s. Fashion is one of their significant areas of expenditure, focusing on high-end products. M&S have attempted to capture this through its Autograph range and by employing wellknown designers such as Timothy Everest. However, potential still remains in this key area.

Leisure Activities:

These days, most people have benefited from an increase in leisure time (due to shorter working hours, increased technology etc.) and casual/sportswear has emerged as a preferred mode of dress. "Increased interest in sports and leisure has been reflected in the increased popularity of sportswear and training shoes as fashion items." (Bohdanowicz & Clamp 1994, p.11) It appears that M&S Menswear has failed to keep pace with this trend.

Many of the casualwear items on offer currently, for example in the Blue Harbour range, will not attract the style-conscious consumer.

Technological

The Internet:

Online shopping and e-commerce have undeniably changed our buying behaviour. M&S have kept abreast of internet shopping developments and offer its male consumer a wide array of its clothing ranges online.

Product Advancements:

The iSuit, as previously described, demonstrates M&S ability to continue to develop products that meet the higher demands of its consumers in this technological age. M&S Menswear have also utilised technological advances in fabric compositions to offer creaseresistant and machine-washable suits in order to compliment the lifestyles of its targetmarket.

Database Marketing:

Many retailers utilise their loyalty cards/own credit cards as a way of obtaining data concerning their customers purchases. In this way, they can specifically target promotional activities to reflect a customers preferences. It appears that M&S have not fully exploited this information source, but could do so through their &More card.

Environmental

Many fashion consumers are becoming more and more aware, and subsequently more mindful of, environmental and green issues. As time goes by, they may query the "need for constant renewal and replacement of clothing to follow fashion." (Easey 2002, p. 36) M&S have reacted skilfully to this by working in partnership with the charity, Oxfam – if any item of M&S clothing is donated to Oxfam for resale, the contributor is rewarded with a £5 M&S voucher to spend in store.

Environmental issues are being integrated into all areas of M&S operational activities, as part of their Plan A. Examples include promotion of Bags for Life, less use of packaging and more energy efficient transport.

Legal

Trademarks:

M&S, in line with all other clothing organisations, must adhere to trademark legislation as and when appropriate. The owner of a registered trademark may instigate legal proceedings to prevent unauthorised use of that trademark.

Labelling:

A retailer must include within their garment labels displaying certain information. "The specific labels that the law actually requires a retailer to include will vary from garment to garment according to a variety of factors including country of origin and flammability of the fabric." (Jackson & Shaw 2001, p.86)

Pricing:

The Consumer Protection Act makes it illegal for businesses to misinform consumers about the price of goods. Additionally, when goods are classed as sale items the previous higher price must be displayed, in order for a customer to have a true assessment of the rate of reduction.

The Future for Marks and Spencer Menswear

This PESTEL analysis suggests that in order for Marks and Spencer Menswear to maintain its relationship with its key consumer, whilst also continuing to strive in the current economic climate, some existing strategies must be retained but other new ones should be implemented.

The relevant policies for today's consumer and market conditions are:

- The Outstanding Value lines and sales promotions.

- Advertising to a younger market.

- Product and process innovation.

- Quality lines, of which Autograph is an example.

- Sizing options, such as the Big & Tall range.

New approaches for the continued success and possible expansion of M&S Menswear could include:

- To broaden its advertising campaigns, building upon the success of the infamous food and womenswear television promotions, to incorporate a greater focus on menswear.

- Furthermore, the advertisement of ranges in mens magazines, for example GQ and in newspaper supplements, would further maximise exposure. As many men embrace technology as a favoured media source, full use of internet and email marketing should also be deployed.

- To launch an equivalent range to that offered to female consumers through the Limited Collection concept, allowing more trend-focused and fashion-orientated garments to be available for men at still reasonable prices.

- To deviate from the traditional dominance of formalwear into the casualwear market, concentrating its efforts in particular on sportswear. The retailer already possess a number of established relationships with sports personalities, such as the England football team, rugby stars Johnny Wilkinson and Martin Johnson, and including them in marketing campaigns could effectively promote and enhance any new brand developed in this area.

- To introduce a personal shopping service in the menswear department of large, significant stores. This particular innovation could attract the older man, i.e. the retailer's current key consumer, who is less comfortable than his younger counterparts in making fashion choices.

- To adopt database marketing to target sales promotion campaigns more specifically to each consumer who uses the &More credit card in store. This could allow the business to improve sales and subsequently maximise on profits, by ensuring customers receive information about products they are most likely to purchase.

Conclusion

To conclude, Marks and Spencer Menswear currently embrace a number of successful communication strategies to maintain their affiliation with their key consumer – middle class males aged 40-60 years of age, seeking quality, value for money products. The retailer has also demonstrated an ability to respond appropriately to external factors.

However, there is still potential to enhance their current relationships, and to create new associations with a younger, fashion-conscious consumer, by adopting some of the proposals, as discussed above. In doing this, M&S Menswear must be mindful not to alienate their dedicated, existing customer base, as they provide a sound foundation for success and future growth.

CHAPTER 11: THE VALUE CHAIN

GIANPAOLO VIGNALI & CLAUDIO VIGNALI

When we consider the use of the value chain we firstly need to consider that the value chain helps to distinguish ones core competences and it is these competences that give a company its uniqueness. Essentially a company must first manage its current competences but also investigate and pursue new core competences as the current ones will be eventually eroded away as competitors decide to adopt certain measures themselves. The successful management of these core competencies will inherently create a competitive advantage but it is important to distinguish early on the differences between core competencies and just competencies.

A true definition for a core competence does not just include the skills required in delivering a service. They are, aformentioned, unique and can be specific to your organisation and can they be protected. This will enable the customer to have an identifiable experience and the utilisation of skills and knowledge (through the application of resources) helps to create a competitive advantage.

The value chain helps distinguish the core competencies of a firm and considers several key concepts including:

• Before the service establishment - the supply chain- control, sourcing, frills or not.

• Inside the service establishment - stocks, labour, culture, work in progress,

• Delivery process- scheduling, labour costs, overheads, techniques/procedures, repair & maintenance

• Service delivery and after - finished experience, complaint handling, relationship marketing.

• Use to determine where the firm has the potential to create and capture value

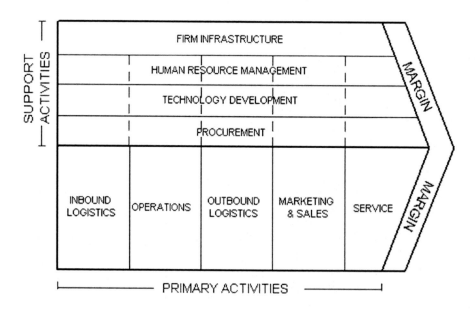

The Generic Value Chain
Kilde: Porter: Competitive Advantage. 1998.

The above diagram illustrates the value chain and shows that each of the primary activiites requires support activities for the succesfull management of this. These vary from organisation to organisation and to varying degrees.

Below is an example of hoe the value chain relates to Topshop:

Primary activities - Activities connected with the creation of the product.

- Inbound logistics – warehousing, material handling, inventory control, etc.

- Operations – Activities that transform inputs into finished products

- Outbound logistics – Activities that store & distribute products to buyers

- Marketing & Sales – Advertisement, distribution channels, all activities that provide the means for the buyer to purchase

- Services – Activities which enhance or maintain the

- Support activities – Support the primary activities and each other.

- Procurement – The function of purchasing.

- Technology Development – Engineering and function development.

- Human resource management – Employees and costs involved.

- Firm infrastructure – General management, coporate affairs and quality management. (Kippenberger, 1997)

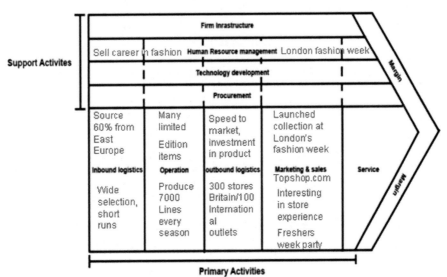

(Porter (1985); Smith,A. (2007);Smith, J. (2007))

CASE STUDY - ZARA

Zara's Mission Statement and Objectives

A mission statement is a brief statement which defines the meaning of the business existence, its raison-d'être, with the intention of promoting the interest of all significant stakeholders; customers, competitors, employees, suppliers, shareholders and governments. It also includes the visions of how the business intends to grow in terms of its products, markets and values, in the future (Burk Wood, 2007). All of the Inditex subsidiaries, including Zara, carry the same philosophy, namely to combine creativity and quality design in order to achieve rapid response to market demands (Inditex, 2008). This statement implies that Zara is market-driven and customer-centric (rather than forecast driven) company, informing stakeholders about the business' customer focus.

Furthermore, in terms of its products, Zara emphasises creativity and design during the product development stage, allowing the business to deliver products specific to the demands of the market. However, Zara not only provides value to its customers through creativity and design, but also through speed-to-market, (achieved through an extremely responsive supply network), which provides Zara with a specific competitive edge. More, Zara's mission is "to be in step with society, dressing the ideas, trends and tastes that society itself has developed" (Inditex, 2008). Zara aims to be design-sensitive, yet not design-led, preferring to be a fast and flexible follower (Wallin et al., 2008; Gallaugher, 2008; Christopher, 2005); supply chain movement is delayed until a demand is realised (Van Hoek, 2001), allowing Zara to sell products which its target market is already buying, rather than introducing unpredictable products which may not sell.

The mission statement is a prerequisite for the development of a set of objectives and performance targets which explain what the business is trying to achieve (Burk Wood, 2007). Zara's main objectives are to get the shortest time to market (Castellano, cited by Thoney-Barletta and Hartman, 2007) as well as to offer quality clothing at affordable prices (Cheng et al., 2008).

Zara's Situational Analysis

The situational analysis forms the basis for the strategic planning process of the business marketing plan. It examines the current situation of the business, the marketing environment, the competition as well as the demand of the target market, in order to highlight any potential problems that may influence the marketing and performance of the business (Burk Wood, 2007). The analysis should be conducted both at an internal level in order to identify the company's strengths and weaknesses, as well as at an external level to identify any opportunities and threats of the external environment (Montana and Charnov, 2000); collectively, the internal and external analysis are referred to as a SWOT analysis.

Zara's Internal Analysis

The internal analysis is necessary for a company to identify its key resources, capabilities and core competencies as well as the structure of its internal system, through which a competitive advantage and strategic competition can be achieved (Drummond et al., 2008). Furthermore, the purpose of the internal analysis is to determine the businesses' strengths, which may be used to capitalise on opportunities in the external environment and to endure any potential threats, as well as to diagnose any opposing weaknesses (Vranesevic et al., 2006).

Zara's Resources and Capabilities

Resources are considered as those tangible and intangible assets owned and controlled by the company, used to create products and services that add value to the market (O'Regan and Ghobadian, 2004). One of Zara's critical resources is its customers. The Zara customer is the main motivation of the Zara business model, creating both the beginning and the end of the supply chain (Inditex, 2007). Zara's target market is not restricted in terms of age, gender or race; regardless whether they are 15 or 40, male or female and despite their difference in culture, Zara customers all have one thing in common, namely a passion for fashion (Inditex, 2008). Another one of Zara's main strenghths is its supply resources; Zara is a backward vertically integrated company, manufacturing approximately 50% of its products in its own manufacturing network, consisting of 22 Spanish factories (Ferdows et al., 2004). Furthermore, 40% of fabrics are purchased from an Inditex partner; Comditel, and the dyestuff is purchased from yet another Inditex partner. The manufacturing facilities allow Zara to keep the compley work requiring a high level of skill within the company itself and only outsources simple, extremely labour-intensive tasks, such as the production of large-volume staple garments to Turkey, Asia and North Africa (Gattorna, 2006). The Zara stores and their locations are also considered as key resources. Zara has 56 stores within the UK, all of which are situated in high-traffic, prime locations. Large and spacious with contemporary interiors, Zara stores are also considered to be communication resources; as Zara does not invest in advertising, it uses its store windows as a key communication tool between the business and its customers (Bund, 2005). Informational resources include the availability of the latest information technology, such as electronic point of sales (EPOS) electronic data interchange (EDI), computer aided design (CAD) and computer aided manufacturing (CAM) (Birtwistle et al., 2006). The human resources focus includes Zara's efficient workforce, in particular those employees within the stores who carry large responsibilities, consisting of approximately 21 individuals (Craig et al., 2004). With a total of 79 517 employees, 3,024 within the UK, 81% consisting of females and 19% of males (Inditex, 2007), Inditex invests in staff training schemes as well as incentives and rewards for employees, in order to minimise staff resistance and increase motivation (Dru, 2002).

Hoskisson et al. (2004, cited in O'Regan and Ghobadian, 2004), define capabilities as a business's ability to combine its resources and skills to achieve a task and improve company performance. Grant (2004) determines flexibility and speed of response as Zara's main capabilities. Zara combines its information resources, supply resources and human resources with knowledge to meet consumer demands. An agile and responsive supply network, delivered through the sharing of information, vertical integration, demandchain management and process alignment (Christopher et al., 2004) , allows Zara to identify emerging trends as well as to design, produce and sell new styles quicker than its competitors (Kroger et al., 2008; Grant, 2004).

Zara's Value Chain, Core Competencies and Competitive Advantage

In order to determine which part of their operations and activities (supply chain entities) add (or may potentially add) value to the product or services intended to meet consumer demands, businesses participate in the value chain analysis, developed by Michael Porter in 1980 (Drummond et al., 2008; Burk Wood, 2007). The value chain divides activities into primary activities and support activities (figure 1); primary activities are those which are directly involved in the production of a product, its distribution and its purchase by the consumer (Kippenburg, 1997). Primary activities include inbound logistics, operations, outbound logistics, marketing and sales and service (Drummond et al., 2008). Support activities support the primary activities and include the company's infrastructure, technology development, human resource management and procurement (Drummond et al., 2008). Although it is important for the business to establish the value which each activity it generates, it is crucial to evaluate their interrelationships. The activities are used by the business to create a competitive advantage as well as to create shareholder value with the aim of offering a level of customer value which exceeds the cost of the activities, resulting in a profit margin (Drummond et al., 2008).

Inbound Logistics: Here, raw materials are received from suppliers. Zara sources 60% of its raw materials from a network of over 200 suppliers in Mauritius, Morocco, Turkey, China, Australia, New Zealand, India, Korea, Germany and Italy (Fernie and Sparks, 2004). The other 40% of fabrics are sourced internally from an Inditex subsidiary,

Comditel, of which most is purchased undyed to allow for any colour changes that may occur once the season has already begun (Ferdows et al., 2002). The procurement support activity ensures that buying offices in the UK, China and the Netherlands maintain Zara's global sourcing policy of souring from a large supplier base in order to minimise the risk of dependency on any one supplier and to increase efficiency (Fernie and Sparks, 2004).

Operations: This activity involves the manufacturing of products. Rather than relying on forecasted demand, Zara manufactures products according to real consumer demand, supplying products to consumers as they require them (Gattorna, 2006). This operation is realised through the support of the technology development activity within the supply chain; a quick response strategy allows Zara's designers to continuously receive information on a daily basis regarding consumer preferences and tastes straight from staff members in the stores, using handheld PDAs (Birtwistle et al., 2006). The support activity of human resource management provides Zara employees with the necessary knowledge, through training and development, to maintain Zara's mission and objectives (Inditex, 2007). Privileged with the task of transferring vital data between the customer and the headquarters, Zara's staff form part of the information loop whereby results are shared (Dru, 2002). Furthermore, as a vertically integrated company, with its own network of 22 Spanish factories, Zara manufactures approximately 60% of its products in-house. The other 40% is manufactured externally, mostly within Europe; however, basics which can be produced in higher volumes are manufactured in Asia (Ferdows et al., 2004). In terms of its manufacturing systems, only capital intensive operations which enhance cost efficiency through economies of scale, such as dyeing, cutting, labelling and packing, are performed in-house (Frankel, 2006; Fernie and Sparks, 2004). Labour-intensive operations, such as sewing, are outsourced to over 400 subcontractors located nearby, with which Zara has exclusive arrangements (Frankel, 2006). As well as producing in smaller batches, Zara more often, applies an operations management style of postponement, whereby Zara suspends inventory commitment until in-season (Ferdows et al., 2004). This enhances the overall value of the supply network by increasing responsiveness to consumer needs as well as a reducing demand uncertainty and costs, achieved through reduced inventory levels, reduced storage costs and fewer potential mark-downs (Boone et al., 2007).

Outbound-logistics: This includes all those activities involved in getting the finished products to the customers. Once the garments have been produced and pressed, labelling takes place within the factory. Attaching price tags and security tags to the garments before reaching the stores saves a lot of time and money, as time that would've been spent labelling by store personnel, is spent selling instead (Capell, 2008). Thereafter, Zara's products are sent to one of the two distribution centres, in Arteixo and in Zaragoza.

The factory and distribution centre in Arteixo are connected via a tunnel through which the merchandise passes. Once received, the products are seperated according to country and store on moving hanging rails (Capell, 2008). Little monitoring is required by workers, as the system is fully automated, ensuring that merchandise spends less than a few hours in the distribution centre before it is freighted to the relevant stores via truck and subsequently arrives in the UK within 24 hours. Deliveries are made to the stores 2-3 times a week.

Marketing and Sales: Marketing and sales involves informing the customer about the products. Zara does not invest heavily in marketing, rather using its stores as the communication link between the buyers and the products. Window displays entice customers to enter the store, whilst a spacious in-store atmosphere prompts customers to browse the entire shop floor. Knowing that most of the products may not be replenished, Zara customers are met by a fear of loss, creating an incentive for them to buy on the spot (Ferdows et al., 2004), hence increasing the number of impulse purchases made within the stores (Christopher et al., 2004).

The value chain analysis is not only used to identify which activities add value to the customer, but also to establish the core competencies which in essence are the source of a business' competitive advantage. Those internal resources and capabilities of a business which collectively act as a source of competitive advantage over rival firms by delivering fundamental customer benefits, are considered as core competencies (Purdue University, 2003). Zara's core competencies lie within its agile supply network; Zara regards its backward vertically integrated supply network as a source of competitive advantage. Although many businesses believe, that rather than being vertically integrated, businesses working in volatile markets, such as the apparel industry, should rather be transformed into virtually integrated ones owning less assets (Ferdows et al., 2004). Zara however disagrees, and argues that it would not be possible to design, manufacture and sell products faster than its competitors, if it didn't have full control over its supply chain (Kroger et al., 2008). Another one of Zara's core competencies lies within its product development and the use of the latest information technology to share information within the supply network, thus enabling Zara to transform design ideas into actual products. It is from these core competencies that Zara's sustainable competitive advantage originates. A sustainable competitive advantage is one that can be maintained over a period of time.

Zara's competitive advantage therefore is its speed to market whereby Zara is able to respond to the ever-changing demands of it customers with constantly adapting product offerings, faster than any of its competition (Mazaira et al., 2003); Zara is able to introduce over 11,000 new products a year and delivers new products to its stores twice a week, with none lasting more than four weeks (Lincoln and Thomassen, 2007). This competitive advantage is valuable, rare, difficult to imitate by competitors and non-substitutable – it did not just happen overnight, but rather derived from significant market orientation and an appropriate business concept (Maizara et al, 2003).

Zara's Culture and Leadership

Zara's corporate culture consists of three layers, namely the company's values, beliefs and paradigm/ assumptions (figure 4) and defines the way in which Zara does business (Cheng et al., 2008). Corporate culture determines the way in which the business' leaders and employees think and behave (Entrepreneur Connect, 2008). Furthermore, Melewar (2003, p. 8) states "The company's corporate culture influences its corporate identity, quality of its products and services as well as its performance."

At Zara, customers are valued as the foundation of the business. The company considers customer orientation and continuous innovation as the principle values of its corporate culture (Inditex, 2007); "The customer is our inspiration and customer service is our goal" (Mazaira et al., 2003). For this reason, the customer is considered as the beginning and the end within the Zara supply network; Zara collects requests and information regarding demand directly from its UK stores, which is then immediately sent to design teams and commercial teams in Spain. By delivering new product to all its UK stores twice a week, Zara is able to respond quickly to its customers. The corporate culture is also reflected in the behaviour of Zara's personnel; store employees ensure that the Zara mission and business model are aligned with its customer service and hence the brands perceived corporate identity (Cheng et al., 2008).

Zara believes that speed to market through vertical integration is the key to superior performance and customer satisfaction. Furthermore, Zara believes that by postponing production and delaying supply chain movement until a demand is realised (Van Hoek, 2001), it is able reduce inventory and overproduction, as well as efficiently supply its customers with the products they require (Gattorna, 2006; Boone et al., 2007). As a result, customers perceive Zara's product range, quality and prices as being consistent with the brands mission of being in step with society and offering quality clothing at affordable prices (Cheng et al., 2008; Inditex, 2008).

Leadership is defined as the process of guiding people in a certain direction in order to achieve goals (Kurnik, 2008); Leaders are required to delegate tasks appropriately in order to achieve company objectives and are considered as major functions of how a company performs (Drummond et al., 2008). Zara store managers employ an autocratic leadership style (figure 8). According to the Tannenbaum and Schmidt, continuum of leadership behaviour (1973), autocratic leaders usually make their own decisions. Although many may criticise this leadership style, it is considered an advantage in situations where quick decision-making is required (Money-Zine, 2007); such is the case in the Zara stores.

Zara's retail managers are given a lot of power in terms of making decisions. Within the fast fashion industry, decisions have to be made quickly, if the business intends to meet consumer demands. If Zara store managers are not made aware of consumer demands as they evolve and react to these appropriately, there is a possibility that Zara will miss a sales opportunity that will probably not be repeated. Secondly, once the products then finally reach the stores, Zara's store managers may find that demand has already started to decline, leading to the occurrence of obsolescent stock and therefore products having to be sold at a discounted price (Ferdows et al., 2004). To avoid this from happening, Zara's retail managers make quick, daily decisions on product alterations and product design; using handheld PDA systems, the information is sent directly to the design team at Zara's head office. Zara's store management consequently makes the idea of real-time inventory and retailing a reality (Dru, 2002).

CHAPTER 12: STOP

TIHOMIR VRANESEVIC, GIANPAOLO VIGNALI & CLAUDIO VIGNALI

Segmentation

A simple definition of segmentation identifies it as a strategy of creating and applying different marketing programmes intended to satisfy similar needs and wants of members of individual groups, i.e. of different consumer segments. Segmentation facilitates the distinction of the market's heterogeneity, as well as the homogeneity of the needs and wants of the different consumer groups. Each consumer group or segment has a unique demand depending on the products price, characteristics, points of sale, and ways of selling it. Therefore, each segment is characterised by a different perception (on the consumers part) of the products and services. Companies strive to market (sell) their products in such a way as to satisfy more or less similar requirements by the same consumer segment. Different companies have different facilities for servicing a variety of consumer segments in the same market.

Having determined the consumer segments, companies need to emphasize the characteristics of the product, and thus win a more favourable position in relation to the competing products and/or companies planning to satisfy the needs and wants of the same segment. This refers to the position in the consumers' mind, i.e. their perception of the product in relation to other products. Thus, product positioning means developing the kind of marketing mix (including all marketing elements) consumers or buyers expect.

It involves adjusting the marketing mix to the expectations buyers have built in their minds. The marketing mix can also influence the expectations aimed at positioning a company's product or service in the future. Product positioning can be viewed as a company's final objective: to manufacture a product, to present it in the way the buyer wants it, or to approximate the product/service to the perception (image) the segment has of the ideal product/service, as a means of satisfying the needs, wants, and requirements. The foundation of product positioning of a product brand is market segmentation. It offers guidelines on how to achieve the optimal position by determining the target group according to the company's opinion.

Having determined the segment to be served, and the product position which is thought to best meet the specific needs and wants of a segment, it is necessary to estimate the size of the segment by estimating the present and future demand. The company will not perform successfully if it underestimates either the present or future demand.

Development Strrategies in Market Segmentation

Development stages in market segmentation depend on the prevailing circumstances in the market, and can be examined through the following states:

- mass (undifferentiated) marketing

- production differentiated marketing

- target marketing.

Mass marketing implies marketing products/services by the same marketing mix in the entire market (to all possible consumer segments). That approach has advantages when the demand is higher than the supply and when the needs and requirements, as well as the methods used to fulfill them, are homogenous and desirable for the majority of consumers. The advantages of this approach (provided that conditions for their application are present) lie primarily in the product's lower costs and the efforts to market it.

The production differentiated marketing approach means that the company enters the market with the intention to offer the consumers an adequate choice, so that they can cluster themselves into groups with preference for certain products. Thus, the significance of this approach rests in the constant innovation of fresh characteristics of the existing product or new products. Consumer segments are not overwhelmingly important here since they are mostly considered to be insufficiently stable, as well as because the basic goal of the company is to offer a variety of choice opportunities so that the consumers alone may decide which product modification suits them best in a given moment and over time. These are the characteristics of the product orientation concept. Target marketing implies determining or, better said, finding out the consumer segment which is the target for servicing, and then designing the marketing mix (including the development of a new or modification of an existing product) which will realise this project, and, needless to say, enhance the company's performance. Determining target markets opens up market opportunities as companies with a specific marketing mix gain competitive advantage over other products, if we take into consideration the consumer segment viewed as target market. Companies create the product, the price, distribution channels, selling methods, and promotion techniques that best suit the specific consumer segments. Instead of wasting their resources (financial and human) on trying to cover the entire market by offering the product in it unselectively, the product is targeted at a determined consumer segment (by a specially developed marketing mix).

As specific needs and wants develop, the marketing concept answers by increasingly detailed segmentation. The consequence of this is the appearance of numerous microsegments, each of them with the different needs and wants, which makes the determination of target markets increasingly difficult. This has also resulted in the emergence of micromarketing, which heralds the final stage — marketing focused on each particular consumer. Thus, the company is obliged to adapt its marketing mix taking into account even individual clients if it intends to cover their needs — both from the fields of endconsumption and business consumption (companies that buy products in order to operate in the market). That process is also referred to as "one-to-one marketing". An example of this approach may be found in Dalrymple and Parsons (1995, p. 177), where the new process of Computer Designed Swimwear is described. Namely, aided by a video camera, a computer takes measurements of the buyer, and when the buyer selects the style and the fabric s/he can buy the model, which can be turned into a suit in less than an hour.

There are three ways to approach the determination of market segments and the measurement of the differences among them. The classical approach is the a priori approach that bases its segmentation method on easily identifiable characteristics, such as geography and demography, which is followed by additional data to enhance the knowledge about members of the individual segments. Additional data may include ownership or usage of certain products, shopping habits, exposure to the media, or different attitudes.

Companies use a priori differentiation of segments to better direct their marketing efforts to individual segments, i.e. target groups selected on the basis of their own insights. That approach to segmentation determines in advance the consumer characteristics known to be important indicators of each consumer segment, its type and number. Nevertheless, we should keep in mind that the segmentation achieved in this way plays only the reconnaissance role, and that any division of the market into too many segments (or too few segments) actually reduces the company's ability to serve it appropriately. A priori segmentation should be considered to be the starting point and a step towards better scrutinising the market and obtaining a general picture of the possible segments. A contrary approach is segmentation aided by market research, which classifies the consumers into groups (segments) on the basis of research and on the basis of some other selected characteristics. These characteristics are not exclusively only demographic or geographic, but also involve specific needs, attitudes, opinions, lifestyles, values, and benefits expected from the product or service. The number of segments is not known beforehand.

Potential consumer segments may also be determined by lifestyle, sets of values, attitudes towards the product or service, benefits expected from the product or service, etc. The procedure is therefore reversed: the starting point is the actual consumer behaviour, and then the possible similarities of the characteristics (e.g. demographic) in those groups are analysed and clustered.

The third approach to market segmentation is a combination of a priori segmentation and segmentation according to groups. The combined approach uses both segmentation criteria; first the population is separated by a demographic characteristic (age, occupation, or similar) depending on the experience-based information, and then the a priori acquired insights are classified into additional groups on the basis of the research results, e.g. the expected satisfaction with the product, needs, etc. In literature the combined model of approaching market segmentation is also referred to as the hybrid model.

In order to discover the market segments in this way, it is necessary to carry out research by collecting primary data and/or by searching for secondary sources of information. Taking into consideration the ideas of numerous authors, including Kotler et al. (1996, p. 354, cf.), the entire process of market segmentation, target segment determination, and positioning can simply be shown through the following steps :

1. determining characteristics, segment selection criteria

2. analysing segments - target segment determination (conditionally viewed, of the market)

3. analysing indicators for determination of segment attractiveness

4. selecting the segment which will be served by products and services - positioning

5. selecting positioning objectives in each of the selected (target) segments

6. determining the marketing mix (including all marketing elements: product, price, sale and distribution, promotion) which will serve the segment and enter the competition in the target market.

Kotler, Ph., Armstrong, G., Saunders, J., Wong, V., Principles of Marketing — European edition, Prentice Hall, London, 1996, p. 354 (cf.). The process is shown in Kotler's later works.

The basic idea of market segmentation is portrayed in the following chart.

Approaches to Market Segmentation

On the basis of the above discussion, the approaches and methods of market segmentation are numerous, but it is also necessary to take into account some purely business requirements for determining the appropriate segments. In addition to the basic assumption that a consumer group is characterised by particular features that separate it from the rest of the market (i.e. from other consumers), the following principles should govern the determination of the segments: "particularity" needs and wants, as well as their satisfying must be unique and different in relation to other market segments, which implies uniformity of their demand.

The basic steps in segmentation and market targeting

| Step 1 | Step 2 | Step 3 |

The Market ⟩ Is Broken Down ⟩ And Grouped ⟩ To Facilitate Target Market selection

A H B		#1	#2	#3		#1	#2	Product
C C		A	D	F				Price
D F G		B	E	G				Sales & Distribution
G F H		C		H				Promotion
B D								Other Marketing Mix Elements
E A E								

Heterogeneous Consumers   Individual Consumers

Reasonably Homogenous Market Segments

Target Market

#3

Source: Zikmund, G.W., d'Amico, M., Effective Marketing, Creating and Keeping Customers, West Publishing Company, 1995, p. 181, adapted.

Process of Market Segmentation and selecting Target Markets

Criteria by which all buyers can be studied and divided into segments are numerous. Most frequent are the ones that are easiest to verify — e.g. age, gender, geographic location — but we should also keep in mind that segments can be determined according to consumers and/or buyers needs, wants, resources, consumer habits, shopping habits, etc.

Naturally, segmentation may also be carried out according to all possible combinations of the particular criteria given above, e.g. by combining the age, gender, and income criteria. The basic groups of segmentation variables include geographic affiliation (location), demographic characteristics, psychographic traits, and the particular consumer behaviours while shopping and/or consuming in a market.

Geographic segmentation

Geographic segmentation implies splitting up the entire market into different geographic units: states, regions, provinces, cities, and even specific parts of cities (neighborhoods). Marketing activities can cover all or just some areas. Here attention is directed at all geographic differences in terms of needs. One possible example would be the geographic segmentation of UK by a car tyre manufacturer. Regions might be England, Scotland, Wales and Northern Ireland or (at a more detailed level) counties or major metropolitan areas. According to the regional differences, the manufacturer will not place same marketing efforts into selling winter tyres in the south and in the northern parts of UK. A global company may identify individual countries (e.g. Austria, England, and Croatia) or even groups of countries (Central Europe, Southern Balkan countries, Northern European countries) as segments which the marketing efforts are directed at. Geographic segmentation points to the possible differences in consumption habits, living conditions, etc. Thus, for example, in Dalmatia warm clothes are sold in smaller quantities, fish and veal are eaten more often, and olive oil is consumed in larger quantities. The differences may be caused due to climate reasons. Companies may conduct segmentation based on climatic similarities, and for example, observe Mediterranean countries as a segment.

Conversely, other companies may decide not to pay too much attention to geographic segmentation, and approach different markets in numerous countries in a more or less similar or the identical way, as is done by Coca-Cola, Levi's, or IKEA.

Demographic segmentation

Through demographic segmentation, the market is divided according to age, gender, income, occupation, education, family size, and sometimes by religious, national, and racial affiliation. Commonly, companies segment their consumers (markets) according to demographic characteristics if they lead to different use, promotion, and/or selling of their products or services. In general, the differences between the segments studied according to those characteristics are clearly visible and easily recognisable.

Segmentation by age

People's needs and wants differ with age; they are different in childhood, youth, the middle, and golden ages. Thus, P&G segments the consumers of its diaper market according to the child's age: more than 7 days old, under a month, under two months, etc. Additional demographic variables may include the child's weight and gender to supply the adequate product to a given consumer segment. It is worth mentioning that, in this case, the consumers are not buyers at the same time: namely, the buyers, or the buying decision-makers are the children's parents. Lego has a similar approach to segmentation when offering its toys by age, which is indicated on the label, e.g. 1-2 years, 3-5 years, etc. Other products may also use this type of segmentation — e.g. children's periodicals, teenager and adult magazines, etc. Users of nursery homes are elderly people, discothèques cater to mostly younger generations, although there are always exceptions.

Segmentation by gender

Segmentation by gender is usually connected with shoes, clothes, magazines, beauty products, etc. Companies often use the advantages of gender segmentation to sell, for example, a typically masculine product adapted to meet the specific needs of women (shaving or hair removing items, and after-shave creams). Consumer segmentation by gender is visible in editors' genders of certain magazines (e.g. Playboy is intended for men, and Cosmopolitan for women, as well as DIY and Hola).

Car manufacturers also recognise the importance of segmentation by gender, and increasingly pay more attention to buyers of smaller cars in particular, such as Peugeot 106 and Twingo.

Segmentation by income

Grouping customers by income is common for products in the area of housing, real estate, automobiles, clothes, etc. This type of segmentation is particularly important for up-market companies, as their goods/services are likely at attract buyers from the upper income brackets. There are also companies that offer low-cost products intending to attract lower income buyers. Car manufacturers may also cluster consumers according to their incomes, offering different car types (e.g. Mini, Economy, Standard, Premium, Luxury, etc.) with different additional equipment.

Psychographic segmentation

In this type of segmentation, consumers are divided according to their lifestyles, personality, and social class, as the same demographic group may be composed of different people in psychographic terms.

Segmentation by social class

Many companies market products based on the awareness of the differences among social groups or classes. Namely, social groups are, among other things, differentiated by their interest in purchasing special products, such as cars or furniture, places for entertainment, leisure activities, as well as all other ways of spending one's income. A possible example is the idea to offer seemingly parallel options for choosing cars for the members of the upper or high class. The members of this consumer group more often than others consider buying certain luxury cars and make their choices among the types of cars that may be quite different by their technical characteristics, but are perceived as similar because of their luxury and prestige features. Although those cars differ considerably, they are bought for the same reasons. Thus, for example the members of the British upper class most commonly choose luxurious cars (Porsche, Ferrari or Jaguar).

Although it is not so prominent, the differences may also be identified in the entertainment spots whose clientele varies according to the social class. Of course, this is less obvious or recognisable in the choice of car makes, but the differences are present regardless of the fact that many are more or less aware of them, or ready to openly admit them.

Segmentation by lifestyle

The starting assumption of this type of segmentation is that consumers have different needs and wants depending on their lifestyles. Thus, for example, the people who want to live a healthy life, and/or are ready to accept the requirements of environmental protection, may be separated as a particular segment. The former will want to buy foods that were manufactured without the use of additives (e.g. preservatives) that are, according to them, harmful, or agricultural produce that was grown without the use of artificial fertilizers. Similarly, this group will probably drink more fruit juices, mineral or spring water, and less alcoholic beverages. Members of this segment will buy products whose manufacturing contributed to the least possible degree to the pollution of the environment (e.g. by releasing poisonous gasses into the air, or by polluting the soil, water, or air).

Similarly to the previous segment, they will be interested in buying, according to them, ecologically grown agricultural products. In line with the lifestyle, it is also possible to isolate a consumer segment that is characterised by affiliation to healthy life, who will most likely to want to drink natural fruit juices and vitamin beverages. This shows that, although all above mentioned segment types may have the same need for identical or similar products, their shopping will be triggered by different motives. It is the role of the marketers to determine the ways of reaching the particular segments, and to illustrate the very characteristics and features of the products they look for and expect.

Segmentation by personality

Personality is a common variable of product diversification that is interesting to different consumer segments. This segmentation is particularly prominent with beauty products and clothes, where fashion designers express and actually sell personalities through their products (Versace, Hugo Boss). The most distinguishable approach in this type of segmentation is probably the years-long promotion of Marlboro cigarettes by the image of a typical smoker known as the Marlboro Man.

Segmentation by behaviour

Behavioural segmentation is based on classifying consumers into groups with relation to their buying habits, attitudes on particular products, frequency, and ways of using the product.

Segmentation by occasion

This is, seemingly, the simplest type of segmentation, and it boils down to observing the consumers according to the special occasion they will buy the product in/for. Thus, for example, all potential buyers of umbrellas will be those persons who do not have umbrellas on a rainy day, given the opportunity to buy it. The buyers of camera films in Dubrovnik in the summer are most frequently tourists who are sightseeing and have run out of film. A potential segment for street sellers of newspapers will be the drivers who have to stop at a traffic light where they are selling their papers and magazines, or the pedestrians who pass by them at the crossroads.

Segmentation by the search for benefits

Numerous buyers seek out personal benefits when buying products, which is another valid basis for segmentation and is based on the awareness of what benefits buyers most commonly seek from products. Kotler et al. (1996, p. 366) quote the toothpaste market segmentation as the example of this type of segmentation. Researchers have identified four basic segments, depending on the benefits the customers seek/prefer: economic, medicinal, cosmetics, and taste (consumer segment derived from the taste preference of their toothpaste).

A similar example is presented by Dalrymple and Parsons (1995, p. 182), who quote the same segment in toothpaste consumers — depending on: 1. taste and appearance, 2. whitening quality, 3. tooth-decay prevention, and 4. price. That approach is based on the assumption that the consumers, depending on the segment they belong to, may differ in terms of their demographic characteristics, special behavioural habits, and lifestyle, but that they may also behave in a similar fashion when searching for benefits for themselves. Among other things, this information may be helpful in creating promotional efforts (sending the appropriate message, selecting the right media for the transmission of the message, etc.). A similar example may be the segmentation of the market for hair shampoos, where it is also possible to differentiate: the economy segment (large packages), the medical segment (depending on the hair type — e.g. for dandruff, greasy, or damaged hair), the beauty segment (colouring shampoos, for shiny or fluffy hair) and the different scent segment (fruity, flowery scent, etc.). It is quite demanding to find out the benefits consumers seek and expect in order to carry out segmentation, but the information obtained by market research is of huge assistance here, as well as everywhere else.

Segmentation by frequency of use

Consumers or buyers may also be grouped according to the frequency they use the product or service. Thus, it is possible to identify occasional, permanent, and exceptionally frequent consumers of some products and services. The literature cites the 80/20 principle, which claims that companies often realise 80% of their revenue from 20% of their best products.

The most appreciated buyers and consumers are predominantly those who contribute to the company's performance. The results of the research carried out periodically by Simmon Market Research Bureau, on the sample of 20,000 respondents over 18 years of age, suggest that it is possible to identify the differences in the meanings of particular consumer segments depending on their frequency of use.

According to the findings, about 28% frequent consumers buy 53.5% of the products. Obviously these extremely frequent consumers ("heavy users") are most important to the company marketing the products. The category entitled "frequency index per person" additionally shows their significance, as it proves that for the 1 dollar spent per month by the occasional ("light") consumer the "heavy" consumers spend on average 4.35 dollars.

Targeting

When the company has established the presence of the different customer segments, it is necessary to decide to which segments to market its products and services. In evaluating the segments, a company must keep in mind the attractiveness (a combination of profitability and simple accessibility) of the individual segments, as well as its capability of responding to the challenge of meeting the needs and wants of the consumers from that segment.

If the company finds out that there are attractive and accessible segments, and that its profit in the long run could be higher than the invested resources (financial, organisational and human), it is necessary to decide which segments to serve, and in what way. The target market includes the consumer segments a company intends to serve, and the process of determining these segments is called target market determination. A company may determine three marketing strategies in order to cover its target market: undifferentiated marketing, concentrated marketing, and differentiated marketing.

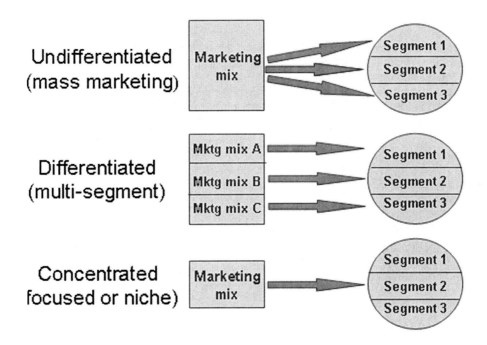

Undifferentiated marketing

With this strategy, a company estimates that it will realise greater benefits if it ignores possible consumer segments, and enters the market with a unique marketing mix. The marketing mix implies all possible combinations of the marketing elements (product, price, promotion, distribution, and ways of selling) that function as a system — causing each other and one resulting from the other. The reasons for that may be found in the fact that companies identify the differences in the segments as insignificant and the needs and the demand as unique — thus, the company develops the marketing mix targeting the greatest number of potential buyers/consumers, according to their estimates. The advantage of this approach lies primarily in lower costs: the identical product, the identical promotion, the identical price policy and the identical sales efforts and distribution in the entire market certainly imply lower unit costs of the product or service. If more companies implement this approach in the same market at the same time, the situation results in ruthless price wars — much to the consumers' delight. It is also worth mentioning that some products may be marketed successfully by undifferentiated marketing owing to the product demand and its nature. An example of this type of product may be domestic salt, whose two types, sea salt and stone salt, will result in two consumer segments depending on the consumers' preferences.

Concentrated marketing

Concentrated marketing implies a company's orientation on one or several — plausibly as similar as possible — consumer segments. This approach is particularly appropriate for companies with insufficient resources for a differentiated approach. Using concentrated marketing, a company gains advantage through the excellent position of its product in the segment it serves. That favourable position is the result of high specialisation and insight into the needs of the segment it serves. All company's efforts and activities are streamlined in that direction. Although that approach is very much due to high specialisation, it also carries great risks, such as market penetration of the competition, attracted by high profits, and market changes in terms of demand (e.g. a manufacturer of typewriters lost the entire market share when personal computers appeared, regardless of its specialisation level).

Differentiated marketing

Differentiated marketing implies a company s approach to the market by covering all segments with a separate marketing mix. The advantages of that approach lie in strengthening the product/service position in the consumer segments. In this way, companies regularly realise higher sales of their products and services than by undifferentiated marketing, as their product positions are firmer, more protected from the competition's attacks; but it is worth mentioning that this approach requires a higher level of investment.

Attraction of target segments

When making any kind of decision connected to the final choice of the target segment, Wilson et al. (1992, p. 276) suggest careful consideration of the following:

- existing market share and market homogeneity

- product homogeneity

- nature of the competitive environment

- market trends and marketing environment

- consumers' needs

- segment size, structure, and future potential, and

- company's resources.

When estimating the different market segments, a company must pay attention to:

- overall attraction of the segment, and

- company objectives and resources.

It is also important to deliberate on:

- the size of the target segments

- growth potential

- expected profitability

- economies of scale, and risk.

When the decision on the potential target segments has been made, the company should decide on the type of conquering strategy to be applied. There are numerous strategies to be chosen from, including:

- single-segment concentration - a highly risky strategy if additional competition for that target segment appears, or if the consumers' attitudes change

- segment specialization
  - by product
  - by market
  - by selective specializations

Five patterns of target market selection

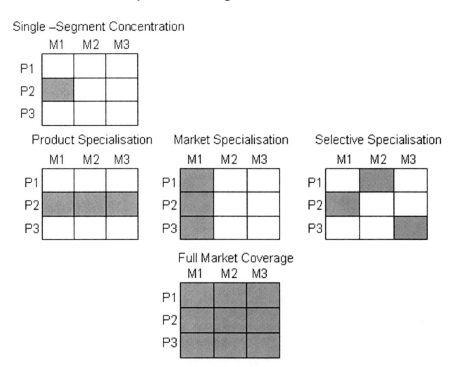

Source: Kotler, Ph., Keller, K.L., Marketing Management, 12th edition, Pearson Education, Inc. 2006, p. 262.

Market segment attractiveness and organisational resource strength

		Organisational Resource Strength	
		High	Low
Market Segment Attractiveness	High	**Best Prospects** Attractive segments that fit well with organisational resources	**Build Strengths First** Attractive markets but with poor fit with organisational resources
	Low	**Poor Prospects** Unattractive segments that fit well with organisational resources	**Worst Prospects** Unattractive segments with poor fit with organisational resources

Source: Hooley, G., Saunders, J., Piercy, F.N., Marketing Strategy and Competitive Positioning, FT Prentice Hall, 2004, p. 299.

In their market appearance and business operation, companies often use the "segment by- segment" conquering approach — the process by which companies try to hide their principal plan (the goal is to reach the supersegment or a greater number of segments), by conquering, attacking or fighting the competitors in only one segment. That strategy was used by Pepsi-Cola to attack Coca-Cola; it first focused on the retail market, and then the food market, targeting the fast food market segment.

Companies must find the adequate relationship between the segment attraction and their own power. In general, a segment active on the market does not have to be an attractive and realistic target segment for a particular company.

Positioning

For a company, segmentation means dividing the market into groups of buyers whose needs and wants are focused on different products, and who can be influenced by separate marketing activities. It is positioning that implies marketing the products buyers expect. It means adjusting all marketing activities (of the entire marketing mix) to the consumers' expectations in the individual segments. The basis for product (or brand) positioning is market segmentation.

Although product positioning is a subjective process in which buyers perceive the product in their own way, companies strive to attribute the products with just the characteristics buyers and consumers of the segments consider important. This paves the way to possible and significant misunderstandings — consumers may deny the product the characteristics attributed by the producer, or the company may believe that the buyers look for something different from what they really expect from the product. Different consumer segments expect and perceive the product's fulfilling their needs in different ways, which is one of the fundamental assumptions in determining the market segment. The very variety of needs and the difference in the perceptions by consumers, members of the different segments, generates verve in the market, and facilitates survival and market success of numerous products that satisfy the more or less similar needs and wants. The advantage of positioning lies in creating and emphasising competitive advantage relation to the other competitors.

According to Kotler et al. (1996, p. 410), quoting Ries and Trout (1981) and Ries (1988), positioning offers three possible choices:

- carrying out activities to reinforce current positions in the consumers' perception. A good example of such approach may be statements like "We may not be the biggest, but we try hardest."

- carrying out activities aimed at taking over the unoccupied area (consumer segment) that has not yet been conquered by other producers, but whose takeover is justifiable by business reasons.

Maps are generated by using relatively complex statistical methods (e.g. multidimensional scaling, factor or cluster analysis) applied through processing of the information collected in research.

Positioning Strategies

Selection and implementation of positioning strategy

Companies most commonly implement combined approaches in choosing positioning strategies for their products and services. On the basis of identifying the possible competitive advantages, and by the consumers' perceptions certain products have in the market, it is necessary to select the strategies that will enable the company to gain advantage, and then consumers should be convinced that just that product will satisfy their needs and wants.

Awarness of the possible competitive advantage

Consumers seek, and most commonly buy, the products that best meet their needs and wants, according to their opinions. The very perception in the consumer's mind that a given product has a particular characteristic which is important to her/him gives it competitive advantage in relation to other products (brands) on the market. Unfortunately, there is a common opinion that consumers may be fooled by making them believe that a product has certain characteristics that are important to them, but which are unjustified.

However, if a company plans long-term survival in the market it should fulfil all its promises. Products differ depending on their characteristics, as well as on the characteristics of the companies that deliver them. Some companies constantly innovate their products, others copy the efforts of other companies, but the typical approaches in product differentiation on the market include:

- product differentiation: based on product characteristics. Companies may offer products of different characteristics. Some companies offer standardised products in which there is little difference, e.g. washing powder may be seen as a generic product, but most producers make efforts to differentiate their products by stressing purpose (for colours or white laundry), effectiveness, packaging, freshness, etc.,

- service differentiation: attempts to offer different services for the purpose of differentiation. The two-year guarantee period may help create a different perception of the product than the product with a one-year guarantee, or even without it. Similarly, guarantees of money refunds in cases of customer dissatisfaction with the expected product characteristics may also serve the purpose of product differentiation,

- employee differentiation: employees and their behaviour may be the basis for a different perception of a product or a service, too. Thus, for example, bank clerks or student administration staff may help build a different image of the basic product (service) which is marketed. Such differentiation certainly requires effort on the part of the company to employ adequate staff, train them to be familiar with the product, to be helpful, responsible, and primarily to want to leave a good impression on the consumers,

- image differentiation: the most sophisticated type of product differentiation, and particularly manifest in situations when more products have similar characteristics and companies offer similar or the same services while marketing the products, when the employees have the same or similar knowledge, and when the staff makes the same or similar efforts into the relationship with the consumers. Image is not built overnight. Companies need to think about long-term image building

- it took a lot of effort to build the image of Nestlé or Reebok to achieve the present positive image with the majority of consumers of their products. Many banks try to be recognisable by reliability and safety, but they cannot manage to fulfil that mission (thus, some banks are more or less justifiably infamous for their lack of reliability).

CHAPTER 13: PROMOTIONAL MIX

TIHOMIR VRANESEVIC, GIANPAOLO VIGNALI & CLAUDIO VIGNALI

Promotional activities are countless and every day we witness the fact that imagination is the only limit. They are quite difficult, if not impossible, to carry out and study in isolation, but they can be classified into groups and analysed in terms of group characteristics. These groups of promotional activities may be viewed as elements of the promotional mix, provided that the elements are clearly differentiated from their factors. In accordance with this, it is possible to identify the following elements of the promotional mix:

- advertising

- sales promotion

- public relations and publicity

- personal selling.

In addition to these generic elements, it is possible to state two more elements that use promotional tools, but differ in the method of communication and the place where the activity takes place. They are:

- point-of-sale promotional activities

- direct marketing"

Everything that was said about harmonising the individual elements of the marketing mix (product, price and distribution) in trying to achieve optimal marketing goals holds true for analysing promotion as a system which consists of certain elements. Direct marketing may be viewed as a more complex marketing activity, which is not limited only to direct mail and activities that require direct answers and reactions by potential customers.

Elements of the promotional mix

Advertising

Advertising is paid, impersonal communication, oriented simultaneously at a large group of people or the public through the usual means of mass communication. According to its orientation advertising may be:

- advertising of products and services ‡" directed at promoting specific products and services which may be bought on the market now or will be available for purchase in the near future

- institutional advertising - aimed at promoting ideas, desirable social behaviour, or the company as a whole.

Advertising may be analysed according to its purposes and goals, as well as the media it uses.

Purpose of advertising

The basic purpose of advertising may be:

- to inform

- to persuade

- to remind.

The purpose of informing implies creating awareness of the product. It includes information about its characteristics in satisfying needs and fulfilling wishes, and, in that way, it attempts to initiate a certain level of demand. The purpose of persuasion is to create, defend, or enhance those advantages the product may have due to its position on the market. This purpose of advertising is often fulfilled in such a way that the advantages are emphasised directly (especially in the USA, but not as much in Europe) or indirectly, in comparison to competitive products or previous methods of satisfying those needs.

Reminding is used when the product has been on the market for a longer period of time, when it is necessary to remind the buyers of all its benefits, and when it is necessary to sustain the customer's trust in order to deter them from turning to buying new products from the competition, which is the orientation of the competition's advertising activity in terms of information and persuasion.

Advertising media

Advertising can also be observed according to the media through which the advertising message is sent. Thus, it is possible to differentiate between the following types of advertising:

- in the press

- on TV

- on the radio

- by outside/external advertising

- by direct mail

- on the Internet.

The share of advertising in the press (magazines, daily papers) is large compared to total advertising. One of the advantages is that advertisements can be focussed/streamlinedt owards a determined target segment, depending on the readers of the paper/magazine.

Additional advantages of the daily press are current relevance, ability to cover the entire market, or focus on a specific region or location — e.g. launching advertisements in issues of daily free papers or in the local weekly papers. The advantage of current relevance may also turn into a negative aspect of the short-lived nature of the daily press, which also affects the ads. As for the magazines, their basic advantage is the possibility of focussing the ad exactly on a determined reader segment; e.g. if hunting equipment is the object of advertising, the sensible solution is to print an appropriate ad in the Hunter's Gazette, a specialised journal for hunters and hunting fans. The situation is similar with other periodicals whose readers have a definite profile (e.g. the Babies). An advertisement in periodicals is characterised by a longer life span than that in the daily newspapers since periodicals "live" at least until the next issue — for a week, for a fortnight, or a month, which may be seen as an advantage, as well as a drawback in terms of updated information.

Advertising on TV, through TV commercials, facilitates massive scale perception and great market coverage. Advertising on TV accomplishes greater effects due to the possibility of repetition. Also, broadcasting of sight and sound is a significant advantage towards perceptibility and memorability of the message, and the very sighting on TV bears a certain prestige affordable only to the largest companies. The greatest drawbacks of TV commercials may be the high cost and the inability to control or determine the target segment.

Radio as an advertising medium is not as expensive as TV, and can be fairly flexible. Since there is a high number of radio stations, it is easy to determine the target segment with reference to the geographical area. The disadvantages of radio as an advertising medium are, unfortunately, as numerous as its advantages. Since radio transmits only sound, the commercials are less perceptible. Also, radio is usually listened to while engaging in some other activity (working, driving, reading, etc.). Therefore, to cover a greater area or a larger target segment, it is necessary to air the commercial a great many times, as well as on a great number of radio stations, which all raises the initially low price. Mass advertising refers to advertising with posters that are put up at certain sites and that are supposed to result in frequent perceptions by potential customers from the target segment. The most prominent type of such advertising are billboards by the road. In addition to these, this group includes advertising on posters attached to trams or taxies or in them, as well as big posters on the front of the city buildings, and at tram, bus, or train stations, etc. Billboard advertising is also characterised by efforts to increase perceptibility through various technological innovations, such as city lights, revolving advertising boards, beamers, music broadcasts, etc. The advantages of this type of outside advertising are relatively high perceptibility — provided that the ad is attractive and simple, which is one of its basic prerequisites — and the potential to put up posters in a great number of places, thus covering a wider area depending on the number of places for posters. The drawbacks include the difficulties of illustrating the basic idea in an adequate way, since the exposure to the advertisement is rather short; for example, passengers in a vehicle passing by a billboard have only seconds to perceive and try to understand the ad. This is partially neutralised by frequent exposure and placing of posters at a number of different spots.

The direct method refers to delivering advertising material (e.g. leaflets) directly to potential customers by mail (direct mailing), by leaving leaflets in post boxes or onwindshields, or by handing them out in public places (e.g. in a public passage or on the street). The advantages of direct mailing lie in the personalisation of the message and the possibility of giving detailed information (e.g. catalogues of products). The drawback is the high price, and the fact that efficiency depends on the list of addresses of true and potential buyers. The advantages of leaving advertising material in mailboxes include high area coverage and relatively low costs, while the disadvantage is the worthless and cheap image of the advertising material.

Advertising by Internet is a novelty facilitated by the development of information and communication technology. Advertising by Internet can be viewed at least from two aspects: sending advertising material directly by e-mail to the potential customer's address, and advertising on Web pages. The advantages of e-mail are personalisation, direct contact, and exceptionally low costs, while the disadvantage is that a growing number of companies have begun to use this advertising method, and that the received messages are beginning to be considered as worthless and distressing (spam), and are erased quickly without being read. Moreover, there is also the fear of computer viruses that may be hidden under the mask of advertising activities on the Internet. The advantages of advertising on the Web are low cost and the possibility of creating an ad that will contain sound and signs, as well as the possibility of linking to other pages with additional, more complex contents. The drawbacks are the need for a list of e-mail addresses of potential customers, and the need for stimulating interest to visit the Web pages containing ads, as well as the still limited number of computers used at home and with Internet connections.

An additional advantage for companies that advertise on the Internet is that by doing so they acquire an image of a company that follows changes in the development of technology and communications. Furthermore, there are numerous other possible, less prominent advertising media, e.g. flying balloons, children's balloons, matches, lighters, pencils, pens, etc. In addition to traditional ways, we may study advertising by mobile telephones, which was first possible by sending text messages and now by sending picture and sound contents.

Research for advertising needs

One of the basic definitions of advertising describes it as communication whose final goal is selling, and the potential buyer is seen through four levels of understanding:

1. awareness/getting to know the potential buyer must be aware of the product or the company;

2. undestanding s/he must understand what the product is for and what benefits it will bring;

3. conviction s/he must arrive at the conviction that the product should be bought;

4. action finally stimulates buying.

Research for advertising purposes is carried out to facilitate the understanding of reactions of potential consumers at all four levels mentioned. The advertising message should be designed to fully bring about the stated effect. Of course, this cannot be achieved by one message. Advertising is in itself a long-lasting process and, as such, may be a path leading from awareness to action. According to Mandic and Vranesevic (2001, p. 434), research for those purposes is oriented mainly towards certain specific areas in order to obtain answers to the following questions:

1. What should a potential consumer be told about the product? That part is seen as research with the purpose of defining the goals of advertising.

2. How to say it? What is the best way to turn goals into words and/or images? This implies all research undertaken for the purpose of defining the advertising message.

3. What are the most efficient forms of transmitting the message? The answer to that question should be supplied by research on the choice of the medium.

Sales promotion

Sales promotion implies all activities steered at increased buying of the product, that are directly connected to the product or its purchase. The basic reasons for the growing popularity and implementation of sales promotion, according to Jefkins (2000), are the need for aggressive competitive promotion at points of sale in big supermarket chains, attracting new buyers, and a more direct connection of manufacturers with the distribution channels, as intermediaries in joint marketing effort towards survival and achievement of realising long-term success. Sales promotion as an element of the promotional mix is becoming more and more important, which is reflected in increased financing for those activities to the level of total advertising costs.

The sales promotion activities may be focused on end-consumers, on intermediaries (wholesale or retail), and on the sales force as their employees. Sales promotion activities steered at end-buyers These activities are designed with the purpose of stimulating direct purchase of products regardless of whether that is initial purchase, repeated purchase, or increased purchase. The basic activities that traditionally fall into the category of sales promotion are:

- free samples of the product

- coupons

- discounts on quantity ("buy 2 get 3"; "25% more for the same price", etc.)

- prize games.

All activities geared towards end-buyers can be considered as pertaining to the activities within the pull strategy of attracting buyers to challenge, support, or increase the demand for the product, and thus to additionally stimulate sales intermediaries to promote that product. The sales promotion activities steered at end-buyers are especially effective, and, although expensive, they are still cheaper than advertising activities.

Furthermore, they have a shorter reaction span and provide a simpler method for measuring results (measured by direct increase of sales). Sales promotion activities steered at sales intermediaries Sales promotion steered at sales intermediaries may be considered a part of the push strategy and is aimed at stimulating their interest in promoting the product. The usual methods are additional discounts on quantity and on frequency of orders, product presentations at points of sale, handing out promotional material connected with the product (pens, pencils, glasses, bags, etc.) and with selling at point of sale (awnings, simple showcases/shelves, refrigerating showcases, uniforms). Another effective method is setting aside financial resources for joint promotion of products and point of sale, or for manufacturers and sales intermediaries.

Sales promotion activities steered at sales force

The purpose of sales promotion activities steered at the sales force is to motivate salespersons to pay more attention to more successful performance in sales. Among such activities, the basic one is connected with training and availability of all necessary training materials (presentations, product characteristics, instructions on correct selling procedures).

Furthermore, these activities may be focused on financial rewards (e.g. percentage from realised sales paid by the manufacturer) or different other rewards, such as incentive trips, the employee-of-the-week awards, visits to the plant, gift products, etc.

Publicity and public relations

Publicity

Publicity is defined as the opinion formed on the market under the influence of any sort of news or articles published in the mass media and connected with the company or the company's activities. In contrast to other activities within promotion, publicity is generally not paid, but it refers to a situation when the mass media, i.e. journalists, consider a piece of information about a company or its products important and/or interesting for publication. Publicity is the result of efforts connected with a company's activities and, if correctly analysed, it is the result of the process of public relations management.

Companies understand the importance of publicity, especially since there is positive and negative publicity. Positive publicity implies affirmative news about the company, e.g. news on acquiring new technology, winning new awards, or personal achievements of employees in sporting or cultural areas.

On the other hand, negative publicity may cause great damage to a company and refers to bad news and negative publicity about a company. An example of negative publicity may be news of employee position abuse, of embezzling practices, of a product being a health hazard, or of accidents in plants. Negative publicity may also include rumours that occasionally start circling within the market on some products causing health problems, which is supported by information obtained through hearsay. There are numerous examples of negative publicity and big companies, such as Coca-Cola and Procter&Gamble, periodically have to launch campaigns to avoid greater damage resulting from rumours (once about, the damage their drink causes to health and, once about, the connection between the company's logo and a satanic cult).

Public relations

Public relations implies all activities steered at analysing and accepting accurately all the company's efforts aimed at achieving and maintaining a positive image of the company as a subject concerned with publicity, and that acts in the public interest. In short, PR could be characterised as the element of the promotional mix which is "in charge" of persuading all that the company, in addition to gaining its own profit and meeting the consumers' needs and wants, fulfils its social objectives, and that it is socially responsible.

The public can be viewed as external (customers, buyers, media, authorities, government, etc.) and internal (employees). Public relations are primarily linked to events and special activities. In a somewhat simplified and adapted version of Mason and Ezzell (1993, p. 561), PR can be classified into three groups of activities connected with2:

• point of sale

• public entertainment scene

• education/training and social services.

Events and activities relating to sales are designed and carried out in order to bringpeople to points of sale, regardless of whether they buy the product or not. This can be achieved through fashion shows, musical event, and singing or cooking competitions with the participation of famous athletes, actors, musicians, or politicians. Activities concerning public entertainment are oriented at sponsorship of cultural, athletic, and social events. Sponsorship may be realised in the form of money, products, or services. Companies can sponsor popular rock concerts (such as American Express sponsorship of the Rolling Stones concert in London), film or theatre premieres or performances, athletic events or athletes participating in them.

Many companies support educational processes by sponsoring equipment (e.g. computers) for elementary schools, universities, or by sponsoring or offering scholarships to gifted students. They may also donate equipment for diagnosing diseases, ambulances or air conditioning systems to hospitals, or sponsor treatment costs for patients. All those activities are intended to fulfil the basic marketing objectives and are in total harmony with the marketing philosophy of business operations. Such events provide the best opportunities for creating positive publicity generated from a news story published in the papers or reported about on the radio or TV. Just because of this recognition of the possible positive or negative impact of publicity, and of the importance of systematically carrying out activities in the public relations area for the overall success in the market, most companies found departments devoted to catering to systematic affirmative relations with journalists and the public in general. The main role of these departments and their employees is to create, and inform journalists of, affirmative activities of the company, which will guarantee positive publicity and positive relations. Mason, J.B., Ezzell, F.H., Marketing Management, Macmillan, 1993, p. 561, adapted.

Public companies may direct their activities of realising and maintaining positive image and relations of the company towards (Jefkins, 2000, p. 245; Wells et al., 2003, p. 461, adapted):

- government institutions

- financial institutions

- intermediaries

- creators of public opinion

- employees (former, current and potential)

- customers (former, current and potential).

In addition to the general public, they all have a certain place in strategic marketing, and companies should hold it important to see what the prevailing assumption about them is in the general public, as well as with individual subjects.

Personal selling

Personal selling is a selling activity that involves the salesperson and the potential buyer at the same place and at the same time. Marketing philosophy views personal selling as much more than a mere transaction of goods for goods (product for money). Personal selling is primarily assisting in the search for a solution and optimal satisfaction of the customer's (buyers, consumers, users) needs and wants at a given moment. Due to its significance in the communication process, in terms of promotional goals, it is necessary to view personal selling within the framework of all elements of the promotional mix.3.

Types of personal selling

Explaining the strategy of the sales force, Kotler (1996) states that it must be allocated, in such a way as to address buyers in the right way, and at the right time. A sales representative can realise the approach to buyers in the following ways:

- sales representative - buyer in person or by telephone

- sales representative - group of buyers at organised sales presentations

- sales team - group of buyers (company employee, sales representative, and sales manager organising a sales presentation)

- sales conference (sales representative and a person from the company's hold a meeting with one or more buyers to discuss mutual problems and possibilities for cooperation)

- sales seminar/workshop (the company's team organises seminar/workshop in the buyers company for a group of technicians on achievements in the sales area).

Once the decision on the selling approach has been made, the company also decides whether it will use its own sales force, comprised of the company staff and field sales personnel, or will the job be given to a contracted sales force, comprised of representatives, sales agents, or intermediaries, who work for commission.

Basic tasks of personal selling

The salesperson should be able to recognise the needs, habits, wants, and purchasing power of permanent and potential buyers. S/he should also be acquainted with the characteristics of the product s/he is offering and that is exhibited in the sales area forming the business nomenclature of the individual shop. To some extent, a selling conversation may be viewed as sales negotiations between the two parties, during which both parties wish to realise and protect their own interests. Sales conversations (negotiations) may be examined according to stages in which they take place, bearing in mind that each one of them has certain goals and characteristics.

Overcoming objections in sales conversation and types of salespersons

In trying to protect their own interests, and in order to achieve their own profits, potential buyers may have different objections in terms of product features or statements by salespersons. The salesperson□s task is to provide answers to the stated objections by offering proof that should neutralise the objections to secure the positive closing of the sales conversation. This is certainly an activity that requires a high level of expertise and a proficient knowledge of many aspects of people's motivation, their characters, and personal traits.

Objections may be numerous, but most commonly they refer to price. An illustration of a response to an objection to a (excessively) high price may be to point out the relationship between price and quality, directing the buyers attention to the products long life, stating that maintenance costs will probably be lower, that the product will achieve a higher price next time it is sold. In addition, it is possible to compare the price with that of the competitions products or present the broken down price, i.e. if a product costs 10,000 money units and the expected duration period is 10 years, the objection on the product□s priciness may be rebuffed by stating that 1,000 money units is not such a high price for a product of such quality.

The evidence and arguments given in response to a buyer's objections need not be exclusively auditive; it is desirable to show visual proof (e.g. graphical illustrations of the products life-cycle movement or the movement of resources necessary for the products maintenance), to show and demonstrate the use of the product and its efficiency in fulfilling the basic purpose — e.g. offering the buyer a chance to test the product (by handling the tool, by drilling a hole in the wall, by test-driving the car, or by tasting or smelling the product).

According to their characteristics and methods of conducting their sales conversations, salespersons can be classified into several basic groups (Bratko, et al., 1996, p. 300, adapted)

- a product-oriented salesperson places main emphasis during the sales conversation on explaining the product features

- a buyer-oriented salesperson places main emphasis of the sales conversation on the buyer liking him/her

- a neutral salesperson conducting the sales conversation on the assumption that buyers know best what they need

- an expert technician in selling who knows and applies modern selling techniques.

Source: Bratko, S., Selling and distribution, Chapter 12, in: Marketing, group of authors, eds. Bratko, S., PreviƒĺiE, J., 2001, adapted.

The sales process - sales conversation (negotiation)

Accessing interested (buyer)	Presence, appearance, attention, knowing wishes and needs of interested (buyer)
Winning trust of interested (buyer)	Product demonstration; interest awakening; basic data and information about goods; pointing out possible differences between various products; pointing out advantage; motivating interested (buyer) to buy
Assisting the interested (buyer) in decision making	Argumentation of important factors; pointing out trendiness, season, durability, maintenance, functional and other features of product; keeping interest of potential buyer for short listed goods (relating to showed interest)
Overcoming (neutralisation) of objections	Neutralisation of possible objections to quality, price, assortment, (choice); acceptance of justified objections; keeping up motivation of interested (buyer); increasing interest towards choice, maintaining 'balance of relation' between interested and seller
Steering sales conversations towards closing the deal	Convince buyer that his/her choice is good
Express necessary attention to buyer when the sales conversation has been completed successfully, as well as when s/he refused buying	

Every approach has certain advantages, but the best type of salesperson would be a person who takes the marketing approach, i.e. who approaches customers differently in view of the circumstances, and who works persistently on establishing and maintaining long-term relations with clients based on delivering values. It is common knowledge, and probably everybodys experience, that a purchase greatly depends on the way in which the salesperson behaves. When studying personal selling, the very basic personal human traits and values have to be emphasised as the decisive factor in the potential buyers evaluation of a salesperson.

The salesperson needs to sail competently towards a happy closure of a sales conversation, taking into consideration the inevitability of achieving and keeping his/her own interests, as well as those of the buyer. A correctly understood sales conversation, in terms of the marketing philosophy, implies active participation of the buyer and respecting mutual interests, as well as the opposing interests of both parties in the sales conversation.

Solomon i Stuart (2003, p. 485) suggest that the management of the sales force (the network of salespersons) may be analysed as a process consisting of:

- defining the goals of the sales network

- determining the strategic framework of sales ‡" structure and size of the sales network

- recruiting salespersons

- training the sales force

- developing forms of motivation and rewarding salespersons

- measuring the performance of salespersons.

The process should be managed in an appropriate manner. Personal selling is both a form of selling and a promotional activity. Managing this process is demanding, but may have an exceptionally positive effect on the selling performance. The situation is reversed if personal sales are not managed in an appropriate way.

Promotional activities at points of sale

Promotional activities at points of sale relate to the different methods and tools by which buyers are directly influenced during the stage of the buying process at the point of sale. These include numerous activities and approaches studied within the framework of other elements of the promotional mix, especially within the areas of advertising and sales improvement. They differ in that they are applied and carried out at certain points of sale, and during a determined phase of the buying process, or directly before making the decision on the choice of product and purchase. Those activities are often the component and supporting part of the entire promotional campaign and are most commonly combined with activitie of other elements of the promotional mix aimed at achieving a synergetic effect. This combined approach is sometimes also recognised as the speed-up process within promotional campaigns. Similarly to the speed-up process, it is necessary to look at approaches in which different companies merge their promotional efforts in

Opinion on salesperson characteristics

The Most Appreciated	%
reliability	98.6
professionalism	93.7
knowledge of the product	90.7
innovation in solving problems	80.5
preparation and presentation	69.7

Source: Peter, P.J., Donnelly, H.J., Jr., Marketing Management, 3rd ed., Irwin, 1992, p. 184, cf. "Purchase Agents Examine the People Who Sell to Them", Sales and Marketing Management, November 11, 1985, p. 39, adapted.

The basic underlying concept of promotional activities at the point of sale is that a great number of purchases are done on impulse. According to Solomon (2002, p. 286), as many as nine out of ten buyers do not plan ahead for at least every third product of all products they buy. According to the same author, unplanned purchases include: chewing gum in 85% of cases, oral hygiene products in 75% of cases, and cosmetics and toiletries in 70% of cases. Wells et al (2003, p. 82) state that 30 to 70% of purchases are made without previous planning. On the basis of this, it is possible to conclude that a great number of purchases are made on impulse, and that it would not make sense to spend millions of dollars talking to people when they are at home and in cars when you could just let them wonder around supermarkets with 30,000 different possible products without anything to remind them to buy just that companys product (Solomon and Stuart, 2003, p. 487). With respect to the share of impulsive buying, the importance of promotional activities at points of sale is clear.

Many tools may be used to carry out promotional activities at points of sale. Jefkins (2000, pp. 126-133) enumerates a total of twenty six — from watches, dustbins, flat or multidimensional models, hanging tags and stickers with prices, etc. to the usual posters, and advertisements at points of sale. Rather than trying merely to differentiate the tools and activities, which are limited only by imagination, it is more important to direct attention to their total impact on the selling performance. Berman (1996, p. 450) cites the results of a research study on the impact of price reductions, classical advertising, and advertising at the point of sale on the sales of electric bulbs. With a reduction in prices, the sales of electric bulbs rose by 9.6%. In combination with advertising on hoardings/ billboards and newspaper ads, the sales of bulbs grew by 137.1%. However, when the reduced prices were combined with advertising at points of sale (posters, hoardings/billboards, models and displays) the sales of electric bulbs grew by 147.2 %.

The simultaneous impact of all activities (reduced price, classical advertising, and advertising at points of sale) caused a record high in the sales of electric bulbs of 430.1%. Although this is a typical product bought on impulse and without previous planning, the above stated figures support the argument on the synergic effect of the mix of different promotional activities, as well as of the importance of using promotional activities at points of sale.

Direct marketing

According to Stone (2002, p. 37), direct marketing is the interactive use of the advertising media with the purpose of momentarily stimulating the buyers reaction in such a way that it can be followed, recorded and analysed, and finally filed in databases in order to be modified in the next campaigns5.

The basic features of direct marketing

The basic features of direct marketing are:

- Interactivity - two-way communication between the company and the customer, by using more media of advertising, which results in a synergetic effect.

- More advertising media - activities of direct marketing usually imply combining activities and media to achieve a synergetic effect.

- Measurability of responses - possibilities of direct quantification of realised sales in relation to the invested.

- Transaction at any location ‡" by using all available media, contact with clients can be realised from any location: by telephone, in a kiosk, by mail, at home, in the shop, etc.

- Order - due to direct order, direct marketing is often called marketing of the direct order, which offers the possibility of establishing a specific, more durable and trustworthy relationship with customers.

Marketing is a philosophy of business operation and, among numerous marketing approaches and activities implementing that philosophy, similarly to personal selling, direct marketing stands out by its features that may be viewed within sales and promotion at the same time. These features are:

- selling to known clients identified by name and address, and with purchasing habits and behaviour

- distribution and/or delivery of products to clients is an important additional value of the product

- the direct marketing market is achieved by the media

- a company has control over products until delivery.

Of all other promotional activities with a mass communication character, apart from personal selling, direct marketing is specific due to its individual and selective approach. Potential and existing buyers are specified not only by quantitative data and socio-demographic features, but also according to their qualitative features and additional attributes, such as their behavioural characteristics while shopping, decision-making criteria, special interests, etc. After such specification, consumers are isolated as separate units, and approached individually.

The specific features of direct marketing, especially in the context of studying it as a promotional discipline, are obvious in its comparative analysis with advertising as part of all-comprising market communication, according to Duncan (2001, p. 10):

- advertising sells the product - direct marketing sells the offer

- advertising creates/molds the market - direct marketing reveals it

- advertising changes behavior - direct marketing forms it

- advertising is emphatically emotional - direct marketing is emphatically realistic

- advertisements strive to be as short as possible - direct marketing strives to be as precise as possible

- advertising design has a function to create/maintain image - direct marketing design is strictly formal, clear, and functional

- advertising creates sales - direct marketing creates buyers.

The nature of direct marketing

The effect (use) and the nature of direct marketing are determined by:

- the choice of product

- defining objectives

- choice of media

- formulating the offer

- using client lists/databases

- determining sales systems

- organising and realising planned activities.

Choice of product

In practice, there is a growing opinion that methods of direct marketing may be used for selling or assisting in selling all kinds of products and services. Price used to be considered a barrier, but now jewellery worth several tens of thousands of dollars is sold by mail, diamonds by bulletins, and computer equipment is sold by telephone. The price barrier is probably more evident at the lower end, where there is not enough differentiation in the price that would allow for the necessary expenses to cover the sales costs by direct marketing. Sometimes only unique or unusual products that are not available in retail shops are believed to be suitable for successful selling by direct marketing.

Similarly, in direct business-to-business (b2b) operations, paper pads, copying paper or other office stationery items are sold successfully by catalogues or telemarketing. Nevertheless, when choosing products, some rules still apply. Firstly, in order to sell the product by direct mail, it should be easily describable by words and picture. Secondly, there must be an additional price difference for paying the typical costs of selling through the direct marketing channel.

It is necessary to point out that end-selling need not always be exclusively accomplished through methods and tools of direct marketing. Direct marketing may also be used for collecting inquiries to be followed by personal selling.

Defining targets

Before developing particular targets it is necessary to establish whether the basic target of collecting orders (i.e. selling) or acquiring information (creating databases and lists) is the turning of potential buyers into buyers. The great difference between these two approaches in direct marketing, influences the nature and characteristics of the activities.

Methods of direct marketing can also be used for maintaining contact with buyers between sales visits. Such a form of communication is not considered the primary goal, but is a very important factor in keeping the customer and his/her loyalty.

Choice of media

Most common media in the service of direct marketing are the following:

- direct mail and catalogues

- printed media

- telephone

- radio and TV broadcasts/programmes

- fax

- electronic mail, etc.

The choice of the adequate medium for launching the determined offer depends on a number of different factors, including the necessary level of selectivity of the audience, space (or time) necessary for presenting the offer, the need for showing the product, and certainly, the level of expenses the company can sustain in view of the expected percentage (or per mill) of answers.

Creating offer

The purpose of every direct marketing program and campaign is to generate measurable reactions that would, in its final phase, result in a sale. The main task of the offer is to stimulate a reaction by potential buyers. The emphasised usefulness for the receiver of the offer will contribute to the sale, or generate lists for a sale during step two, or increase the turnover in the shops. Elements of creating a good offer are:

- unit of sale

- price

- payment terms (cash, credit, instalments, etc.)

- obligations (what is expected from the buyer)

- transportation and delivery

- warranties

- additional values (special arrangements, free trials, gifts, prize games)

- time - duration of offer.

As has already been mentioned, direct marketing does not merely include the generation of answers, but also the carrying out of orders, qualification of inquiries, etc. The system of execution includes order processing, inventory control, service, etc. It is no less important than the offer or the packaging, because customer satisfaction is a direct result of careful handling of his/her order. An unsatisfied customer will probably not answer positively to the next promotional efforts of the salesperson.

Customer bases

In order to be sure that the offer will reach the right hands, it is necessary to have a good list of potential buyers, in addition to choosing the right medium. One of the basic differences between direct marketing and other promotional approaches and activities is to use buyer databases. The imperative of efficient direct marketing is a high-quality and up-dated database on buyers. The information on the best buyer, on the type of product/ service bought previously, and on the frequency of buying, make up the secret arms on the market, and should include at least the following data (Stone, 2001, p. 45):

- the customers/buyers name and family name

- postal address, including the post code

- telephone number

- source of inquiry or order

- date and purchasing details of the first inquiry and order

- data on last purchases, frequency of buying and paid amounts

- historical monitoring and estimate of reliability and respect

- relevant demographic data for individual users (age, gender, marital status, data on family, education, income, profession, etc.)

- relevant business data for companies (business buyers; activity, size, income and revenue, number of employees, etc.).

Promotional activities should be based on market segmentation and target segments. For the purposes of segmentation and directing targeted promotional activities, direct marketing uses databases, i.e. a list of existing and potential consumers. A good buyer database may offer competitive advantage to a company, as well as strength since it facilitates penetrating the target market.

Selling systems of direct marketing

The choice of a suitable selling system depends on the nature of the product, the number of available products, and the complexity of information to be presented before the decision on buying is made. In direct marketing, there are six basic methods of selling:

1. One shot method

This method defines an offer for sale of a product in only one transaction. When the goods are ordered, paid and delivered, the transaction is closed. This method is most commonly used for products that are relatively simple and for services that do not require demonstration or personal selling effort. This is a way of selling products of low value, as well as those of very high value.

2. Two step method

First, additional information on the product or service is offered, e.g. brochure, catalogue, or personal selling. After that enquiry follows qualification and their conversion into selling. A combination of the press, mail, telephone, and personal selling is used. This is a method of selling high-quality and complex products that require longer consideration, personal information, or a demonstration. This method is also used for creating a list of addresses to which future promotional efforts will be directed.

3. Catalogue selling

A catalogue is a tool for offering a certain product assortment, offering the buyer an opportunity to choose one or more products. The offer in catalogues is valid for months or sometimes even longer than a year. This method is applied to a wide range of products offered to a target public. The catalogue is, by concept, the most similar to retailing, which offers a wide range of goods, and invites the consumer to make a selection.

4. Subscription

This method implies a continued offer during a certain period of time. It is usually paid in advance, and most commonly is used for reselling magazines.

5. Club

Club refers to offer and continuous delivery of products according to an automatic shipping schedule. Payment is due at the time of the receipt of the goods, and the buyer needs to invest only minimum effort to cancel. This system is most commonly used for selling books, CDs, insurance services, and special telephone services.

6. Continued

This method offers specified series of products, shipped in regular intervals over time. The buyer can usually cancel the shipment at any moment, and payments are made in instalments. Most commonly this method is used in the book publishing industry.

Organization and realization of the planned

As mentioned before, direct marketing does not include only generating responses, but also the supplying of orders and following up any inquiries. The implementation system encompasses the processing of orders, inventory control, maintenance, etc. This system is not less important than the offer or promotional packaging, since the customer's satisfaction is a direct result of careful handling of his/her order. A dissatisfied customer will not respond to the next promotional effort by the seller.

Before any serious activity of direct marketing begins, the company must be sure it is able to:

• respond promptly to requests for information

• deliver the order without delay

• make adjustments and corrections helpfully, and whenever problems occur

• send bills efficiently, and serve the customer kindly.

The above stated show that direct marketing can be an efficient tool for achieving all the usual targets and effects of promotional activities (awareness, knowledge, liking, preference, persuasion, and buying), bearing in mind the fact that direct marketing pays special attention to buying.

Determining the Promotional Mix

The determination of suitable elements of the promotional mix will influence the successfulness of a company's entire marketing mix on the market. The decision on which elements to use, and to what extent, depends on numerous factors relating to:

• the market

- the product, and

- the company.

Market factors can be studied in view of the target segment of potential buyers towards which promotional activities are oriented. Different promotional mixes are considered to be suitable for end-consumption products, on one hand, and for those for business consumption, on the other. The end-consumption market will use mass communication media to carry out its promotional activities (e.g. advertising in magazines and on TV), while the business consumption market still prefers personal selling and direct communication. In making this decision, it is certainly necessary to estimate which promotional activities will be best received by the target segment of the market. The target market rarely reacts exceptionally well if the promotional activity is limited to only one element of the promotional mix. Furthermore, it is necessary to make allowances for the level of development of communication channels and product distribution channels. If product distribution channels are insufficiently developed, it is possible to state, for example, that personal selling will be particularly efficient, especially personal selling by visiting homes of potential buyers and organising live presentations of products. The previously mentioned classical text book examples of personal selling are Avon (cosmetics) and Zepter (dishes). Similarly, the decision on the domination of either the pull or the push strategy will affect the choice: for example, advertising in the mass media will be more successful within the pull strategy.

Product-related factors may be viewed as opportunities for product differentiation in connection with other products or the possibilities of brand differentiation. On the other hand, it is also possible to communicate likeness to competitors products and brands. Special characteristics of products related to taste or scent may influence a greater implementation of activities in the area of product improvement (e.g. free samples and product tastings or testings). High value products will require more expensive implementation of promotional activities. Similarly, the lifecycle phase a product may be going through will also have an impact on the promotional element. Thus, for example, in the introduction phase, an end-consumption product will use, to a much greater extent, advertising and product improvement for awareness-raising purposes than in the business consumption product, in which case publicity and personal selling will be more suitable. In the maturity phase, end-consumption and mass consumption (e.g. cosmetics and foods) promotional activities at points of sale will be more often used than in other phases of those products' life-cycles.

In addition to the stated, the greatest impact on the promotional mix is generated by the company, i.e. the people who manage it. According to their estimates, push or pull strategies will be used, or both simultaneously, at a determined combination of activities. The managers knowledge of and information on promotion will determine the choice of promotional elements, as well as of promotional activities. Finally, the choice of promotional elements, the activities within the individual elements, and the intensity and comprehensiveness of their implementation are strongly under the impact of the budget the company allocates for promotion, as one of the elements of the promotional mix.

Determining the Promotion Budget

The total financial means for promotion are influenced by many factors that determine the necessary promotional activities and their intensity with the goal of achieving the desired target. Some of those factors are: the size and the reliability of the target segment - in terms of the number of potential buyers and their following of certain media (radio, TV, press), the products innovation and differentiation, the level of demand for the product, and the product's lifetime, in terms of the necessary purchasing frequency.

It is difficult to determine an optimal promotion budget, since market inclinations are extremely changeable. Therefore, a great number of managers believe that the promotion budget will never be sufficiently optimal, and that it will never be clear whether more or less resources should have been allocated for promotional activities with relation to the wanted targets. It is because of this awareness of the significance of promotion in a products success that promotional activities should be planned painstakingly, and carried out with clearly determined goals within promotional campaigns. Those goals may be direct achievement of a certain level of sales, but they may also be the creation and the change of attitude to a product, or reaching a certain level of awareness of the product. Such promotional targets may also result in increased sales — although not directly.

The methods of determining the promotion budget are different and, as mentioned before, depend on numerous factors, including the managers knowledge. To name just a few, the following methods (Mason and Ezzell, 1993, pp. 517-518, adapted) may be cited here:

- percentage-from-sale methods

- in-harmony-with-set-target methods

- competitor-investment-related methods.

The application of the percentage-from-sale method is widely practiced; it is simple to understand, and easy to calculate. According to this method, the budget is determined in a percentage amount, depending on total sales, realised in the past or expected in the future period. The implementation may be connected to past data of the product levels, with an explanation that it was achieved by known investments for promotion. The desired future level of sales, according to this approach, should keep the same ratio, and thus it is simple to calculate the necessary budget.

The advantage of this approach is simple calculation and clear connection between the invested and the expected results, through the relationship of the invested resources and the gained profit. The shortcomings to this approach refer to its static and linear nature, as well as to the fact that market circumstances are not taken into account. Also, changes in demand for a product may require spending different amounts on promotional activities per product unit rather than the regular 3 pounds per product as scheduled.

When harmonising the promotion budget with the objectives a company wants to accomplish in the next period for different products, the necessary resources for promotion are estimated. The resources for promotion must agree with the set objectives, as well as with the companys financial strength. The advantage of the second method is that it also takes into consideration the variety of objectives and studies the necessary resources for their realisation, which is not linear as the percentage-from-sale method, but is analysed by forecasting market circumstances in the following period. This certainly requires that the manager to invest greater efforts into estimating the probability of achieving objectives.

CHAPTER 14: THE INFLUENCE OF PRODUCT DISPLAYS ON CONSUMER BEHAVIOUR IN THE FASHION INDUSTRY

DAMIAN O'REILLY & KATIE DODDY

In this study we examine which of the four product display types, hanging, rail, folded and mannequin (Kerfoot, et al. 2004) are most likely to increase approach behaviour from the store's target customer. We examine the effect each product display can have on consumers' approach or avoidance tendencies and as a result their browsing and spending behaviour. We conclude that certain display types (hanging and rail) increase customers' approach behaviour and as a result, their propensity to browse. A better understanding of the impact of product displays can result in more efficient utilisation of retail floor space and ultimately, increased spending by the customers.

The Stimulus Organism Response Paradigm

The study was conducted through the Stimulus, Organism, Response paradigm (SOR). Mehrabian and Russell (1974) recognised a Stimulus-Organism-Response (S-O-R) paradigm. The model offers a description of intervening variables and resulting behaviours of the stores customers. Spangenberg, Crowley and Henderson (1996) noted that in the retail environment, the S-O-R paradigm can be applied, where atmospherics are the stimuli (s) that cause a consumer's evaluation (o) and cause behavioural responses (r) as approach or avoidance behaviour. The stimulus factors in the Mehrabian and Russell Model are physical features (e.g. product displays) of the environment. The emotional states generated by the physical environment are pleasure, arousal and dominance, with the resulting reaction of approach or avoidance behaviour (Mehrabian and Russell 1974, Russell and Pratt 1980, Donovan and Rossiter 1982). The secondary research examines atmospherics and in particular product display types and approach-avoidance behaviour theory which stems from Mehrabian-Russell's (1974) Pleasure, Arousal and Dominance Model (PAD). The study uses displays as a moderating variable to the reaction of approach behaviour in the fashion retail sector.

The Stimulus

Kotler (1973) used "atmospherics" to describe the conscious designing of space to create certain affects on users of that service environment; the effort to create an ideal environment which will elicit desired emotional reactions from users, in turn enhancing their satisfaction.

The Importance of Atmospherics

Markin et al., (1976) recognised that the proximate environment that surrounds a shopper is never neutral; the retail store is a bundle of cues, messages and suggestions which communicate to shoppers. Kotler (1973) noted that in some cases the atmosphere is more important to consumers' shopping decisions than the product itself. Kotler (1973) suggests spatial aesthetics be used similarly to pricing and advertising in influencing the consumer purchase decisions.

An important aspect noted by Kotler (1973) is the difference between the intended atmospherics and perceived atmospherics. Bitner (1992) highlighted the fact that managers continually plan, build and change an organisation's physical surroundings in an attempt to control its influence on patrons, but often do this without fully understanding the impact of a change on customers. For that reason researchers encourage further research in the area of environmental cues.

Kotler (1973) notes the atmosphere is most valuable where the product is purchased or consumed in the atmosphere, and/or, where the retailer has atmospheric design options. Within this article Kotler (1973) states that atmospherics become more relevant as the number of competitive outlets increases, or competition becomes more fierce; and particularly in industries where the product and/or price differences are small. Finally, Kotler (1973) recognises that atmospherics are more relevant as an asset when product introductions are aimed at distinct social classes or life-style buyer groups. These factors are evident within the fashion retail industry.

Kent (2003) notes that visual appearance matters as much as functionality with respect to impulse purchases and when targeting the customers' wants rather than needs. Hart and Davies (1996), in discussing non-food retailing, noted that shoppers may develop a unique relationship with a store's ambience: the location of the product could encourage greater browsing and product displays may predispose consumers to buy on impulse. Newman and Patel (2003) studied Topshop and The Gap and perceptions of target markets towards their atmospheres. Their study demonstrated the importance customers place on a fashion stores atmosphere. Newman and Foxall (2004) point out that fashion retailing is a dynamic and competitive industry and those atmospheric elements, particularly the arrangements of stock, fixtures and fittings are the fashion retailers' tools to delight their customers.

Atmospheric Elements

Turley and Milliman (2000) point out that the category breakdown of atmospherics allows managers to begin to identify and tailor the appropriate atmospheric elements, to communicate a desired image or environment to their target market, and induce the desired result from their shoppers. Turley and Milliman (2000) go on to break down each of the five sections into sub sections.

In this chart product displays are recognised within the elements of point of purchase and decoration variables. Within point of purchase and decoration variables is the subsection of product displays. Studies have generally found that more prominent displays can significantly influence sales.

The Display

Sheri Waters (2008) highlights the fact that an attractive product display can draw customers over, promote a slow moving item, or highlight new stock. Buttle (1984) states that a display must attract a shoppers' attention and that the product shown must be easy to pick up and look as if it is selling well.

Kent (2007) remarked that displays should go past the window and onto the shop floor to design a better selling space to target customers. Donellan (1996) remarked that displays increase interactions between customers and products, Hu and Jasper (2006) remark that shopping has become a leisure activity and Carbone, (1999) recognises that it is important retailers create cues to draw the customer into a more fulfilling experience, especially in time of heightened competition.

Atmospherics in Fashion Retailing

Kerfoot, Davies and Ward (2003) studied numerous atmospheric elements in a fashion apparel retail setting. The researchers found that the atmospheric elements most strongly related to purchase intentions were presentation styles, product displays, path finding and lighting. Kerfoot et al., (2003) found that while the liking of the display does not totally determine a purchase it does make it four times more likely.

Displays in Fashion Retailing

Lea-Greenwood (1997) recognised that retailers often create their displays based on inadequate information and are weak at researching the area. While further research has been done in the area, product displays still need more analysis. Kerfoot et al., (2003) believe that the use of product displays has an important role in shaping the service environment and should be examined by management.

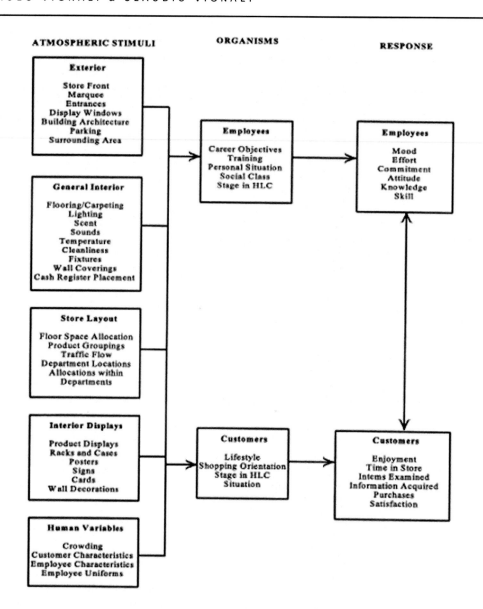

The Influence of Retail Atmospherics by Turley and Milliman (2000)

The Response

McGoldrick and Pieros (1998) explored the issue of the social-psychological significance of store space through these hypotheses:

- Space is an important modifier and shaper of behaviour (Markin et al.,1976);

- The retail store as a proximate environment affects behaviour by a process of stimulation (e.g., customers lower their voices on entering a bank);

- The retail store affects customers' perceptions, attitudes and images (e.g., Baker et al., 1994; Grewel and Baker 1994; Akhter et al., 1994), customers learn while they perceive;

As a result space utilisation and store design can be deliberately and consciously programmed to create desired customer reaction.

Considering these theories by McGoldrick and Pieros (1998) it is important, as Bitner (1992) states, that the first consideration when designing the atmosphere is to understand what is the desired consumer reaction: incorporate the environment, the organism and their possible responses; and the likely resulting behaviours. With cognition the environment can create or add to the beliefs about a place, its products and the people in it (Bitner 1992). Also the fact that the perception of the environment influences how people categorise the organisation means the environment serves as a differentiation tool (Bitner 1992).

Emotional Response

The perceived service area may elicit emotional responses that then influence behaviours. The environment elicits two emotional qualities: pleasure (to displeasure) and arousal (to non-arousal) (i.e. the amount of stimulation or excitement). Bitner (1992) concludes that pleasure increases approach behaviours, and arousal - except when combined with unpleasantness - increases approach behaviours; the perception of greater personal control increases pleasure, complexity increases emotional arousal; compatibility, natural elements and the absence of nuisances enhance pleasure; and finally, perception of the service environment and associated positive (negative) emotions can lead to positive (negative) feelings associated with the organisation, its people and its products.

Emotional States

The Pleasantness-Unpleasantness dimension in the Mehrabian-Russell Model (1974) relates to the degree to which the consumer feels happy, pleased, satisfied, or content in the environment. The Arousal spectrum from high-low distinguishes between feelings of stimulation, excitement, or hysteria and arousal and relaxation, boredom or sleepiness. The Dominance to Submissiveness spectrum relates to the extent to which a person feels in control, influential, important, and autonomous or on the other hand passive and lacking control (Mehrabian and Russell, 1974). Pleasantness and Arousal dimensions were very beneficial in describing the atmosphere in an environment, however, the dominance spectrum was not found to have a predictable or significant effect on the respondents,

Approach or Avoidance Behaviour

The Mehrabian and Russell Model (1974) noted that shoppers respond to an atmosphere with one of two responses, approach or avoidance. Mehrabian and Russell (1974) further suggested an interaction between pleasantness and arousal in determining individual approach-avoidance behaviour. In pleasant environments, an increase in arousal was argued to increase approach behaviours, whereas in unpleasant environments, an increase in arousal was suggested to motivate more avoidance behaviours.

Donovan and Rossiter (1982) found a positive relationship between pleasantness and arousal and intentions to remain in the environment and to spend more money in the store. Baker et al., (1992) found an increase in pleasantness and in arousals influence the consumers' intention to buy and the amount of visits. Mattila and Wirtz (2001) found that a combination of pleasantness and arousal leads to increased levels of approach behaviour and as a result an increase in impulse purchases. Donovan et al., (1994) reported that in unpleasant settings arousal was associated with what they labelled as 'un'-spending.

Donovan and Rossiter (1982) found that in-store stimulated pleasure was positively associated with consumers' willingness to buy and store-induced arousal influenced the time spent in a store and willingness to interact with sales assistants.

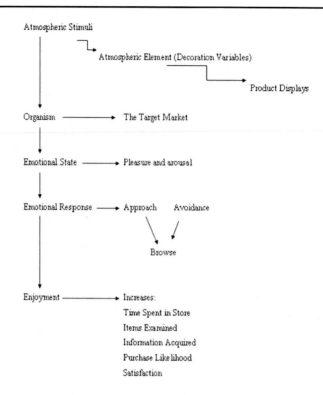

Model adapted from Mehrabian-Russell Model (1974)

Following Mehrabian and Russell (1974) and Donovan and Rossiter (1982), it was hypothesised that:

- Pleasure experienced within the store would be positively correlated with unplanned time spent in the store and unplanned purchasing;

- Arousal is positively correlated with unplanned time and purchasing in pleasant environments (i.e., for those reporting pleasant experiences), but inversely correlated in unpleasant environments.

It was further hypothesised that:

- The emotional variables of pleasure and arousal experienced in the store would contribute to extra time spent in the store and unplanned spending independently of the cognitive variables of perceived merchandise quality, variety, specials, and value for money. (Donovan et al., 1994)

Mehrabian and Russell (1974) noticed that consumers react - depending on their preference or lack of preference - to an environment from the pleasure-arousal-dominance factors, in approach or avoidance behaviours.

Moye and Giddings (2002) identified that approach behaviours are the reaction showing a consumer's willingness to stay in the environment, often leading to browsing in it, which can also lead to them verbally expressing preference for that environment. Avoidance behaviours are described by Moye and Giddings (2002) as showing a desire to leave an environment, rarely resulting in browsing behaviour.

Donovan and Rossiter (1982) noted that consumers' approach-avoidance behaviours can be related to in-store browsing and repeat shopping frequency, as well as time and money spent in that retail outlet. Turley and Chebat (2002) noted that approach behaviours are positive responses to an environment, including a desire to explore it and a willingness to stay for relatively long periods. Also, browsing behaviour is likely to directly impact on both planned shopping and impulse purchasing behaviours

In contrast, avoidance behaviours are associated with negative reactions to an environment, including the desire to leave and not return. Lovelock and Wirtz (2004) use the basic theory that pleasant environments result in approach behaviour and unpleasant environments result in avoidance; arousal levels amplify approach or avoidance behaviour.

Approaching or Avoiding Fashion Displays

Kerfoot et al., (2003) classified four methods for fashion retailers to present their products:

- Hanging (hanging front-facing),

- Folding,

- Rail-based (side rail) and

- Mannequins

They found that hanging the items was considered the most attractive presentation technique. This was because the product was readily visible, and it also reduced the need to rummage. It was also noted that the respondents showed preference for hanging because it made it easier to visualise the outfits and mix and match items available.

Folded items were viewed as neat but the display technique made it difficult to visualise the product and some respondents noted that if the display looked too neat they avoided it. Kerfoot, Davies and Ward (2003) found that in fact a surprising number of respondents said they would not browse if they felt it would disturb the display.

Rails as a form of product display received negative responses, leading to avoidance behaviour. Respondents said that they were irritated by this presentation technique because the customer could only see the sleeve.

Mannequins as a form of product display on the shop floor received a positive response in the study. The interviewees liked mannequins as they were able to see an entire outfit and how it might look on a person. These comments did not surprise Kerfoot et al., (2003) as they state that the results support the previous suggestions that mannequins can lead to multiple purchases (Kotler, 1973; Levy and Weitz, 1996; Morganstein and Strongin, 1992). Respondents in the study also remarked that mannequins were very visual. These positive responses which went as far as to report dissatisfaction with displays not featuring mannequins support why their use has been deemed to stimulate browsing. Moye and Giddings (2002) recommend a simple and easy store layout free of clutter to appeal to the older customers.

Difficulties with Managing Product Displays

A study carried out by Cunningham and O'Connor (1967) showed that consumers did not react to changes in product presentation styles and price changes in the way that management assumed, which highlights the fact that management do need to consider product displays more carefully. The results showed that reduced prices did not lead to as great an increase in sales as did more prominent display types. Bitner (1992) states that management often design their service areas but frequently do this without understanding the impact of those changes on their customers.

Donovan and Rossiter (1982) noted three reasons why it is especially difficult to measure effects of store atmosphere:

- Such effects are basically emotional states and thus difficult to verbalise,

- They are transient and therefore difficult to recall;

• They influence behaviour within the store, rather than external behaviour such as store choice.

Baker, Grewal and Levy, (1992) note that one of the limitations of the Mehrabian-Russell (1974) model is the lack of a classification system for specific environmental features.

Conclusion

In conclusion, the store environment impacts on the customer in three ways: cognitively, emotionally and physiologically; these responses will result in feelings of pleasure, arousal and dominance at different levels, which will result in approach or avoidance behaviour (Bitner 1992). Approach behaviour increases the consumer's likeliness to browse which will increase the chance of a purchase by four times (Kerfoot et al., 2003). Therefore by creating an environment that can impact positively on in-store behaviour it will cause approach behaviour which will increase the likeliness to browse and therefore to purchase. As Turley and Milliman (2000) highlighted, this increases time spent in stores. This will not only increase the likeliness of more sales, but also decreases the time available to the consumer to spend in other stores.

Methodology

In conducting research the authors considered a qualitative approach to be the most appropriate. However, it is important to realise that the results from this form of research are subjective because they are not numerical and so cannot stand up to statistical testing (Malhotra and Birks, 2007).

As Kerfoot et al., (2003) note qualitative research is most appropriate for the central topic of product displays, as it has not been investigated thoroughly and the aims of the research focus on developing an understanding of the stimuli that cause particular responses in the consumer. It is therefore necessary to explore respondents' feelings and views in relation to a particular presentation and as a result a more open approach is needed. For this study the authors conducted semi-structured interviews with twenty-five respondents. The authors used photographs of the four different types of product display with the respondents. The interviews were conducted outside the retail environment thereby eliminating potential influences and biases on the interviewees: such as store atmospherics (See below).

Interviewing

Advantages of interviews:

• The interview can be tailored depending on the respondent/situation.

• Both the researcher and respondent can explore questions and negotiate topics.

• The response rate is higher than to surveys.

• Misunderstandings can be checked immediately.

• More than one issue can be covered per interview.

• Peer group pressure is not an issue.

Disadvantages of interviews:

• High time and money costs.

• Potential problems of interview bias from direct contact between researcher and respondent.

• A need to build up a relationship between the researcher and the respondent.

• May be difficult to prove validity and truthfulness of information gathered.

(Lang and Heiss, 1991)

Participants

• The Retailer

A small boutique in south of Dublin City was used for the research. It is a popular boutique in the area, selling a range of brands including Save the Queen and Marco O Polo. The boutique's owner describes the store's regular customers as stylish women, typically ranging in age from thirty five and up, who follow fashion and like up-to-date trends.

A boutique retailer was used because atmospherics as a tailored strategic tool is more applicable to a smaller retailer with a more focused target market as they have many of the elements Kotler (1973) noted as increasing atmospherics importance.

• Interviewees:

The twenty-five respondents were selected based on a description by the store of their target market, but who have not studied or worked in the retail industry. The interviewees were chosen so that they did not previously have direct contact with the interviewer but who were highly recommended. This deals with issues two, three and four above (Lang and Heiss, 1991).

The Interviews

In total twenty-five semi-structured interviews were carried out. Each interviewee was met separately, shown all four photographs together to measure approach and browsing preferences, and then each photograph individually. The questions covered:

• Liking/disliking of the display types.

• Approach/avoidance tendency.

• Likeliness to browse/search.

• Why the display elicited these responses.

• Identification of what was and was not attractive.

• Reason for wanting to browse.

In order to gather information respondents were asked to rank forms of display based on which they would be most likely to approach, to the least likely, if not avoid; the same was done for browsing behaviour. Respondents were asked to imagine each display at the same distance on entering the store; all other elements remained constant in each photograph therefore responses were based solely on the form of display used. Order of the layout and individual photographs shown varied to ensure that this did not influence the response.

The Photographs

A professional photographer took images of each of the four display types, hanging front facing (Photograph 1), rail (Photograph 2) folded (Photograph 3), and mannequin (Photograph 4). These were used in the interviews to determine the respondents' preferences. The photographs were used by the respondents to compare and contrast each of the display types and then comment on each display individually. Each photograph was blown-up to approximately two foot square.

Hanging front facing (Photograph 1)

Rail (Photograph 2)

The Benefits of using Photographs

Photographs of the displays were used because they eliminate bias towards a display because of other atmospheric stimuli. The clothes, lighting, background and hangers stayed constant for each display; therefore none of these aspects influenced the respondents' decision. By using photographs the human variables were excluded as no people or crowds were featured. External variables were also excluded, as all the photographs were taken inside the shop. General interior variables were not included in the study, and these factors were excluded where possible or else controlled. P.A. usage, scents, width of aisle, and temperature were not an issue by using photographs. Flooring, colour schemes, wall composition, paint and wall paper and ceiling composition were constant and featured in the photographs at a minimum. The merchandise, cleanliness and lighting were kept constant in each photograph.

Layout and design variables were kept to a minimum by keeping photographs centred on the featured display. By doing this, work station, equipment and cash register placement; waiting areas and rooms, space and design allocation, department locations, traffic flow, racks and cases, waiting cues, furniture and dead areas were not featured. The grouping of the merchandise is kept consistent in each photograph. Point of purchase and decoration variables are also excluded bar the area of product displays which is the area being studied. Point of purchase displays, signs and cards, wall decorations, pictures, art work, usage instructions, price displays and teletext were all excluded from the pictures. The hangers used were wooden as were aspects of the mannequin. The shelves, table and rail displays were all a mixture of iron and glass. The shop and brand names used were kept from the respondents and any labels on the clothes were covered so that these aspects could not be an influencing factor. As a result, the product displays are the only influencing atmospheric in the respondents choice as they are the only elements in the photographs that change.

Folded (Photograph 3)

Processing the Information Gathered

Miles and Huberman's (1994) data preparation and analysis steps were followed.

- Data Reduction: Reducing, abstracting and transforming information from the volume of data.

- Data Display: The information is organised and compressed to show conclusions.

- Conclusion and Verification: Conclusion is verified depending on the subjectivity of the data collected.

Notes taken during the interviews were studied and themes from the interviews were highlighted as part of the thematic analysis that is recommended (Kerfoot et al., 2003). The themes were used to analyse the effects of the product display types on liking, approaching and browsing.

Mannequin (Photograph 4)

The Results

Bitner (1992) states the first step in designing an atmosphere is to determine what the desired reaction is. By using product displays that the target market finds most attractive the retailer could elicit a positive emotional response as the reaction would be positive to the environment.

Emotional Responses

The results from this study show clear emotional responses to displays with 40% of respondents using "hate" to describe folded displays and 52% of respondents using love to describe hanging displays. Clearly hanging displays elicit positive emotional responses resulting in pleasure which, according to the Mehrabian-Russell Model, is more likely to result in approach behaviour. On the other hand folded displays result in displeasure for almost half respondents, which according the Mehrabian Russell Model encourages avoidance.

56% of respondents said they liked mannequins, and 88% of respondents like the hanging form of display, because they give them ideas for style and trends. This demonstrates that these forms of display result in stimulation and/or excitement for customers and as a result have high levels of arousal thereby encouraging approach and browsing behaviour. Physiological remarks made on the display types include feeling uncomfortable disturbing folded products and a fear of knocking over mannequins. These would result in displeasure and the response of avoidance behaviour. It could be argued that by seeing the hanging display that was expertly put together for them, customers feel more important and dominant in the environment. On the other hand when the clothes are folded, and the customer prefers not to unfold them, it may be because of the sales assistants' effort put into the display and therefore customers feel submissive in the environment and therefore will not approach. However, this is more speculative as the respondents were not studied in the environment and so this suggestion would need much more investigation to clarify.

Likely Outcome

Donovan and Rossiter (1982) found a positive relationship between pleasantness, arousal and intentions to spend more time and money in that environment; and Baker et al., (1992) found an increase in pleasantness and arousal influenced consumers' intention to buy and return; Mattila and Wirtz (2001) found that a combination of pleasantness and arousal leads to increased approach behaviour resulting in impulse purchases and Donovan et al., (1994) reported that in unpleasant settings arousal was associated with what they labelled as 'un'spending. Based on these findings it is vital that management tailor their displays to be as pleasant for consumers and elicit arousal from them in order to increase time spent in the store and sales,

Favourites

The findings prove that the hanging and rail based forms of display are favourites with the target market. With no negative remarks and few constructive criticisms, hanging displays achieved the most positive response. Rail displays received criticisms that should be taken into account for the target market, and while mannequins did not receive the praise previous literature such as Lea-greenwood (1998), Kerfoot et al., (2003), Kotler (1973), Levy and Weitz (1996), and Morganstein and Strongin (1992), would suggest, they are liked by the target market and should be used, taking criticisms into account. Pleasure and arousal can be elicited using each of these forms of display and so the retailer would create the ideal shopping environment with greater utilisation of these displays. However, folded forms of display create low levels of pleasure resulting in avoidance. It should be noted that results on the rail form of display in particular were quite different to the similar study carried out by Kerfoot et al., (2003). The different result could be, at least to some extent, due to the different target market studied in each, and so highlights the fact that it is important that the retailer realises its own target markets preferences.

Implications

Newman and Foxall (2004) recommend that in order to differentiate themselves fashion retailers should use tools, such as arrangements of stock, to delight customers.

Folded Displays

As folded displays were not viewed this way by the target market the study recommends it only be used when necessary. The results would imply that retails should aim to use another form of display wherever possible over the folded form, and when necessary use slanted shelving or tables for displays. Management could also consider displaying products that are easier to see from a side angle and to move, therefore touch and browse, such as bags, jewellery and other accessories.

Hanging Front Facing Displays

Sheri Waters (2008) states that an effective display can attract a customer and so promote a slow moving item or advertise new stock. As hanging was the most well received form of display retailers should use this method for this purpose.

Hanging Side Rail

This form of display was viewed less favourably by the target market segment, however, it was still relatively liked it can still be used but perhaps for older stock.

Mannequins

Due to the fact that the majority of interviewees enjoy looking at mannequins retailers should use these to give customers ideas on new trends and to show the latest stock. However, retailers could look at using hanging displays instead of some in-store mannequins because as one quarter of respondents remarked it offers the best of both worlds, mannequin style outfits but with the benefits of being able to browse a rail display.

Using the Displays

By using hanging, rail and mannequin displays retailers create a pleasurable environment and in many cases elicit arousal, therefore creating the ideal shopping experience. It is important that retailers take in to account the critique given by respondents to ensure pleasure levels are as high as possible.

It seems important that retailers strike a balance with the display types. As the majority prefers the hanging form the author recommends this form of display be used the most, followed closely by rail displays. Mannequins should be used to show the latest trends on offer and they could even be limited to use in window displays. Finally, retailers in this market should minimise the use of shelving wherever possible and, when it is a necessity to fold, retailers should use slanted shelving or tables.

In-Store Effect

By applying these findings practically and rotating stock, an increase in sales is likely and management could control stock levels more efficiently. The store would be able to reduce the number of product options held as satisfaction with the products featured, and as a result sales, would increase. As a result there would be lower levels of discounted stock and write-off stock thereby generating higher profits. These implications would also result in less space being required in the stock room allowing the retailer to expand the selling floorspace.

Conclusion

While Kerfoot et al., (2003) found that their study did not cover the area of visual merchandising and the affective responses adequately and in enough detail, the author believes that by concentrating on the area of product displays and carrying out a qualitative study, it has been shown that the target market has a strong opinion on the different forms of display and that these are not always in line with the beliefs of the stores designer. While the study was for a specific market it highlights the need for every retailer to study what forms of display would be most effective for their own outlets.

Turley and Milliman (2000) recommend that the retail environment should be arranged with the particular consumer in mind. Turley and Milliman (2000) note that smaller retailers, who aim at narrow target markets, will be more able to offer a tailored atmosphere. As Lea-Greenwood (1998) recommends the effective use of displays in a retail fashion context can differentiate a retailer from its competition.

Carbone (1999), states that by creating customer cues the retailer will draw the customer in to a more fulfilling shopping experience. This was definitely the case with the respondents reactions to hanging and even rail based displays saying they "love" them and enjoy the shopping experience they present.

Using the Results

With the current industry structure it is important for every retailer to use every asset available to them to compete. A major differentiation tool is atmospherics and given the current economic climate retailers should have more awareness of its potential benefits.

The results show that the correct use of display to cater for the target market will result in approach and browsing behaviour (Mehrabian and Russell, 1974). While this does not necessarily result in an increase in sales it does make it four times more likely (Kerfoot et al., 2003), and as Turley and Milliman (2000) note it will increase the consumers time spent in the store, which leaves the consumer with less time available to spend in other stores.

The improved store layout will reduced staff hours needed on tidying the store as folded displays take the longest amount of time to remake. The staff can also spend more time on less repetitive and more enjoyable aspects of their jobs such as customer service and visual merchandising. The retailer will create a more enjoyable working environment improving the entire ambiance of the store.

Further Research

Turley and Milliman (2000) stated that more effort is needed to explain, predict and control the consumers' reaction to atmospheric elements. Within the area of displays a study on the form of folded displays would be beneficial to a retailer. As respondents often remarked that slanted shelving or tables were a preferred method of display over eye level flat shelving, further inquiry into the different forms of displaying folded products could help influence approach behaviour further.

Also the study focuses in on one section of the fashion retail industry, boutiques, and concentrates on a specific market segment, thirty-five plus age group. It is important to note, as Turley and Milliman (2000) state, an atmospheric element that produces certain responses from one group may elicit entirely different responses from another target market. Gulas and Schewe (1994) found that reactions to environments vary by age and Yalch and Spangenberg (1990) found variation by gender. The authors recommend retailers to carry out their own study for their specific area in retail and their market segment in order to appropriately design their selling space.

It is important to note that product displays are a subsection of one of the five elements of atmospherics (Turley and Milliman, 2000) and it is crucial that retailers use every element, and their subsections, of atmospherics to the best of their ability to create the ideal selling space.

CASE STUDY 1: A HIGH-STREET RETAILER

When the above recommendations are applied to a low price fast-fashion high street retailer many benefits can accrue. Firstly, customers are encouraged to shop the entire store being drawn from one display to the next. The consumer is more likely to browse each display and therefore, not only more likely to buy but more likely to make multiple purchases. The retailer's target segments become more profitable. With each display easier to shop: with clothes hanging: in size order and easy to see, the displays are less damaged from customer rummaging and also easier and faster for the retail staff to tidy as it is quicker to re-hang clothes rather than to refold. The problem of stacks of clothes being overturned in order for customers to find a specific size is also avoided. The extra time spent in the retailers store because the customer is drawn to multiple displays leaves less time available to the customer to spend in other stores. Another benefit for the retail staff is that the display will be a lot faster to refill. When the rails run low the staff member could fill a runner rail with stockroom supply and refill from that rail. Hangers could be reused to hang excess stock on delivery or if there was an sufficient collaboration between suppliers and retailers the clothes could arrive on the recycled hangers. From the stock room point of view (while rails do take up more space than shelving) there would be less lost stock as the piles would not become jumbled and half full boxes would not get lost among other departments' stock. Rails would also be easier to refill in the stockroom and the clothes are less likely to fall and injure someone than a stacked pile or boxes. There would also be less of an issue with dust and damage due to paper (boxes) stored for long periods.

Finally the environment creates a more enjoyable shopping experience for the customer as it is easier to see stock; to browse the display: and as the entire store is tidier, sizes are easier to find and it increases on-shelf-availability; an issue that is often neglected within the fashion industry. Also it would make the staffs' job easier with them no-longer having to refold clothes, hanging stock is easier to transport and rearrange and customers less likely to make a mess. More time can be spent on the more enjoyable - and arguably more important - areas of retailing such as customer service and visual display management. With less staff time spent on folding clothes the retailer could also save money and wages with the likely outcome being less staff hours required, certainly on overtime store recovery during busy periods.

CASE STUDY 2: A HIGH-END FASHION RETAILER

When the above recommendations are applied high end retailer many similar benefits can be seen. As in the case study above, consumers can be drawn through the entire store by being attracted to various displays. The consumer will be more likely to browse each display and therefore, not only more likely to buy but more likely to make multiple purchases, thereby increasing profitability and satisfying the retailer's target market. Satisfied customers can become loyal customers and loyal customers have a greater propensity to spend in their favourite retail outlets. With each display easier to shop: with clothes hanging: in size order and easy to see, the displays are less damaged from customer rummaging and also easier and faster for the retail staff to tidy with it being a lot quicker to re-hang clothes than to refold. The time saved can be used to offer further customer services which is a major draw for high end retailers. The fact that the retailer can use the stockroom space as floor space is a significant advantage for the high-end retailer as their locations are usually in the more expensive rental areas. As a result, it is even more important to use every square foot to the best advantage.

The store layout will be easier to alter for promotions, seasons and sales. The tasks of the staff can be better defined as they will spend less time folding clothes and more time on customer service and visual display management. Staffing levels in smaller retailers is difficult with many having multi-functional roles. Better displays will assist the store assistants in locating stock quickly for customers and also being able to engage with more customers.